Wise Counsel

ABOUT THE AUTHOR:

Dr. Darrell Richard Ferguson (B.A. Moody Bible Institute, M.S.L., D.R.S. Trinity Theological Seminary) is the founding Pastor of Agape Bible Church in Thornton, Colorado, host of the daily radio broadcast Food For Your Soul, and author of *What's So Great about God? A Daily Journey through the Attributes of God* and *Forgiveness and Reconciliation*.

Wise Counsel

Applying the Word of God to Life's Problems

Darrell R. Ferguson

food
for your
soul

*Treasuring God's will by
teaching His Word*

www.FoodForYourSoul.net

Wise Counsel
published by Food For Your Soul Press

© Copyright 2011 by Food For Your Soul Ministries. All rights reserved.

Second Printing December, 2011

Cover Design by Tracy Ferguson
Editors: Rosemary Ferguson, Marie Grow, Virginia Wages, Bill von Schulz
Illustrations: Faith Ferguson

Printed in the United States of America

Library of Congress Control Number: 2011934856

CONTENTS

INTRODUCTION

Every Christian needs counseling. Not everyone needs formal, weekly sessions with a professional counselor, but all of us need exhortation, encouragement, comfort, rebuke, instruction, warning, and wise advice.

Additionally, every Christian *is* a counselor. Whether you think of yourself that way or not, the fact is, when you talk to your friends about their struggles or sins or suffering, or when you give advice, you are counseling. That is God's design. The biblical commands to exhort, encourage, comfort, rebuke, instruct, warn, and offer wise advice are directed to *all* believers.

Sadly, in most of what is being written about counseling today, whether it be in biblical counseling circles or in the world of psychology, the emphasis is on training certified counselors or therapists. There is certainly nothing wrong with highly trained counselors functioning in an official capacity. But there is a lack of instruction designed for the average Christian—the person who has neither the time nor the inclination to pursue a degree or intensive certification, but who has friends and family members who need help in the course of everyday life.

Any Christian with a reasonable ability to understand God's Word can be a good counselor. God requires that we let the Word dwell in us richly enough that we can teach and admonish in all wisdom (Col.3:16). That does not mean we all have to be in a formal teaching role in a Bible study. Teaching is simply explaining to a person how to apply relevant principles from Scripture. We do that in informal ways all the time. All counseling is teaching. It is a Bible study with just one student. And you can do it!

Romans 15:14 I myself am convinced, my brothers, that you yourselves are full of goodness, complete in knowledge and <u>competent</u> to instruct one another.

The goal of this book is not to give detailed instruction on what to say in every counseling situation. It is rather to introduce you to a way of thinking about problems in relation to God's Word that will enable you to offer wise counsel in any circumstance, and to serve as a reference to help you find a starting point in helping those who seek counsel.

PART 1 THE BASICS OF COUNSELING

CHAPTER ONE
JOINTS OF SUPPLY

God's Purpose Statement for Your Church

If you were asked to draft a purpose statement for your church, what would you write? More importantly—what would Jesus write? He would say exactly what He already said in Ephesians 4:11-16.[1] In the Greek it is one, long, complex sentence, and yet it can be summed up in a single word: *maturity*.

Ephesians 4:11 It was he who gave some apostles, some prophets, some evangelists, some pastors and teachers, to prepare God's people for works of service, so that the body of Christ may be <u>built up</u>[2] 13 until we all reach unity in the faith and in the knowledge of the Son of God and become <u>mature</u>, attaining to the whole measure of the fullness of Christ.[3] 14 Then we will <u>no longer</u> be <u>infants</u>... 15 Instead, speaking the truth in love, we will in all things <u>grow up</u>... 16 From him the whole body, joined and held together by every supporting ligament, grows and <u>builds itself up</u> in love, as each part does its work.

God's purpose for the Church is repeated in every verse.

12 built up

13 mature,

14 no longer infants

15 grow up

16 grows and builds itself up

No doubt about it—God's purpose statement for your church is all about maturity. And the reward for reaching maturity is staggering—"the

---

[1] This passage is perhaps the most direct statement in Scripture on God's purpose for the Church.

[2] Author's translation.

[3] All Scripture quotations are from the NIV unless otherwise noted.

whole measure of the fullness of Christ"! What could be more important than receiving a great measure of all that Christ has to offer?

This is not to say maturity is the only goal. The Church is also called to function as God's Temple, as Christ's Bride, as God's Household, as a holy priesthood, etc. But the emphasis in Scripture is on maturity, because it is only when the Church is mature that we will succeed in all those other roles. Reaching maturity, then, is the central objective of the Church.

How to Reach Maturity

The question of how to attain maturity is answered in Ephesians 4:16.

Ephesians 4:16 From him the whole body, joined and held together by every supporting ligament, grows and <u>builds itself up</u> in love, as each part does its work.

God Won't Do it Without You

Physical growth takes place only when the lungs bring in oxygen, the heart pumps blood, the nerves send their signals, and all the various parts of the body carry out their roles. Each Christian is a unique organ of the body of Christ (Ro.12:5), so the body cannot grow to maturity unless each part is functioning. But what if someone opts out? What if one member decides to worship God on his own and chooses not to get involved with the functioning of the body? Will God bypass him and see to it that his part gets done another way? Will the growth of the body happen through the primary cause (which is God), even in the absence of a secondary cause (which is the individual part of the body supplying the rest of the body)? No. A word-for-word translation of verse 16 makes that clear.

Ephesians 4:16 From whom the whole body, joined together and held together through every ligament of supply according to working in measure each individual part,[4] makes the growth of the body toward upbuilding itself in love.[5]

---

[4] κατ' ἐνέργειαν ἐν μέτρῳ ἑνὸς ἑκάστου μέρους
[5] Author's translation.

The phrase, "according to working in measure" points to proportion. The whole process takes place only in proportion to the working of each individual part. So if the individual part does not do its work, God will not override that. He will allow the body to be diseased and disabled in the whole area surrounding that dormant body part. God will not allow the body to grow except in proportion to the functioning of the various connective parts. That is why Ephesians 4:16 says the body builds *itself* up. God will not do it without you.

Most Christians would give a hearty "Amen" to Psalm 141:4.

Psalm 141:4 Let not my heart be drawn to what is evil, to take part in wicked deeds with men who are evildoers; let me not eat of their delicacies.

We all want victory in our fight against sin. But how many of us say "Amen" to the next verse?

Psalm 141:5 Let a righteous man strike me--it is a kindness; let him rebuke me--it is oil on my head. My head will not refuse it.

The psalmist knew that the answer to his prayer in verse 4 would come in large measure through the one-another ministry—through the reproof and admonition of some other believer.

The Work of Ministry: Joints of Supply

What comes to your mind when you think of the work of the ministry? Singing on the worship team? Running the sound board? Serving in the nursery? Cleaning the building? All those *support* the work of the ministry and are therefore important, however, they are not the primary kind of ministry that Paul has in mind here. In verse 16 we get a picture of what the upbuilding ministry looks like.

Ephesians 4:16 From him the whole body, joined and held together by every supporting ligament, grows and builds itself up in love, as each part does its work.

The phrase, "joined and held together," means to be closely fitted together and to relate harmoniously together. The parts work together in harmony, which is best illustrated by the human body. Every part of the body has to work interdependently with the rest of the parts. No part functions independently. Joshua Harris is right: "Lone rangers are dead rangers."[6] If you take out your liver and set it out on the table, it will die (so will you). But more importantly, even if it could be kept alive somehow it could not possibly fulfill its function, because its only function involves working in conjunction with the rest of the parts of the body. Outside the Church you are like a liver on a table—you cannot possibly fulfill your purpose for existing.

It is no surprise, then, that special attention is given to the connective tissue of the body.

Ephesians 4:16 joined and held together by every supporting ligament

The word translated "ligament" is not a precise medical term. It is simply a term that applies to all kinds of connective tissue—including ligaments, tendons and joints, as well as nerves, veins and arteries. The word translated "supporting" means *supply* or *provision*. The people of Paul's day had enough medical knowledge to understand that the connecting organs in the body *supplied* the various parts of the body with what they needed.

With every breath you take and every beat of your heart, nutrition and oxygen are carried throughout the body to supply each of the organs. When they receive that nutrition and oxygen they carry out their function and the body grows. That, says Paul, is how your ministry works. When you do these works of service or ministry, your work in the church functions like an artery—to supply something to the other members of the church.

To supply what? Grace from God. Your ministry is to serve the function of taking the Bread of life and the Water of life and delivering it to the rest of the body. God offers grace, but He wants that grace delivered personally—through a human being—through *you*.

If your ministry is setting up chairs or shoveling snow or cleaning up, that is of great importance, but if that is all you are doing it is not enough. Even the preaching ministry—if that is all the preacher does, falls short of the kind of close, interdependent, grace-supplying connection that verse 16 is describing. Each Christian's ministry is to function like an artery.

---

[6] Harris, Sex is not the Problem: Lust is, 131.

It also functions like a ligament or a joint, because the interaction between the body parts takes place only where there is contact. We cannot fulfill our calling at a distance. We must be in contact with one another.

Are you functioning as a supplying joint? Or are you a dislocated limb? Are you an arm that is doing nothing for the body because it is out of its socket?

Unless your church is very small it would be impossible to have the kind of immediate, close, intimate connection that verse 16 describes with everyone. No single artery supplies every part of the body. But every artery supplies *some* part of the body. No artery is a dead end. Look around at the people in your church next Sunday. Several of those people are your responsibility. If Judgment Day were tomorrow would you be ready to give an account for that? Are some of those people not as strong as they should be because you are a clogged artery?

When a church becomes weak, lethargic and sick it is often a symptom of some clogged arteries. Clogged arteries walk in, sit down in the pew and watch, say a few hello's, and go home. There are cells and organs in that body that are in desperate need of oxygen and nutrition that are being choked off from their source of life and sustenance because the flow from God to them is being blockaded by the clogged arteries who cannot be bothered with needy people.

Keep that in mind when you criticize the church or someone in the church. There are people who will point the finger at some sick, dying body part and say, "Look at that pathetic organ. It is not functioning as it should be!" and they become so offended that they drop out of ministry or even leave the church. The next time you find yourself pointing an accusing finger ask yourself, *could it be that this body part I am criticizing is weak and sick and dying because I cut off the flow of grace to that person by being unfaithful in my ministry?*

The "One Another" Ministry

Perhaps at this point you are thinking, *An artery? That's such an abstract metaphor—what does it even mean in real life?* If you want to answer the question of how the parts of Christ's Body are to relate to one another you need only look up the phrase "one another" in the New

Testament. What sort of interactions are we to have with one another? Mostly we are to love. At least sixteen times in the New Testament we are commanded to love one another. Beyond that we are to...

Carry each other's burdens (Gal.6:2)

Teach and admonish one another (Col.3:16)

Encourage one another and build each other up (1 Thess. 5:11)

Consider how we may spur one another on toward love and good deeds. Let us not give up meeting together, as some are in the habit of doing, but let us encourage one another (Heb.10:24-25)

Confess your sins to each other and pray for each other (Jas.5:16)

Be kind and compassionate to one another, forgiving each other (Eph.4:31-32)

Stop passing judgment on one another. ... do what leads to peace and to mutual edification. (Ro.14:14,19)

That is a small sample of the many ways we are to function as arteries supplying grace to one another. Pick out a person in your church God has placed within your reach. If God has called you to be the "joint of supply" to bring His grace to that person, then you are responsible to carry out the one-another commands toward him or her. If he is suffering, comfort him. If he is weak, strengthen him and encourage him and spur him on to love and good deeds. Build him up and edify him. If he is in unrepentant sin, rebuke him. If he is repentant but stuck in bondage to a sin, instruct him from Scripture about how to break free. If he lacks motivation, admonish him. If he is discouraged, refresh him. Teach and instruct him with all wisdom.

Those are our responsibilities, and counseling is simply the verbal aspect of all that. When you use your mouth to encourage or instruct or rebuke or supply what the person needs in some way, you are counseling.

The most common biblical word for that is *parakaleo*. The NIV generally uses the word "encourage" to translate the Greek word *parakaleo* when a person is the object of the verb.

Hebrews 3:13 But encourage one another daily, as long as it is called Today, so that none of you may be hardened by sin's deceitfulness.

Hebrews 10:25 Let us not give up meeting together, as some are in the habit of doing, but let us encourage one another—and all the more as you see the Day approaching.

Romans 12:8a if [one's gift] is encouraging, let him encourage.

When the word *parakaleo* is used this way it simply means offering a person what he needs. Sometimes that means giving a respectful rebuke (1 Tim.5:1) or a call to repentance (Lk.3:18). Other times it means offering refreshment or rest.

Encouragement Involves Begging or Requesting

When *parakaleo* is not followed by an object[7] it means "to beg or request." The word implies a sense of urgency in the heart of the one doing the encouraging. In these cases the word is translated "appeal," "urge," "plead," "beg," and "implore."

In order for a counselee to recover from a problem, there are things he will need to do. If he lacks the motivation to do these things, then it is your job to attempt to motivate him. It is not loving to coldly inform him about what he is supposed to do with a "take it or leave it" attitude. If you really love someone, you must be willing to expend a certain amount of energy to bring him to do the right thing.

Acts 2:40 With many other words he warned them; and he pleaded (*parakaleo*) with them, "Save yourselves from this corrupt generation."

Peter did not just say, "Turn or burn" and then scoot off to his next speaking engagement. He preached a moving, passionate, powerful sermon; called them to repentance, and then "with many other words" he went on to *plead* with them to do what was right.

Preparation

All this can sound pretty intimidating. Perhaps you are thinking, I can't do all that. I don't have the knowledge or the giftedness or the training. I am not a counselor—nor do I want to be. That is not my gift.

Lack of giftedness, however, is not an excuse for neglecting this ministry. Every Christian is called to counsel. The "one-another" commands are not restricted to especially gifted people; they are given to every believer. God did not say, "Let the Word of Christ dwell in you richly, teaching and admonishing one another with all wisdom—unless

---

[7] This happens about 70 times in Scripture.

you lack the training and ability, then you can just sit on your hands and let the person wither on the vine." Not everyone has the gift of faith, yet we must all trust God. Not all of us have the gift of mercy or helps or giving, but we must all be merciful and serve and give.

If we lack the knowledge or training we must simply do what Colossians 3:16 commands—let the Word of Christ dwell in us richly. Every Christian is responsible before God to saturate his or her heart with God's Word so that we can teach and admonish with all wisdom. It is the goal of this book to help you do that.

Saturate Your Heart with Scripture

There are two parts to preparation for this ministry. The first is daily saturation with God's Word. No one can walk around with full, comprehensive knowledge of what the Bible says about every possible problem or issue. All of us, however, can fill our hearts with Scripture on a daily basis so there is something there for the Holy Spirit to work with.

When you meditate deeply on the Word every day it is amazing how often a problem comes up that "just happens" to relate to the passage you are thinking through. You pick a psalm or a proverb or a principle from the prophets or epistles or gospels; you study it and think hard about the ramifications of it for life, and soon after that you run into a person who is struggling, and that passage you have been thinking about turns out to be just what the Doctor ordered for that person's struggle.

Counseling Deep Problems

Another part of letting the Word of Christ dwell in you richly involves more systematic, targeted study. Some problems are especially difficult and require more than just the typical off-the-top-of-your-head encouragement. A person has been wrestling with an issue for decades, and the simple solution you offer after a two-minute conversation is something they thought of years ago. What do you say to someone who has fought against an addiction for twenty-five years and is still on the losing end? Or someone who is suicidal? What about someone with "clinical" depression—or who is cutting herself—or who has a life-threatening problem like anorexia or alcoholism? How about someone struggling with homosexuality? Or someone completely paralyzed with apathy? If you are meditating on God's Word, then the counsel you can give after a brief conversation will be valuable, but it probably will not be enough. They are going to need some more extensive help from you. It is my prayer that the chapters ahead will equip the reader with the basic fundamentals for counseling any problem.

Whether through this book or your own study of Scripture, one thing is clear: it is your responsibility to instruct and encourage those who need help. Are you prepared? Do you know where to take someone in Scripture to show him what God's Word says about overcoming fear or solving a temper problem? Remember, Colossians 3:16 is a command from your Creator directed not to your pastor or the church staff counselor, but to *you:*

Colossians 3:16 Let the word of Christ dwell in you richly as you teach and admonish one another with all wisdom.

In all counseling, whether it be counseling those in pain or counseling those in sin, we must instruct from God's Word. Every believer in Christ is responsible for becoming skilled enough in God's Word to be able to help others.

What If We Fail?

Are you reluctant because this seems too difficult, or you feel you are not cut out for it, or you are not convinced it is all that important? As you consider whether or not you are going to devote yourself to learning how to excel more and more in teaching, admonishing, encouraging, reproving, and comforting; ask yourself two questions. First, what happens if we fail to carry out the commands of Ephesians 4?

Maturity Is at Stake

According to Ephesians 4:14, if we fail at this we will be infants, who are...

... tossed back and forth by the waves, and blown here and there by every wind of teaching and by the cunning and craftiness of men in their deceitful scheming.

An immature church is like a little child. The people are spiritually gullible. They are indecisive. They are easily distracted. They are selfish. And most of all they are incredibly vulnerable because they have no discernment. For that reason they tend to be worked over by the deceivers. They are theologically unstable and fall into all kinds of deadly error because they are drawn into every fad that comes along.

If God's design is for strength to come through constant, regular encouragement from individuals, but that is not happening, would it be any surprise if many of the people in the church developed a great number of serious problems? Wouldn't you expect a high number of addictions, emotional problems, behavior problems, and attitude problems? If the flow of God's grace is choked off, should we not expect that the people in the church will lack strength, encouragement, hope, joy, comfort, inner peace, faith, motivation, or any of the other things that God designed to come through the "one-another's"? Sadly, that is exactly what we see. The explosion of the psychotherapy industry in recent years even within the Church is a symptom of a dramatic failure in this area.

Eternal Life Is at Stake

What happens if we fail in the one-another ministry? Countless psychological and emotional problems, ongoing defeat and bondage to enslaving sins, and, in the long-term—ultimate disaster.

Matthew 24:12-13 Because of the increase of wickedness, the love of most will grow cold. 13 But he who stands firm to the end will be saved.

Hebrews 3:12-13 gives us an idea of how a person's love for God grows cold.

12 See to it, brothers, that none of you has a sinful, unbelieving heart that turns away from the living God. 13 But encourage one another daily, as long as it is called Today, so that none of you may be hardened by sin's deceitfulness. 14 We have come to share in Christ if we hold firmly till the end the confidence we had at first.

We must stand firm to the end, because there is a real danger of becoming hardened by sin's deceitfulness and developing a sinful, unbelieving heart that turns away from the living God. That is a very real threat. Think for a moment about the people within your influence at church—one of those individuals for whom God is holding you responsible to be the supply of His grace. What can you do to make sure that person is not one of the "most" whose love will grow cold? What will be the deciding factor that will cause that person to persevere to the end and not become hardened by the deceitfulness of sin and turn away from the living God? The answer is in Hebrews 3:13.

But encourage one another daily, as long as it is called Today, so that none of you may be hardened by sin's deceitfulness.

The thing that will prevent the brothers from becoming hardened by the deceitfulness of sin is daily encouragement from you. The word "encourage" is the Greek word *parakaleo*, which is a term that summarizes all the "one-another" commands. If we encourage one another by carrying out the one-another commands on a daily basis, that is what will keep us from falling.

What happens if we fail? Not only do we fail to reach maturity as a church, and not only do we miss the attainment of the whole measure of the fullness of Christ, but many brothers and sisters will become casualties in this war who otherwise would not have. People's lives are at stake! This is a matter of eternal life and death.

What If We Succeed?

The reward of reaching maturity, on the other hand, is amazing:

Ephesians 4:15 Instead, speaking the truth in love, we will in all things grow up toward him who is the Head, that is, Christ.

As the church matures, love for one another increases and truth abounds. The church fills up with warmth and compassion and care. And that combination of truth and love causes the church to become more and more like Christ until finally we attain to the whole measure of the fullness of Christ—a large portion of all that Christ offers.

Counseling Unbelievers?

How does all of this apply in the case of unbelievers? It doesn't. Counseling is for Christians. If an unbeliever comes to you with an emotional, behavioral, or marital problem, what that person needs from you is not advice on how to have his path to hell become smoother. He needs the gospel. No matter what problem a non-Christian has, the first step is to turn to Christ. And until that step is taken no other step means anything.

CHAPTER TWO: INTEGRATION OR BIBLICAL COUNSELING?

The debate over how we should counsel in the church is often heated and passionate because proponents on both sides genuinely care about people who are hurting. One side believes the most effective way to help people is by integrating principles from secular psychotherapy with principles from the Bible (the integration approach). The other side calls for using the Bible alone [8] (the *Nouthetic* [9] or biblical counseling approach).

This is an extremely important debate. 1 Corinthians 1 condemns the use of human wisdom in spiritual matters. Integrationists would argue that the use of psychology in counseling is not the sort of thing Paul had in mind when he spoke of human wisdom. Are they right? If not, the consequences are dire to say the least. Paul goes so far as to say that if we mix human wisdom in with the gospel it will actually *empty* the cross of its power!

1 Corinthians 1:17 For Christ did not send me to baptize, but to preach the gospel--not with words of human wisdom, lest the cross of Christ be emptied of its power.

The debate over the use of psychology centers mostly on two basic questions:

1. Are all psychological problems spiritual issues?

2. Is human wisdom useful for solving spiritual problems?

---

[8] That is not to say that the biblical counselor is opposed to the use of common sense or all human reason. On the contrary, those elements of psychology can be quite helpful (see below under *The Role of Legitimate Psychology.*

[9] This term comes from the Greek word *noutheteo*, which means "to admonish, instruct, or warn." The theory behind Nouthetic counseling is that whatever Scripture means when it says, "admonish one another"—that is what counseling should be.

1. Are All Psychological Problems Spiritual Issues?

Three Categories or Two?

Integrationists tend to draw distinctions between psychological/mental problems and spiritual issues. For a medical problem, go to a doctor. For a spiritual problem, go to a pastor. And for a psychological problem, go to a psychologist or psychiatrist. A person trained only in the Bible, they insist, is no more qualified to address a psychological problem than he is to perform surgery. The Bible is sufficient in the areas it addresses—spiritual areas, but it gives no instruction on how to remove a gall bladder or cure major depression. Biblical counselors are simply in over their heads when counseling severe psychological problems.

This distinction between psychological issues and spiritual issues is widely accepted in our culture, but could it be that it is a distinction without a difference? Is there really such a thing as a psychological problem that is neither physical nor spiritual? Are there emotional or behavioral or mental issues that Scripture does not address?

How one answers those questions depends on his understanding of the doctrine of the sufficiency of Scripture. Both sides of the counseling debate agree in general terms that the Bible is sufficient. The question, though, is, "Sufficient for what?" Clearly Scripture is not sufficient for rebuilding a carburetor or performing a tonsillectomy, because it does not address auto mechanics or modern medicine. Can the same be said about psychological problems?

Sufficient for What?

2 Timothy 3:16-17 All Scripture is God-breathed and is useful for teaching, rebuking, correcting and training in righteousness, so that the man of God may be thoroughly equipped for every good work.

A person armed only with the Bible would be partially equipped at best if he were diagnosing and treating cancer. But anything that calls for spiritual teaching, sins that need rebuke, moral problems that need to be corrected, and anything that is a part of training in righteousness—for all of that a person armed only with Scripture is "fully equipped," even without any knowledge of psychology.

The term *work* is a broad one. "Every good work" encompasses every good task, every good deed, every good endeavor, and any and every good activity. Without question this term would include overcoming any sin. Breaking free from an addiction, overcoming wrong behaviors, gaining self-control, finding joy, peace, or hope, making wise decisions—all the things for which people seek counsel—these are all included in the phrase "every good work."

The phrase "thoroughly equipped" speaks of one who is ideally suited to a task. The only time the Christian can stumble or fail in a good work is if there is a deficiency either in his knowledge of Scripture or in putting what Scripture says into practice. Failure is never due to Scripture being insufficient, nor is it due to failure to learn some psychological theory. Scripture alone, without any supplement, can make us ideally suited for every good work.

Had Paul stopped at this point the statement would be astonishing enough, but lest the reader still entertain doubt about how thoroughly equipped the one with Scripture really is Paul adds one more term. In addition to being perfectly suited for every good work the person equipped with Scripture is "complete,"[10] which is an intensified form of the word "thoroughly"[11] and is in the most emphatic grammatical form possible.[12] Paul selects a strong word, uses it twice, puts it in the strongest tense and modifies it with the word *every*. What else could have been done to make this statement more absolute?

The word translated "thoroughly"[13] is actually an adjective rather than an adverb: It means *able to meet all demands, qualified, fully ready, perfectly fit, proficient*. It describes a person perfectly suited for a task, and it appears at the beginning of the sentence for emphasis. The entire passage focuses on being utterly and completely sufficient.

It is essential to recognize that this term applies to everyone—including those with no training in psychology. To the degree you are

---

[10] *exartismenos.*
[11] William D. Mounce, Word Biblical Commentary vol.46 Pastoral Epistles, Thomas Nelson Publishers, Nashville, 2000, p.571.
[12] Perfect, passive participle.
[13] Greek *artios.*

proficient in handling God's Word you are well equipped and ideally suited for any and every spiritually good activity. The Word of God is utterly sufficient for any person with any conceivable spiritual need in every culture in every context in all times.

Are Psychological Problems Addressed in Scripture?

One major argument of the integrationists is that the Bible is not sufficient to address twenty-first Century psychological "diseases" because they were not known back in Bible times and are therefore not addressed in Scripture. But they were known in Bible times. The only part that is modern is the Freudian lingo that casts emotional and spiritual problems in medical-sounding jargon. This jargon has had a dramatic impact on the way most people think about psychological problems. Terms like "psychosis" and "neurosis" make emotional problems sound like diseases, and as a result most people believe the problems that have technical labels are very much like medical maladies. Just as a doctor can use sophisticated equipment to diagnose a tumor, so the psychologist can discern mental "diseases" that an untrained layman would have no way of diagnosing or treating.

But the psychologist has no diagnostic equipment. There is no machine that can scan a person's soul to discover a disorder. The only way the experts can discover if a person is depressed is if that person tells them he feels depressed. The soul is invisible, so the counselor is 100 percent dependent upon the reports of the counselee to discover what is going on inside. And two thousand years ago people behaved in just as many problematic ways as today and reported the same kinds of feelings that counselees report today.

Does the Bible address behavior and feelings? Absolutely. The only thing that is different is the terminology; today there are novel theories and new labels for age-old problems. And the new, scientific-sounding terminology does not shed any new light. Quite the opposite. In Chapter 4 we will see how modern psychological jargon tends to obscure the nature of the problems of the soul. But when the jargon is set aside in favor of biblical terminology the fog clears away.

Any issue that is addressed by Scripture should be regarded as a spiritual issue. If the Bible teaches principles about anger, then those principles should be applied to all struggles involving anger. The same holds for fear, anxiety, irresponsibility, pride, sorrow, apathy, rebelliousness, suffering, and every other problem to which God's Word speaks directly. Does the Bible address the issue of depression? It does not use the term "depression," but there is a great number of passages that speak of discouragement, sorrow, joylessness, lack of hope, despondency, and being downcast. What psychological problem is not addressed in Scripture? God's Word speaks about emotional distress, errant behavior, bizarre behavior, selfish behavior, fear, sorrow, weakness, rejection, obsession, attitudes, moods, the thought life, self-control, enslaving sins, deception, and every other issue related to problems that have been labeled "psychological."

The truth is there is a spiritual component to *every* problem (and every blessing). No matter what comes our way, God calls us to respond in a godly, Christ-honoring way. Even actions as mundane as eating and drinking are to be done for His glory (1 Cor.10:31). Every issue in life, then, is a spiritual issue.

If there is also a physical component then it is a dual problem. For example if the person is angry because he suffered a broken leg he should see a medical doctor to address the problem with his leg and turn to Scripture to address the issue of his anger.

But is there a third category? After a medical doctor has done all that can be done to help with the physical part, and a biblical counselor has applied God's Word to the person's thoughts, attitudes, affections, inclinations, decisions, or behavior; is there anything left for a psychologist to do?[14] It is at this point where integrationists and biblical counselors part ways. The integrationist says, "Yes, there are some cases of mental disease in which no biblical principle will help, and only principles from secular psychological theory will help." The biblical counselor insists that once Scripture has been applied to the heart of the soul, human wisdom can add nothing of any value.

Some integrationists have accused biblical counselors of being shallow—applying simplistic, trite, clichéd solutions to deep and serious problems. But in some cases this attitude is due to the shallowness of the

---

[14] The question of how to determine which aspects of a person's problem are spiritual and which are physical will be addressed in detail in the chapter on medications.

integrationist's knowledge of Scripture. Ask the average counselor, "What does the Bible say about fear?" and usually the best he can say is something like, "We shouldn't live in fear. We should trust God." Or maybe he can quote a Bible verse with the word "fear" in it. If someone can quote twelve verses with the word "fear" in them, we tend to think he has a deep knowledge of Scripture when in reality his understanding of each of the twelve verses may be quite shallow. If a person is crippled with fear, simply telling him "Fear not" will not help much. What is needed is specific information about how to eliminate the fear, and steps he can take to gain control over his thought life. If all the Bible did were supply basic commands about what is good and bad but offered no instruction about how to change the heart, it would be shallow; and we would have to depend on human wisdom to figure out how to make changes. But that is not the case.

It is no surprise that integrationists and many other Christians would think this way about Scripture because so much of the preaching of God's Word perpetuates the idea. A pastor preaches on a verse that says "fear not," then reverts to human wisdom for all the practical "how to" instruction. This practice tacitly teaches people to think of the Bible as a mostly unhelpful book of platitudes that does little more than state the obvious (how much insight does it take to tell a fearful person, "fear not"?). To use the Bible, then, to address serious, life-threatening problems seems irresponsible and simple-minded, according to the integrationist.

It is my goal in the pages ahead to demonstrate that Scripture does indeed have detailed instruction on both the ideals and the "how-to's."[15]

What about Physiological Causes?

What about problems that have a physical component? Suppose a person's sorrow or anger or bad mood is related to hormones or chemicals in the brain? Does this negate the sufficiency of Scripture to address those problems? Not at all. The connections between the soul and the body are incredibly complex; and our emotions, thoughts, and

---

[15] The technical term that theologians have given to this study is "Practical Theology."

behaviors are influenced by countless factors—including physical ones. The sufficiency of Scripture, however, is not restricted by causes. Our bodies have an effect on our feelings, and our feelings have an effect on our bodies. Just as higher or lower levels of various hormones or chemicals can affect feelings, so feelings can affect chemicals. However, if the solution for hormone-induced anger or sadness were different from the solution for other kinds of anger or sadness, surely the Lord would have given some indication of that in His Word. Speaking in blanket terms, as Scripture does, about fear or weakness or joy or anger would be reckless if different varieties called for different solutions.

The truth is, only God knows the role chemicals play in human emotions. Theories about chemicals in the brain are not the hard science they are made out to be. There is no way to test the brain for high or low levels of various chemicals during mood changes. And even if there were, there would be no way to know if the chemical change caused the mood change, or the mood change caused the chemical change, or some other factor caused both. God made us as complex beings with complex connections between the material part of us and the immaterial part. Thankfully, knowledge of how it all works is not necessary. All we need is to follow the guidance our Maker gave us in His Word.

Is the biblical counselor in over his head when it comes to serious psychological problems? Not at all. It is the psychiatrist/psychologist who is in over his head. Imagine a computer that develops a software problem. The psychiatrist or psychologist is like a repair man who attempts to correct the problem by opening up the computer and moving wires around, applying electrical surges at various points, etc. The biblical counselor is like the repair man who simply looks at the repair manual and presses the buttons the manual says to press for that problem. The first approach will do more harm than good—even in the case of an especially brilliant repairman. The second approach requires only that the repairman be able to read and follow instructions. God has given us clear instructions for dealing with the problems of the soul, and it is reckless to ignore those instructions in favor of tinkering around in the soul via human wisdom. The human soul is infinitely more complex than any computer, which is why psychology, for the most part, has not worked in solving even the most basic problems for which people seek counsel.

Psychotherapy Hasn't Worked

The primary false religion of our culture is scientism—the belief that only scientific truth is really true. A culture that worships at the shrine of the test tube is uneasy with any spiritual reality, so there is great eagerness to explain the human mind naturalistically. When Freud applied medical-sounding terminology to his theories about issues of the soul, it made them seem scientific, which makes them sound true in the ears of those who regard science as the standard of reality. Ironically, this has resulted in the general acceptance of the ideas without scientific testing or verification.

When the philosophies of psychology are tested scientifically the results are far from impressive. Studies have repeatedly shown that the recovery rate for people with psychological problems is higher for those who do not receive psychotherapy than it is for those who do.[16]

This should come as no surprise. Theories based on a humanistic, naturalistic, godless view of spiritual things will lead to a system devoid of spiritual truth, a system that cannot possibly solve spiritual problems.

What *is* surprising and shocking is the virtually unchecked enthusiasm with which the church has embraced such secular, psychological theories. Christians in great numbers have embraced psychology with both arms. The majority of degrees awarded by Colorado Christian University were degrees in psychology. Denver Seminary, Talbot Seminary, Trinity Evangelical Divinity School, Liberty University, Moody Bible Institute, Fuller Theological Seminary, Dallas Seminary—all are convinced the Bible must be integrated with secular psychological theory. And as a result, most Christian counselors are integrationists.

If psychology worked at all, the church today should be more righteous, well adjusted, self-controlled, godly, and mentally healthy than at any time in history. Ours is certainly the most psychologized

---

[16] Dr. Ed Bulkley has documented many of these studies in Chapter 3 of his book, *Why Christians Can't Trust Psychology*. Eugene, Ore.: Harvest House, 1993.

generation ever. But are there fewer people today with various types of disorders or forms of depression than ever before? Quite the opposite. The legacy of modern psychology has been the destruction of one of the most valuable protective gifts God has given us—the conscience.

Destruction of the Conscience

Psychologists are remarkable people. I have great respect for those who are willing to devote themselves to listening to people and helping them with their problems. The problems for which people seek counsel are often very serious, and to subject oneself to that kind of sorrow on a regular basis requires unusual compassion. Most psychologists, no doubt, are wonderfully kindhearted people. I believe, however, that the principles taught by secular psychology have caused considerable harm.

Sigmund Freud was an atheist whose goal was to provide mankind with a naturalistic explanation for matters that seem spiritual. Guilt feelings over sin, the craving for righteousness, and other various needs of the soul tend to drive people to God. By taking the matters of the soul and couching them in terms that make them sound decidedly non-spiritual, God is no longer needed. Sin and righteousness no longer exist—just psychosis or mental health.

Freud probably never dreamed his efforts would be as successful as they were. It is difficult to calculate how dramatically psychological theories have influenced how most people in the western world interpret human behavior. Unproven and improvable (and un-falsifiable) theories have been adopted wholesale by our legal system, education system, our literature—even by the medical community. They have shaped the ethics of our culture and our entire approach to addressing human problems. With the exception of Darwin, one is hard pressed to find any individual more successful in his goal of bringing about the secularization of culture. Problems that should drive a person to realize his need for divine forgiveness and supernatural transformation are now thought of naturalistically, and in a morally neutral context.

Most Christians understand that it is wrong to grumble and complain. But when grumbling is described with the world's terminology ("venting"), it suddenly sounds acceptable. It is not uncommon to hear a person say, "I just need to vent a little bit," but that person would never dream of saying, "I just stopped by to grumble and complain." The term "venting" is calculated to communicate something about the nature of the behavior. Distress is pictured as some kind of exhaust building up in the heart that simply needs to be released. Who could be faulted for that?

When Scripture speaks of lacking self-control or being controlled by the flesh that terminology points to the sinfulness of the character flaw. But the psychological term for the same problem ("compulsive") is morally neutral. What shame is there in being compelled?

Worry and fretting sound like sins, but how could it be wrong to be "stressed"? If too much weight is placed on a bridge and it becomes stressed, that is not the bridge's fault.

All cowards are consigned to hell in Revelation 21:8, but the same behavior described as "insecurity" suddenly loses all culpability.

Discontent is sin, but coping actually sounds noble.

Enslaving oneself to a sin sounds bad, but who could be blamed for catching a disease called "addiction"?

Instead of fornicating, people "live together." What could be better than things like living and togetherness?

Instead of prideful, arrogant, self-centered, hard-heartedness against God, people are "independent" and "self-reliant." Rather than lacking conviction they are "open-minded." The sins of pride and self-love are referred to as "healthy self-esteem." People become bitter, angry, resentful, or self-pitying and it is all recast under the morally innocent term "emotionally wounded." Why repent over being wounded? Soldiers receive a purple heart for getting wounded!

Instead of "won't" we say "can't." (I *can't* forgive, I *can't* love my spouse, I *can't* resist this sin…"). Instead of hard-heartedness we say we have "emotional issues." Instead of covetousness or greed we talk about our emotional "needs." Instead of cowardliness we say "insecurity." Fear of man is "co-dependence." Selfish demands are "rights," and sinful responses to the violation of those rights are simply "defense mechanisms." Instead of prideful self-absorption we have an "inferiority complex."

Some other examples:
- "sickness" or "disease" instead of *sin*

- "alcoholic" instead of *drunk*
- "subconsciously" instead of *ignorantly*
- "in denial" instead of *unrepentant*
- "rapid cycling" instead of *double-mindedness*
- "coping" instead of *discontented*

This is not to suggest that all secular psychologists or integrationist counselors have the goal of secularizing the culture. In many cases these terms are embraced simply to avoid having to sound judgmental or risk the counselee falling into discouragement or anger because of being made culpable for some of his problems. It can be a great encouragement for the counselee, however, to know that his problem is indeed addressed in Scripture, and there is a glorious solution. Yes, it is painful to realize there is moral blame. However, that pain is like the pain of getting an honest diagnosis from a doctor who also has the medicine to cure the disease. Better to experience the distress of learning about the severity of a curable disease than to remain blissfully ignorant and refuse the medicine.

Decisions Are Made by the Spirit, Not the Body

Our naturalistic culture tends to think of a human being in a mostly (if not completely) mechanistic way. A human being is nothing more than matter, and the only difference between a person and a worm is the complexity and arrangement of the cells. As a result, it is common for people to think there is a physical *cause* in control of our decision-making. That is, certain decisions are determined by the chemicals in the brain as a first cause.

The Bible, on the other hand, teaches that the immaterial part of man dictates to the brain what it will decide or choose. Your spirit is the part of you that makes decisions; your brain simply carries out those decisions.

These radically opposing philosophies lead to radically different ways of addressing bad behavior. The naturalist says, "If my brain keeps making bad decisions, the solution is to adjust the chemicals in the brain until the problem is corrected." However, the Bible teaches that when we make bad decisions, the problem is in the heart, and that is where the corrections need to be made.

Consider alcoholism as an example. Drinking too much is either a decision or a disease. If it is a disease, like the flu, then the person does not have any control over whether he has it. If that is the case, then it must not be sin. If it is a decision that comes from the heart, the person is guilty. Most Christians would agree that it is sinful to get drunk, even for an alcoholic, but they are much slower to say that it is a sin for a depressed person to be in a bad mood, or for a bipolar person to make sinful choices while in a manic state, or for an anorexic to run ten miles, or for an overeater to indulge in gluttony, or for someone with an anxiety disorder to worry.

Are the decisions to do wrong things the result of the spirit choosing sin, or the brain simply misfiring? Is all wrongdoing sin? Or is there some wrongdoing that is justified because it is caused by chemicals in the brain? 1 John 5:17 is clear: "All wrongdoing is sin." And where does sin come from—the brain, or the heart? Jesus was very clear on this point.

Mark 7:21-22 From within, <u>out of men's hearts</u>, come evil thoughts, sexual immorality, theft, murder, adultery, 22 greed, malice, deceit, lewdness, envy, slander, arrogance and folly.

Most people would agree that body parts other than the brain cannot cause sin. One's hair or elbow or pancreas—none of those could ever force him to sin. But because of the influence of evolutionary theory and worldly psychology on the church, many Christians are open to the idea that perhaps your brain *could* cause sin. Their reasoning is that because some people are hostile, mean, negative, or overcome with worry when they are off medication, but not when they are on medication, perhaps those sins are caused not by the person's heart but by chemicals in the brain.

If that is true then Jesus' statement in Mark 7 is not true. Either sin originates in the heart or it does not. If we believe the words of Jesus we must accept that physical matter cannot generate a spiritual reality. All sin originates in an immaterial part of one's being.

The body is the vehicle that carries out the decisions of the spirit. How that happens is a mystery. In one sense, it is mind over matter. The mind is an immaterial entity. The brain is made of physical matter.

When a person makes a decision, that decision takes place in his mind first, and then somehow his mind is able to cause physical things to happen in the brain (it makes the synapses fire and releases certain chemicals). For this reason, any psychological problem that involves sin is a spiritual problem. No matter what physical issues may be involved, if there is sin, it is a spiritual issue.

Even if it could be shown that depressed people have lower levels of serotonin in the brain, it would not prove the depression is caused by the serotonin level. It may be that the depression caused the drop in serotonin. Or perhaps some other factor caused both. A person with the flu experiences nausea and fever. He may speculate about whether the nausea is caused by the fever or the fever by the nausea, when in reality both are caused by a third factor (a virus). If someone experiences physical changes as well as emotional changes, it may be that both are caused by a third factor—a spiritual one.

There is no question that nonmaterial things can affect the physical body. For example, imagine you are colorblind and you see a plump, juicy lemon on the counter. Thinking it is an orange, you take a big bite. Immediately your eyes squeeze shut, your whole body tenses up, and the corners of your mouth tighten. After reading that scenario you likely have more saliva in your mouth than you did before reading it—a chemical "imbalance" in your mouth. The cause of your saliva imbalance was decidedly immaterial—just a series of concepts communicated through symbols on a page, which were decoded and understood by your mind. If a scientist had been monitoring the saliva levels in your mouth, noted the change, then postulated that the chemical change was the *cause* of your thoughts about lemons—he would have it backwards. The thoughts caused the physical change.

Whatever the interplay of causes and effects, we must understand that no physical problem can cause sin. If a person were exactly like Christ—if his heart were completely sinless and totally righteous—he would never sin, even if he had a brain injury or a chemical imbalance or a change in hormones.

2. Is Human Wisdom Useful for Spiritual Problems?

The answer to our first question is an emphatic, "Yes—the Bible does indeed address "psychological" issues. The second basic question in this debate between biblical vs. integrationist counseling has to do with the role of human wisdom. The integrationist argues that while spiritual growth comes *mainly* through Scripture, it can also come from other sources. It might come through special revelation (the Bible) or it might come through natural revelation (that which God reveals through the creation). Psychology, it is argued, falls into the category of natural revelation. All truth is God's truth, so whether it comes through natural revelation or special revelation, either way it is revelation from God. It is through scientific investigation that mankind has discovered how to repair lungs and livers and brains—why not minds and hearts souls? Christian psychologist Gary Collins articulates this point:

> Surely there are times, many times, when a sensitive, psychologically trained, committed Christian counselor can help people though psychological techniques and with psychological insights that God has allowed us to discover, but that he has not chosen to reveal in the Bible …. The Word of God never claims to have all the answers to all of life's problems.[17]

Natural Revelation and Human Wisdom

It is true that natural revelation is from God and must not be ignored. However, there is also such a thing as human wisdom, which is roundly condemned in Scripture when applied to spiritual matters.

1 Corinthians 1:17 For Christ did not send me to baptize, but to preach the gospel--not with words of human wisdom, lest the cross of Christ be emptied of its power.

Human wisdom is never to be integrated with God's Word. Adding human wisdom to Scripture does not augment the Bible, but rather empties the cross of its power! Clearly that must be avoided at all cost.

---

[17] Gary R. Collins, Can You Trust Psychology?, Downer's Grove: Intervarsity Press, 1988, 96-7.

What is the difference, then, between human wisdom, which must be avoided; and natural revelation, which must be heeded?

Psychology is Not Natural Revelation

Not everything discovered through human investigation rises to the level of natural revelation. The doctrine of natural revelation is drawn mainly from Psalm 19:1-4 and Romans 1:18-21. These texts reveal three important principles about natural revelation. For a piece of information to qualify as natural revelation it must 1) be universally known, 2) be essential for salvation, and 3) be taught in Scripture.

1)   Universally Known

General revelation is obvious and universally understood (but suppressed) by all people in all times in all places.

Romans 1:19-20 What may be known about God is plain to them, because God has made it plain to them. 20 For since the creation of the world God's invisible qualities--his eternal power and divine nature--have been clearly seen, being understood from what has been made, so that men are without excuse. ... they knew God ...

Psalm 19:1-4 The heavens declare the glory of God; the skies proclaim the work of his hands. Day after day they pour forth speech; night after night they display knowledge. There is no speech or language where their voice is not heard. Their voice goes out into all the earth, their words to the ends of the world.

Natural revelation, then, is God's communication of truth about Himself to all persons at all times and in all places.[18]

2)   Essential for Salvation

The second unique factor in natural revelation is that the rejection of it results in damnation.

Romans 1:18-28 The wrath of God is being revealed from heaven against all the godlessness and wickedness of men who suppress the truth by their wickedness ... God's invisible qualities .... have been clearly seen, being understood from what has been

[18] Millard Erickson, Christian Theology, Grand Rapids: Baker, 1998, 178.
H. Wayne House, Charts of Christian Theology and Doctrine, Grand Rapids: Zondervan, 1992, 21.
Bruce Demarest, Walter A. Elwell ed. Evangelical Dictionary of Theology, Grand Rapids: Baker Book House, 2001, 1019.

made, so that men are without excuse. For although they knew God, they neither glorified him as God nor gave thanks to him, but their thinking became futile and their foolish hearts were darkened. .... Furthermore, since they did not think it worthwhile to retain the knowledge of God, he gave them over to a depraved mind.

Unbelievers are damned because they reject what God has revealed in natural revelation.

3) *Not Unique*

A third criterion for something to qualify as natural revelation is that everything that is revealed through the creation is also stated in Scripture. The doctrines that are specifically mentioned in the passages on natural revelation are:

- God's divine nature
- God's eternal power
- The glory of God
- The work of His hands

Each of these doctrines is taught explicitly in the Bible. There is nothing that nature reveals about God that cannot also be found in Scripture. The Bible is a much better source of information about spiritual things than nature alone.

There is a great amount of information that can be obtained through human investigation that, while helpful, does not fall into the category of natural revelation because it is not universally known, not essential for salvation, and not taught in Scripture. The fact that God exists and that he is the powerful, glorious Creator is natural revelation. It is evident to all people everywhere, when that revelation is rejected a person is under condemnation, and it is verified in the Bible. But the doctrines of psychology fall short of being in the category of natural revelation on all three points. Theories about Selective Serotonin Reuptake Inhibitors are not immediately obvious to all people at all times, and no one will be consigned to hell for rejecting Rogerian counseling techniques or Dialectical Behavior Therapy. And, as Gary Collins admits, the principles of psychology are not found on the pages of the Bible.

Psychology, then, is not in the category of natural revelation. And even if it were natural revelation, still it would not be adequate for addressing the problems of the human soul.

Psalm 19 has been called "the psalm of the two books," because the first half addresses natural revelation ("**The heavens declare the glory of God**…"), and the second half speaks of special revelation ("**The Law of the Lord is perfect**…"). Does natural revelation point to the glory of God? Yes, but that is all it can do. The rest of the psalm is a contrast. Only God's Word in Scripture has the power to transform the human soul. All the promises in that psalm that have to do with benefits to the soul come in the second section, not the first. Scripture, not nature, revives, renews, and restores the soul; it makes the simpleminded wise; it brings joy to the heart and light to the eyes; and it is sweeter than honey (vv. 7-11). God's Word has a healing, restoring, life-giving effect on the soul. It gives wisdom and guidance. It is essential for the very daily sustenance of the believer. It functions for us spiritually like food and drink function for the physical body.[19]

Is all truth God's truth? Perhaps, but not all truth is God's *Word*. There is a vast difference between the word of man and the Word of God—even when both are true. The mere fact that something is true rather than false does not mean it has the same power to feed, nourish, strengthen, and sanctify the soul that God's Word has.

Furthermore, the information we receive about God through the creation is much less specific than the information in Scripture. A person can gaze at the stars and know there is a powerful God, but nothing in the stars will explain the doctrine of imputed righteousness through faith, or how to overcome the flesh by walking in the Spirit. Nature shows us general truths; Scripture teaches us specifics in detail. The Bible is superior to natural revelation because it supplies us with propositional truth about God rather than mere implications. Examination of the trees and rivers and stars reveals *implied* truths about God, but Scripture gives us direct statements. There is a greater chance of error in interpreting implied messages from a tree than explicit

---

[19] Mt.4:4, Dt.32:47, 1 Pe.2:2.

statements in a Bible verse—especially when dealing with the complexities of human feelings, thoughts, and behavior.

Integrationists, however, reverse this. They would characterize the counsel of God's Word as being general and the wisdom of psychology as being specific. The Bible gives the general principle, such as "Avoid fear of man," and then psychology takes it from there and reveals the specifics of how to accomplish that in practical terms. This approach actually places psychology above Scripture in the sense that it is more detailed and specific.

Human Wisdom is Useless for Spiritual Matters

If the wisdom gathered from psychological studies is not natural revelation, what is it? The biblical term for it is "human wisdom," and it does more harm than good in spiritual matters.

Can human investigation and reasoning discover true things? Yes. And those things can be helpful for temporal applications, but when applied to spiritual things human wisdom is not commended in Scripture:

1 Corinthians 1:19,21 "I will destroy the wisdom of the wise; the intelligence of the intelligent I will frustrate." ... 21 For since in the wisdom of God the world through its wisdom did not know him, God was pleased through the foolishness of what was preached to save those who believe.

Paul points out that human wisdom is not even sufficient to know God in the first place (v. 21). For that reason, Paul made every effort, in his preaching, to avoid mixing God's Word with human wisdom. Those who argue for integration have often failed to take into consideration Scripture's very strong words against human wisdom when applied to spiritual matters. The pursuit of human wisdom is the pursuit of that which God has promised to frustrate and destroy (1 Cor.1:19). Far from adding to the effectiveness of Scripture, human wisdom is not even sufficient to enable a person to know God relationally at all (1 Cor.1:21).

Furthermore, God's Word cannot be obtained through human investigation (1 Cor.2:11). Human wisdom, when applied to building a car, brain surgery, rocket science, or some form of manipulating matter is very valuable; but when applied to a spiritual reality is worse than worthless. It serves as a contamination, not an improvement to

Scripture. It leads to self-imposed worship, false humility, and harsh treatment of the body,[20] is hollow and deceptive taking one captive,[21] and leads to bitter envy, selfishness, disorder, and every evil practice.[22] There is absolutely no need for human wisdom in spiritual matters. Every spiritual truth that it is possible for us to know is in the Bible.

The only wisdom we preach is the wisdom revealed in the Gospel. No matter how smart a person may be, it is impossible to figure out what is on the mind of God through human reasoning—or even through natural revelation. The only way to know the thoughts of God is through Scripture.

1 Corinthians 2:11-12 ... no one knows the thoughts of God except the Spirit of God. We have not received the spirit of the world but the Spirit who is from God, that we may understand what God has freely given us.

The theories of psychology, like all human wisdom, are comprised of both truth and error. Truth mixed with error can be worse than pure error. The Bible is not only the most specific source of truth about spiritual things, but it is the *only* source of truth that is without error. The only way to know a spiritual truth *for sure* is if it is taught in the Bible.

The Role of Legitimate Psychology

Is there any legitimate place for psychology? Should we even bother studying human behavior at all? Yes. Scripture calls us to apply wisdom, and one element of wisdom is observing life and drawing conclusions about the way things tend to go. There is nothing wrong with psychologists making helpful observations about tendencies in human behavior. For example, if a researcher or psychologist or observant parent discovers that newborns often stop crying when wrapped tightly in a blanket, that is helpful information that is not in the Bible. If a person has a problem with overeating, and common sense says that it may help if he busies himself with enjoyable projects during the times of day he is normally tempted to overeat, that kind of observation can be a great help. To the degree that psychology restricts itself to making

---

[20] Col. 2:23.
[21] Col. 2:8.
[22] Jas. 3:14-16.

helpful observations about human behavior it can be a legitimate part of the pursuit of wisdom.

Schools of psychotherapy, however, have gone far beyond the mere observation of tendencies in human behavior and have developed systems and theories that contradict biblical principles. And it is to these that the biblical counselor objects. Both sides embrace common sense. The division arises over the tendency of integrationists to accept secular, worldly, psychological philosophies or systems that reason beyond what Scripture says about spiritual truths.

What is the role, then, of common sense, reasoning, and observations of typical behavior in counseling? Those aspects of wisdom can be useful in the application of biblical principles, as long as several important guidelines are observed.

Suppose a man finds that he is so self-absorbed when he gets home from work that he tends to ignore his family, and a counselor suggests that he use the stop light down the street from his house as a memory cue to remind him to think of principles from Scripture about selfless love, so he is reminded about it just before arriving home from work each day. Or he suggests taping a Bible verse about humility on the dashboard of his car. There is nothing in the Bible about stoplights or dashboards, so both suggestions are human reasoning. Such counseling is not necessarily a sinful reliance on human wisdom, however. Human reasoning in counseling is useful when all of the following guidelines are followed:

1) It must simple enough to test.
2) It must not violate Scripture.
3) It must not be based on unbiblical assumptions.
4) It must have the goal of applying some specific biblical principle.
5) It must not be elevated to the level of Scripture.
6) It must not be the source of one's hope or confidence.

The idea of placing a Bible verse on the dashboard fits each of those principles in the following ways:

1) It can easily be tested. Unlike the complex theories of psychology, it is very easy for this man to give it a try and see if it helps. If it does not, he can drop it and move on to something else.

2 and 3) Placing a Bible verse on the dashboard does not violate any Scriptural principle, nor is it based on worldly assumptions.

4) An essential component of putting the Word into practice is finding a way to *remember* the biblical truth (Jas.1:25). And this is an effort to apply that biblical principle. The principle did not come from human wisdom. It came from James 1:25. The human reasoning is simply an effort to apply that biblical principle.

5) The suggestion is not elevated to the level of Scripture. If the man thinks it is a bad idea, the biblical counselor does not accuse him of sin or look down on him in any way.

6) The counselor makes it clear to him that this idea carries in it no transforming power. By itself it has no ability to generate love or any other virtue in his heart, and it has no power to keep him from sin. If it is used as a method of applying a biblical principle it is good. But if not, it is worthless.

When Should We Refer?

When should a layperson refer someone to a professional psychologist? *Never.* In fact, the more severe a person's problem, the more damage is caused by placing him in the hands of anyone who gives worldly advice or who tries to address spiritual problems with human wisdom. The deeper and more difficult the problem, the more desperately the person needs God's Word—and the greater the harm that can result from relying on human wisdom. If you have a Bible and you know how to interpret and apply it, you hold in your hand that person's greatest hope for recovery.

There may be times when you need to refer someone to a medical doctor (see Chapter 3) or to one who has more biblical knowledge than you, but there is never a time when you will help someone by putting him in the hands of one who uses human wisdom to solve spiritual problems.

As God's children we are forbidden from going to the world for spiritual counsel. The first sentence of the first Psalm tells us, "Blessed is the man who does not walk in the counsel of the wicked." We are not to sit, stand, or walk in the counsel of unbelievers. Why would we seek guidance from people who, according to Scripture, are spiritually blind and do not even know God?

Counseling the "Deep" Issues

Most integrationists are convinced that the Bible is fine for small, superficial, shallow, easy problems; but big, deep, difficult problems should be referred to the psychological professionals. This tendency stems from one of the most fundamental doctrines of psychotherapy—Freud's theory of the unconscious. Perhaps the most extensive impact Freud's teaching has had on modern psychology is the almost universal acceptance of the idea that behaviors are dictated by the unconscious (or subconscious)—an area of one's mind that is for the most part accessible only to the trained psychotherapist. Thoughts, feelings, memories, and experiences are said to be repressed—pushed out of the conscious mind, and shoved into a part of one's being that is deep beneath the surface, but that controls thoughts, behavior, and feelings.

While very few psychotherapists in our day call themselves "Freudian," and there are about as many different approaches to psychotherapy as there are therapists, the one belief almost all of them have in common is the theory of the unconscious. The phrase "Freudian slip" is commonly used even outside of psychological circles (the phrase refers to a slip of the tongue that is thought to reveal a person's true, repressed beliefs).

Perhaps one reason the doctrine of the unconscious is so pervasive is the fact that it is not falsifiable. It violates the first principle in the list above—there is no way to test it. If the unconscious explains everything a person says and does, then no scientific test could possibly disprove the existence of the unconscious. And more importantly, no idea put forth by an expert can be questioned. If the counselee has no access to her own unconscious, but the expert therapist does, the counselee must accept what the expert says. If he tells the counselee that she was abused as a child but does not remember it because the memory was repressed, she has no basis for disputing his claim. Whether the abuse happened or not, the counselor can never be shown to be wrong. The appeal of such a system is obvious. Not only can the counselor never be proved wrong, but the counselee is *utterly* dependent on the experts.

There is nothing unbiblical about the idea that there are varying levels of consciousness or awareness. Clearly we attend to some things more than others. The idea that our problems are so deep that our own conscious mind has *no* access to them, however, is decidedly unbiblical—as is the theory that thoughts, actions, and feelings are controlled by repressed thoughts and experiences from one's past.

It is possible to have a belief or attitude without consciously thinking about it all the time. For example, a person may have a resentful attitude toward someone without realizing it. But if it is brought to the person's attention, the person will be able to see it. There is no such thing as a problem in the unconscious mind that one has no way of perceiving. No problem goes any deeper than the heart—and *the individual has access to his own heart.*

Confidence in God's Word

A wise counselor will not only have enough confidence in God's Word to rely on it alone for wisdom, but will also strive to infuse that confidence into the heart of the counselee. Many people believe they cannot overcome their problem. They may have been led to believe that certain sinful behaviors or attitudes are part of their "condition," and the resulting pessimism can cause a reverse placebo effect. The person can become so convinced that the problem is too deep for Scripture that his heart is not receptive to what Scripture offers. It is crucial, then, for the counselor to continually reassure the person that he or she always has the power to do what God calls us to do, no matter what the circumstances.

1 Corinthians 10:13 No temptation has seized you except what is common to man. And God is faithful; he will not let you be tempted beyond what you can bear. But when you are tempted, he will also provide a way out so that you can stand up under it.

There is no problem so severe that it can override this promise. The Christian is never in a position where he *has* to sin. God's Word offers real hope for all spiritual problems!

The sad reality is many Christians place more confidence in the psychiatrist's degree and training than in the Word of God. They assume the psychiatric experts must be correct, and the Bible must be critiqued in light of their theories. Such an attitude is not only a denial of the sufficiency of Scripture, but it will lead to nothing but confusion since there is no consensus among the psychologists. There are some three hundred different schools of psychotherapy and counseling in the United States alone.[23] And most psychologists do not follow any of them—they mix and match ideas from the various schools. It is folly to lift the world's chaos of confused theorizing above God's holy Word.

Psalm 119 provides us with a dramatic picture of what spiritual growth looks like. Consider the profound implications for the biblical counselor regarding the sufficiency of Scripture:

- Verses 9-16 - the cleansing, purifying effect of God's Word. It purges sin from the heart.
- Verses 25-32 - the renewing effect of Scripture. It preserves life (v. 25), renews thinking (vv. 26-27), renews strength (v. 28) and restores us to the right path (vv. 29-32).
- Verses 41-48 - the empowering effects of Scripture. It enables us to stand against those who oppose us (v. 42), it gives hope (v. 43), it enables us to walk in freedom (v. 45) and to speak without shame even before kings (v. 46).
- Verses 49-56 - the hope that comes from Scripture. It enables the child of God to endure suffering. It brings comfort, encouragement, and joy in hard times.
- Verses 97-104 - the wisdom that comes from God's Word. It makes the believer wiser than his teachers—wiser than people who have more experience, training, and education.
- Verses 105-12 - the direction that comes from God's Word. It is a lamp to our feet and a light for our path. It protects us from the snare and shows us the right way to take.

---

[23] If psychology were a hard science there would not be so many different approaches. There is only one "school" of thought regarding aerodynamics, because if a designer builds an airplane based on a different school of thought, his plane never gets off the ground!

- Verses 121-28 and 153-60 - <u>the deliverance that comes from God's Word</u>. It rescues from trouble and, ultimately, brings salvation.

This overview does not even scratch the surface of what Psalm 119 has to say about God's Word. It is the longest chapter in the entire Bible (176 verses) and every verse is about the power of God's Word. After receiving all that this psalm describes, what more could the soul possibly need?

CHAPTER THREE: COUNSELING THOSE IN PAIN

Your friend is going through some terrible physical or emotional suffering, or is overcome with grief over sin or some great loss, and comes to you for help. She does not have a specific behavior that needs to change; she just needs to know how to handle it. How do you give biblical counsel?

Those who are suffering have two needs: comfort and strength. Some parts of the suffering can be alleviated; others cannot. *Comfort* soothes and restores joy in the areas where pain can be reduced or eliminated, and *strengthening* enables and empowers the person to endure the portion of the pain that must continue.

Comfort

Definition

The most common Greek word for encouragement *(parakaleo)* appears nine times in the New Testament in a context of sorrow. In that context it means *to comfort or console*. Comfort reduces the person's pain.

Sorrow is a disruption of joy. A person is walking along the path of joy some painful ordeal slams into him and knocks him off that path down into the deep, dark pit of sorrow. Comforting means coming alongside the person in that pit, taking him by the arm, and helping him make his way up the steep trail toward renewed joy.

The "coming alongside" part is crucial. The word *parakaleo* literally means *to approach*, or *to be next to* the person. It is a word that speaks of personal nearness. Comfort is not merely helping a person get back to joy; it is helping the person get back to joy *by being near him.*

The person who is in the torment and agony of sorrow is often unable to call to mind anything comforting. He may have a great deal of information in his brain that would be comforting or encouraging, but in the pit of sorrow that information just seems to be locked up in some remote, inaccessible place. God's design in times like that is for a brother or sister in Christ to come close and speak words of tenderness, hope, compassion, and instruction. Even the trained theologian, in times of pain, needs someone else to come near and tell him things he already knows. Pain has a way of clouding the mind to the point where the person is unable to call to mind the principles he needs from the Word of God. Never hesitate to speak even the most basic and elementary principles of comfort from God's Word to the suffering saint.

The person who is in pain needs help doing the hard work of putting his current, specific sorrow into perspective so he can apply the appropriate balm from God's Word to this particular wound. Not just any principle from Scripture will comfort. He needs the right medicine for this ailment.

Comforting a person requires a tender, gentle heart.

1 Thessalonians 2:7,11-12... we were gentle among you, like a mother caring for her little children. ... 11 [W]e dealt with each of you as a father deals with his own children, 12 encouraging, comforting and urging you to live lives worthy of God, who calls you into his kingdom and glory.

First, Paul compares himself to a gentle mother of little children, then four verses later he uses himself as an example of encouraging, comforting, and exhorting others as a loving father deals with his own children. There is no greater illustration of compassion than a loving parent who is deeply moved by the pain of a suffering child. This is our model for comforting one another.

One key element of comfort is refreshment.

2 Corinthians 7:13 By all this we are encouraged. In addition to our own encouragement, we were especially delighted to see how happy Titus was, because his spirit has been refreshed by all of you.

For Timothy, comfort came in the form of refreshment. The term "refreshed" *(anapauo)* is a beautiful word; it literally means *to be made to rest*. Sometimes a person simply needs rest. In his spirit he may be fighting, straining, struggling, embroiled in turmoil and strife—close to the breaking point, and more than anything else he needs someone to come alongside him and speak *refreshing* words from Scripture that enable him to draw near to the one who said, "Come to me all you who are weary … and I will give you rest" (Mt.11:28).

Resistance

Comforting the afflicted is difficult for a number of reasons, not the least of which is the person's own resistance. Ironically, there is something in us that tends to resist comfort when we are in the pit of sorrow.

Psalms 77:2 When I was in distress, I sought the Lord; at night I stretched out untiring hands and my soul refused to be comforted. [24]

The beginning point of comfort, then, is helping the person become willing to be comforted. This calls for great wisdom and sensitivity because grief is appropriate for a time and should not be taken away from the person prematurely.

Proverbs 25:20 Like one who takes away a garment on a cold day … is one who sings songs to a heavy heart.

Grieving can be like a garment. After a horrible loss there is a period of time when the soul just wants to wrap up in a blanket of sorrow and stay there for a while. That is God's design. But it is also His design for times of refreshment and healing to come. There is a time when we must let go of that garment and begin the long, hard trek back up out of the canyon of despair toward the path of joy.

The Motive for Comfort: Compassion

Another factor that makes the ministry of comfort difficult is that it requires taking upon oneself a measure of suffering. The counselor must be willing to leave the path of joy and jump down into the dark pit of despair to come alongside a needy, broken sufferer and actually bear a portion of the load of this suffering.

This is the purpose of compassion. Only a compassionate heart is a powerful enough motivation to drive us to the heavy lifting of the ministry of comfort.

---

[24] See also Gn.37:35 and Jer.31:15.

Colossians 3:12 Clothe yourselves with compassion, kindness, humility, gentleness and patience.

Compassion is a powerful motivation because it is painful. Compassion is the pain a person feels on someone else's behalf that compels a response of mercy. The Greek word for compassion is *splagkna*, which literally means *entrails*. The pain of compassion is felt in the midsection. You see someone in great pain and you feel it in your stomach. Compassion makes you a partner in suffering with the person.

The physical pain of compassion is caused by the secretion of acids that irritate the lining of the intestines. Why does the body inflict pain on itself simply because someone else is suffering? It is a God-given mechanism to assist us in loving one another.[25] The Creator ordered our physiology to express His great heart of compassion. Our capacity for compassion is one of the ways that we are created in His image.

Pain motivates. A person with a rock in his shoe may be too lazy to stop and get it out if the rock is not bothering him. But if it is causing sharp pain he will be take the time to remove it. God instilled in our bodies a pain mechanism (compassion) to help motivate us to be willing to remove the "rock" from our brother's shoe as we begin to feel the pain ourselves.

Compassion arises when one places himself in close proximity to the one suffering and allows that suffering to penetrate his heart. The temptation for the counselor, then, will be to avoid getting that close (and thus bypass compassion). When a brother at church is being plowed under by a devastating trial that has no quick fix, the Christ-like counselor will resist the urge to remain at arm's length, pat him on the back, say "I'm praying for you," and sail out the door without giving it another thought. God calls us to *clothe* ourselves with compassion (Col.3:12).

Attempting to comfort a sorrowing person if your heart is unmoved by the suffering will almost certainly fail. Enter into the pain as much as

---

[25] One wonders how the evolutionist would explain how such a process evolved. It seems that compassion would be the last thing that would make one member of a particular species more likely to outlive those with whom he is in competition for food, mates, etc., for survival. Compassion promotes the survival of the weakest.

possible so you feel something of the grief before you attempt to offer advice.

How to Comfort

Find Comfort for Yourself from God

Once you feel the proper compassion, then what? As you watch the tears stream down and hear the heartbreaking heaves of sobbing from someone who has lost a loved one or has been crushed by some unbearable sorrow, what is the procedure for comforting that troubled soul? The answer is in 2 Corinthians 1.

2 Corinthians 1:3 Praise be to the God and Father of our Lord Jesus Christ, the Father of compassion and the God of all comfort, 4 who comforts us in all our troubles, so that we can comfort those in any trouble with the comfort we ourselves have received from God.

That passage is often misunderstood. Many have taken it to mean if a person suffers some calamity, that person will then be enabled to comfort others who suffer that same calamity. Since he has been through a similar trial he will be able to empathize, and will automatically be able to bring comfort to others who suffer the same kind of hardship.

That is not what the passage says, nor is it even true. There are plenty of people who have lost a loved one or who have been diagnosed with cancer or who have suffered terrible heartbreak in a relationship who have no idea how to comfort someone else who goes through the same thing.

Furthermore, the passage does not restrict the comfort to those who suffer the same kind of trial. Just the opposite—it promises that we will be able to comfort those "in any trouble."

Why is it that some people who have suffered are able to comfort fellow-sufferers, and others are not? It is because the ability to comfort is not automatic just because you have suffered. The ability to comfort others comes *only when you have received comfort from God*. Look at the text again:

2 Corinthians 1:4 ...we can comfort those in any trouble <u>with the comfort we ourselves have received from God</u>.

The person who suffers but fails to receive comfort from God will not have any increased ability to help others find comfort in God.

Many people never do find comfort in God. They endure some terrible trial and respond by drowning their sorrows in some indulgence or distraction, or they find comfort from some other earthly source, but they do not know how to take their Bible off to some quiet place and seek hard after God and receive comfort from Him.

My ten-year-old niece, Bree, once took in a stray kitten that was close to death and nursed it back to health. The cat became the family pet. They named it Sugar, and Bree loved it. Morning, noon, and night Bree would say something about how cute Sugar was. One day Bree was horrified to see a dog attack and kill Sugar. Bree was crushed. The first thing she did was to go into her room and open her Bible and read Psalm 34 about how God is close to the brokenhearted. A couple of nights later her parents were praying with her and Bree said, "God, thank you for giving me that feeling You gave me in my heart when I asked You for comfort." There are thousands of people around the world who watched their beloved pet die who have no idea how to show another fellow-sufferer how to find comfort from God because they never received comfort from God. If you suffer a loss, those are not the people you want to come knocking on your door. You want someone like little Bree, who will be able to come alongside you in your grief, show compassion because she understands what it is like, but then not stop at showing compassion, but to also put a Bible in your hand and say—"Here's what God showed me":

Psalm 34:18 The Lord is close to the brokenhearted and saves those who are crushed in spirit.

"And after God reminded me of that verse I prayed and poured out my heart to Him and asked Him for comfort. And when I did I felt a feeling of peace inside me. And even though I was still sad, I could feel God comforting me and giving me strength and hope, and I could tell the presence of God was close to me, and He was drawing near and touching my heart and healing it."

Those who suffer a loss need more than just someone who can empathize. They need someone who has succeeded in finding comfort from God and who can take them by the hand and show them how to find it. Giving comforting ideas that ought to work in theory, very often does not work. What does work is showing a brother or sister a tried and true process of seeking comfort from God that has worked in your life.

So how do you find comfort from God in your sorrow? Comfort comes when God grants an experience of the nearness of His presence.[26]

Zephaniah 3:17 The LORD your God is <u>with</u> you ... he will <u>quiet</u> you with his love.

Hosea 5:15, 6:1-2 ... they will <u>seek my face (presence)</u>;[27] in their misery they will earnestly seek me." 6:1 Come, let us return to the LORD... <u>he will bind up our wounds</u>. 2 ... he will restore us, that we may live in his presence.

It is when we experience the nearness of God's presence that our troubled hearts are quieted, our wounds are bound up and healed, and joy is restored.

Psalm 16:11 You reveal the path of life to me; <u>in Your presence is abundant joy</u>; in Your right hand are eternal pleasures.[28]

Psalm 21:6 Surely you have granted him eternal blessings and <u>made him glad with the joy of your presence</u>.

Psalm 4:6-7 Many are asking, "Who can show us any good?" Let <u>the light of your face</u> (presence) shine upon us, O LORD. 7 You have filled my heart with greater <u>joy</u> than when their grain and new wine abound.

Conversely, when God withdraws His presence (or turns His face away), the results are anxiety, sorrow, wasting or melting away, dismay, and internal anguish (Ps.32:1-2, 88:14-15, 30:7, Isa. 64:7).

The comforting, soul-satisfying, joy-producing effect of God's presence is one of His attributes. It is part of His nature, which means it would be impossible for a person to experience the presence of God and not be comforted, refreshed, and filled with joy. Unlike earthly pleasures, it is not a matter of taste. No matter who the person is, it is

---

[26] God exists everywhere. He observes and knows everything (Jer. 23:24), and is upholding and sustaining every molecule in the universe (Col. 1:17). When Scripture speaks of God's presence, however, it refers something more than His existence. The Hebrew word for presence is the common word for face. The "presence" (face) of God is not a reference to His mere existence in a place; it refers to God turning His face favorably toward a person. It is personal and relational. You are in God's presence when God has turned His attention toward you in a way that enables you to have a favorable, personal interaction with Him.

[27] The Hebrew word PANEH is translated either "presence" or "face." When used of God there is no difference. The face of God and the presence of God refer to the same thing.

[28] Author's translation.

impossible for a human soul to experience God's presence and not be fully satisfied (Ps.16:11).

The Path to His Presence

So how does one draw near to the presence of God? Bree had it right—turn to the Scriptures! Paul did not say, "Encourage each other with human wisdom." He said, "Encourage each other with these words" (1 Thess. 4:18). Titus 1:9 requires that an elder in the church must hold firmly to the trustworthy message as it has been taught, so that he can encourage others by sound doctrine. If you want to be qualified to encourage others, study God's Word, not the theories of man.

Psalm 19:7-8 The law of the Lord is perfect, <u>reviving the soul</u>. ... 8 The precepts of the Lord are right, <u>giving joy to the heart</u>. The commands of the Lord are radiant, <u>giving light to the eyes</u>.

Psalm 119:76 May your unfailing love be my <u>comfort</u>, <u>according to your promise</u> to your servant.

Psalm 119:82 My eyes fail, looking for your promise; I say, "When will you comfort me?"

Psalm 119:92 If your law had not been my delight, I would have perished in my affliction.

It must be noted at this point that the goal in opening the Scriptures is not merely gathering comforting thoughts and concepts. The goal is to use the Word of God to have an actual personal interaction with God Himself. The reason it is possible to read (and understand) a psalm one day and receive no comfort, and then read it another day and receive great comfort, is that the comfort comes not from the act of reading, but from the presence of God.

God has promised never to leave or forsake His people[29] and to be with them always, even to the end of the age,[30] so there is one sense in which God is always with His people. There is another sense, however, in which God was sometimes far from His people.[31] The promise that He is always with His people means fellowship with Him is always *available*. There are times when greater fellowship is available than

---

[29] Dt.31:6.
[30] Mt.28:20.
[31] Ps.101:2, 13:1.

other times, but *some* fellowship with God is always available to the believer. There is never a time when seeking fellowship with God would be a fruitless effort.[32] God promises success when His people seek Him.[33] The genuine, earnest seeker should always expect a response from God.[34]

This is wonderful news for the grieving heart because it means there is never a time when joy and satisfaction of soul are out of reach—even in the midst of great pain. Any time a believer is not experiencing satisfying joy, it is always because he is not experiencing something he could be experiencing—fellowship with God.

While it is true that God is always with His people in the sense that fellowship with him is always available, there is another sense in which it is possible for a believer to be far from God. While fellowship with God is always possible, His people are not always experiencing fellowship with Him. To experience fellowship with Him the believer must seek it, as David did in times of dryness and distance from God. Such seeking requires considerable effort. In Psalm 63:1, David provides an indication of the degree of effort that is required in seeking God during a time of relational distance: "Earnestly I seek you." The term "earnestly"[35] implies a certain degree of difficulty, as one does not earnestly seek that which is easily found. Finding fellowship with God requires nothing less than *wholehearted* seeking. "But if from there you seek the LORD your God, you will find Him if you look for Him with all your heart and with all your soul."[36] God is a great and awesome king, and He will not be belittled by allowing Himself to be found by half-hearted seekers.[37]

The way to receive comfort from God, then, is by seeking His presence by means of His Word. The Scriptures open the seeker's eyes

---

[32] Isa.45:19.

[33] 1 Chrn.28:9, 15:2, Pr.8:17, Lam.3:25, Heb.11:6.

[34] J.A. Alexander, *The prophecies of Isaiah*, (Grand Rapids: Zondervan, 1977), 186.

[35] שָׁחַר here and ἐκζητέω in Heb.11:6

[36] Dt.4:29. See also Jer.29:13, 1 Chron.22:19, Ps.78:34, 119:2,10.

[37] Mal.1:6-14.

to the glory of God in ways that draw him close to the healing, comforting, joy-giving presence of God.[38]

The following are some particularly comforting passages:

Psalm 5—Protect me!
Psalm 16—God is my only good
Psalm 18—God responds to my trouble with creation-rattling zeal
Psalm 23—The Lord is my Shepherd
Psalm 25—I look to You for satisfaction, guidance, redemption
Psalm 32—Blessed is the forgiven sinner!
Psalm 34—God is near to the brokenhearted
Psalm 36—The Lord is the source of all good
Psalm 37—Do not fret over the successes of the wicked
Psalm 42-43—I long for God, my soul is downcast
Psalm 46—God is our refuge and is more powerful than any threat
Psalm 51—Have mercy on me, a sinner!
Psalm 62—My soul finds rest in God alone
Psalm 63—I long for God in a dry and weary land
Psalm 77—Comfort from recalling God's past deeds
Psalm 84—I long and faint to be in Your presence
Psalm 90—You are our home, satisfy us with Your love
Psalm 91—God will protect you
Psalm 93—The Lord reigns!
Psalm 103—Praise Him for forgiving, redeeming, restoring love!
Psalm 121—God will watch over you
Psalm 125—The LORD preserves His people
Psalm 131—I have stilled and quieted my soul hoping in You
Psalm 139—You know me thoroughly
Lamentations 3—His mercies are new every morning
Isaiah 40—Comfort for God's people
Isaiah 42—The Compassionate Messiah
Isaiah 55—Come, all you who are thirsty!
Isaiah 57:14-21—Comfort for the contrite

---

[38] Do not think of this as a kind of magical incantation. Experiencing the presence of God comes only as a result of correctly interpreting the Scriptures and responding in faith to the truth that is revealed.

Matthew 5:1-13—Blessed are the needy and persecuted

John 13-15—Let not your hearts be troubled

Romans 8—Nothing can separate you from His love

2 Corinthians 4:6-18—Our frailty glorifies Him, and our suffering accomplishes glory for us.

Revelation 3:7-13—Hold on until I come!

For promises addressing specific kinds of suffering see Appendix 1: "Promises to Trust When…"

The Nature of God

Nothing is more important in comforting the grieving soul than understanding the combination of God's goodness and His sovereignty. Those two attributes enable the child of God to rejoice in any suffering.

Few chapters in the Bible are more comforting to the suffering soul than Lamentations 3. The writer of Lamentations was suffering full-blown, clinical depression. And he describes that depression in such vivid detail that one wonders if anything could ever bring him out of such despair. Half-way through Chapter 3, however, his depression suddenly gives way to hope! What was it that had the power to bring him from the pits of depression to the dawn of hope? It was something he called to mind.

Lamentations 3:21 Yet this I call to mind and therefore I have hope...

The words that follow are words about the nature of God. Particularly striking are the words in verse 33.

Lamentations 3:32-33 Though he brings grief, he will show compassion, so great is his unfailing love. 33 For he does not willingly bring affliction or grief to the children of men.

It is God who <u>brings</u> the grief. He did not just allow it—He sent it. However, He did not do so "willingly" (literally, not "from the heart"). What could possibly compel God to do something He does not want to do? Why would He bring grief into your life that He does not want to bring into your life? The only thing that can compel God to do that is His love. Just as a compassionate EMT cringes when he does some painful procedure on an accident victim to save his life, so God cringes when His own love for you requires of Him something that causes you pain.

God would never needlessly bring suffering. There must be a reason. Furthermore, that reason must be great enough to justify the degree of suffering. God would not use excruciating pain to achieve some small benefit that could be achieved some other way.

Think of the torture God is putting Himself through by requiring you to suffer. What would it be like to watch your own child suffer this much? It would be agony for you if you love your child. And God loves you more than you love your child, so watching you suffer is more painful to the heart of God than we can even imagine. Why would God put Himself through the torture of watching one of His beloved children suffer unless the benefit were many times greater than the suffering?

This is a hard principle for many people to accept because they cannot imagine what benefit could possibly come from their suffering. Such people must be reminded that God is not limited by what we can imagine! Picture a man who is in a terrible car accident that breaks all his ribs and causes massive internal injuries. As the EMTs scramble to help him, they ask the man's wife to assist. "Press down on his chest wound while I do this procedure—otherwise he will die." His ribs are broken, so this causes excruciating pain. In the delirium of his suffering the man has no idea what is going on. All he can see is that his wife is inflicting terrible pain on him. He has no idea why, but not even a flicker of anger rises in his heart toward her, because he knows her so well, even though he has no explanation for why she would do this, he knows without a doubt that she would never do something like that unless it was the most loving possible thing for him. That is how we look at God in times of suffering. It is not necessary to be able to imagine how this suffering could be a good thing. It is only necessary to know God well enough to know that He would never do anything other than that which is most loving and beneficial for His children.

Now consider this—how great a benefit would it require for you to be willing to put someone you love through this suffering you are going through? Maybe you have endured 20 years in a terrible marriage, or decades of physical pain, or horrific abuse as a child. What benefit would be enough for you to be willing to put your child through that much suffering? Perhaps your answer is, "I can't even think of any benefit so great that it would be worth it."

Now think about God. His love for you is greater than your love for your child, so God's agony in watching you suffer is far greater than the agony of any parent. And God has full power to bring this suffering to an end at any moment. So why doesn't He? <u>The only explanation is that the benefit that is being achieved by this suffering is so great that it is worth <i>this much</i> suffering!</u> And that means it must be a benefit that is far more wonderful than anything you can possibly imagine (since you cannot imagine a benefit that would be worth it). How grand must be the purpose of this suffering for God to be willing to go through the agony of watching you suffer when He does not want to!

The greater the suffering, then, the greater must be the purpose God is accomplishing through that suffering. The sorrows and troubles we face in the process of serving God are more than worth it because they accomplish outcomes so glorious that they cannot even be compared to our sufferings.

Romans 8:18 I consider that our present sufferings are not worth comparing with the glory that will be revealed in us.

We can give the suffering saint this guarantee: "When you see what this suffering accomplishes for you, you will say, 'I am <i>so glad</i> that suffering happened!!!'"

This principle is a wonderful comfort to those who are suffering, but it is only a comfort if they understand both God's goodness and God's sovereignty. If the person believes God is good but does not control all things, then this suffering might not have any meaning at all. It may just be a fluke that happened outside of God's control. And if the person understands God's sovereignty and not His goodness, he may think God is doing it but it is not ultimately a good thing. It is crucial for the suffering Christian to understand that God controls all things <i>and</i> God only does good things.

Psalm 62:11-12 One thing God has spoken, two things have I heard: that you, O God, are <u>strong</u>, 12 and that you, O Lord, are <u>loving</u>.

Isaiah 46:10-11 My purpose will stand, and I will do all that I please. 11 ... What I have said, that will I bring about; what I have planned, that will I do.

Ephesians 1:11 In him we were also chosen ... according to the plan of him who <u>works out everything in conformity with the purpose of his will</u>

Deuteronomy 32:4 He is the Rock, <u>his works are perfect</u>, and <u>all</u> his ways are just. A faithful God who does <u>no wrong</u>, upright and just is he.

It is also important to understand that our comfort comes not from thinking about the fact that it could have been worse ("Well, at least *that* didn't happen…"). The Christian sufferer must understand that it is the suffering itself that brings about the good things.

2 Corinthians 4:17 Our light and momentary <u>troubles are accomplishing</u> for us from excess to excess an eternal weight of <u>glory</u>.[39]

Notice that it is not that God brings about glorious things in spite of the suffering, but rather in the suffering itself that accomplishes the glory.

And for that reason Paul regards his suffering as "light" (referring to weight) and "momentary" (referring to time). Such a description sounds absurd coming from Paul, whose sufferings were extreme to say the least. But they were extreme only in comparison to other things in this life. Compared to what is coming in the age to come (which is the focus in this passage), this life's suffering is indeed ephemeral and small.

Comfort for the Contrite

There are many different causes for the sorrow in the lives of God's people. Sometimes it is caused by great loss, other times by fear, relational troubles, physical pain, disappointment, or unfulfilled desire. But the most painful suffering of all for the believer is the suffering of guilt. There is nothing that causes more damage and nothing the child of God hates more than his own sin. And yet, tragically, it is this kind of sufferer that many Christians are the least willing to comfort.

Should our compassion be withheld when someone's suffering is due to his own sin? Not at all! God has compassion on our sinful condition. In fact, it is to His compassion that we appeal when we ask for forgiveness and restoration after we have sinned.

Psalm 51:1 Have mercy on me, O God, according to your unfailing love; according to your great compassion blot out my transgressions.

If our sinful condition generates compassion in the heart of God, why not in the hearts of God's people? Many times it is because of anger. The person's sin caused pain for those around him, so those people have no compassion.

---

[39] Literal translation.

In other cases it is because of the misguided idea that it is the Church's job to punish sinners. It is not. Never is the Church instructed to punish a repentant sinner or "teach him a lesson." This applies to friends and spouses as well. Chastisement is God's job, not ours.

Another common excuse for withholding comfort is a concern for justice. The fear is that if the repentant sinner is comforted he will be "getting away with it." Again—God will make sure no one gets away with anything. He is perfectly capable of bringing consequences for sin without our assistance. God does sometimes use people as His tools of chastisement, but He also punishes those very people if they are eager to be used in that way (Jer. 50-51).

Our task as God's people is not to punish or teach lessons, but to be the instruments of comfort and restoration. In Corinth, when a man had sinned, been disciplined, and then repented, Paul urged the church to forgive him and restore him to fellowship:

2 Corinthians 2:7 Now ... you ought to forgive and comfort (*parakaleo*) him, so that he will not be overwhelmed by excessive sorrow.

The unrepentant sinner must be reproved and rebuked, but the *repentant* sinner is to be comforted and restored, not punished. The enemy is letting loose all his crippling, discouraging, demoralizing accusations on the person, and that person probably feels it is wrong for him to defend himself, so he allows himself to be pummeled to the ground by the enemy. It is our job to step in with the life-giving, redeeming, restoring promises from Scripture about God's forgiveness to keep our brother from being destroyed by the enemy through "excessive sorrow."

When a person is crushed with guilt and regret, remind him of the sufficiency of the cross. The price Jesus paid was enough for that sin! Remind him of the eagerness with which the father ran to embrace the prodigal son in Luke 15. Comforting passages from God's Word about forgiveness are easy to find. Some especially wonderful ones are Psalm 103:8-14, Isaiah 57:15-19, Micah 7:8-9, Psalm 30:4-12, Psalm 53, Psalm 32:1-7, and 1 John 1:9.

Strengthening

As important as comfort is, it is not the only thing the suffering person needs. God has given us the power to reduce and even eliminate some kinds of pain, but not all of it. In some cases, a great deal of pain will remain. So in addition to comfort, the suffering person also needs strength.

It is hard to imagine the despair that must have gripped David while he was running for his life from King Saul—God's anointed whom David honored and respected. It was then that Jonathan caught up to David at Horesh and did something which serves as one of the great illustrations of biblical counseling in Scripture.

1 Samuel 23:16 And Saul's son Jonathan went to David at Horesh and helped him find strength in God.

That is the role of the biblical counselor when a brother is suffering.

Acts 15:32 Judas and Silas, who themselves were prophets, said much to encourage and strengthen the brothers.

1 Thessalonians 3:2 We sent Timothy, who is our brother and God's fellow worker in spreading the gospel of Christ, to strengthen and encourage you in your faith....

1 Thessalonians 5:11,14 Therefore encourage one another and build each other up, just as in fact you are doing. ... 14 And we urge you, brothers, warn those who are idle, encourage the timid, help the weak, be patient with everyone.

The word translated *timid* is literally *little-souled*. It refers to someone with a weak, timid, or frail spirit who needs to be fortified, built up, and strengthened. The weak person does not have the strength to do what he should do (for example, to seek godly counsel). Sometimes strengthening the timid and weak begins with taking the initiative to pursue them and offer encouragement, even when they have not asked for it.

Authoritative Encouragement

In order to infuse strength into a weak brother or sister the counselor must encourage compassionately, humbly, skillfully, wisely, and authoritatively. The authority with which God has called us to encourage one another is an often neglected, yet crucially important principle in our efforts to strengthen one another.

It is often assumed that unless the counselor has personally experienced the same kind of trouble the counselee is enduring, he is in no position to offer comfort, strength, or instruction. This belief has bred a generation of pain snobs. Pain snobs are people who think you have nothing to offer them because you have not experienced what they have experienced. (*You can't comfort me because you don't know how I feel.*)

It is a good thing to recognize that the person's suffering might be beyond anything you have experienced. We really ought to cut people some slack when they are suffering, and we need to realize that doing the right thing might be much, much more difficult for them in their situation than it is for us. However, no matter how extreme their suffering, it is not beyond the reach of the power of God's Word.

"But don't I have to first earn the right to be heard?" No—unless what you are offering is human wisdom. If you are going to urge someone to put his savings into a particular investment, or if you are giving medical advice, the value of your counsel is related to your expertise in those areas. But if you are merely repeating something that someone else has said, your expertise is irrelevant. The only thing that matters is the expertise of the one you are quoting. Therefore anytime you tell a person something directly from the Bible, you have every right and responsibility to do so with authority because you are quoting God. To the person who says, "You don't know how I feel" we respond, "You're right, but God knows how you feel, which is why instead of giving you my wisdom I am only going to offer you God's Word."

This principle applies whether the goal is comfort, or strengthening, or exhorting.

Authoritative Comforting

When counseling a person who has experienced something horrible, such as the loss of a child, the counselor does not have to sheepishly say, "Maybe this will help but probably not …" The comfort offered in Scripture is, without any question, the kind of comfort a hurting human soul needs. It is God's comfort. The promises of God *will* do him good if he believes them.

Authoritative Strengthening

When a person is crushed under the weight of some trial and is so weak and fragile that the task of strengthening him enough to be able to bear the load seems impossible, the faithful counselor will remember that the Word of God in the hands of the Holy Spirit is more than enough to strengthen any child of God enough to carry the load God has placed on him.

Colossians 1:9-11 ...we have not stopped praying for you and asking God to fill you with the knowledge of his will through all spiritual wisdom and understanding. And we pray this in order that you may live a life worthy of the Lord ... <u>being strengthened with all power according to his glorious might so that you may have great endurance and patience.</u>

Authoritative Exhorting

Not only do we have the right to offer people comfort and strength from God's Word, we have the responsibility to *command* them to accept God's Word.

Titus 2:15 Exhort and rebuke <u>with all authority.</u>[40]

What about a situation where someone has been abused, raped, or tortured? Do you have a right to demand that the person respond in a godly way? Obviously it would be wrong to do so in a harsh, uncaring, or insensitive way. We must always maintain compassion—especially when a person has endured great suffering. We must also recognize, however, that we have no choice but to humbly, gently, and lovingly *require* of people what God requires in Scripture. We are not justified in editing or dialing back what God has said because of our own self-styled ideas about what is truly compassionate. If God delivered something in His Word as an imperative, and we morph it into a suggestion, we are false witnesses who are misrepresenting God's Word.

A doctor who knows for sure he has the medicine for your sickness does not tap-dance around the solution offering apologies and caveats. He simply says, "Take this!" Instruction from the Word of God is what a suffering person needs. He may not want it, but it is the best thing for

---

[40] Author's translation.

him and it is wrong to withhold it, or to offer it as something less than what it really is. We must tell people the truth about what God requires. So in that sense, we must "demand" what God demands. Anytime you proclaim the Word of God, whether it is from behind a pulpit or sitting on a couch with a friend, you have the responsibility to proclaim it with authority.

Willingness to Suffer

One of the most important ways to infuse strength into the suffering soul is to provide a biblical perspective on suffering. For the world, suffering is an intolerable, unacceptable intrusion into life that must be eliminated at any cost. This makes sense for them. This life is all they have, so if it is spoiled with suffering then all is lost. But we are citizens of another kingdom, and our comfort is there, not here. Furthermore, God has promised that all our suffering achieves grand, eternal purposes that benefit us and glorify Him.[41]

If a person thinks of suffering as an intolerable intrusion, ongoing suffering will be unbearable. When a person thinks, *I must feel better. My only hope for happiness is to find a way to escape this pain!*— enduring long-term suffering with no end in sight becomes overwhelming. The anxiety of worrying about the inability to escape the pain, and the fear that relief may never come, compound the pain of the suffering when the person believes that relief is essential for happiness. In some cases depression lingers on mainly because of the fear of not being able to recover from the depression! Some people have actually recovered from depression simply by saying, *Father, if this is what You have for me right now, I will accept it from Your hand. If You say this is what I need for now, then it's OK for me to feel this way.* Where there is a clear understanding about the crucial role suffering plays in the Christian life, that knowledge alone can help a great deal in enabling the person to endure it.

1 Peter 4:12 Dear friends, do not be surprised at the painful trial you are suffering, as though something strange were happening to you.

---

[41] Ro. 8:17, 28, 2 Cor. 4:17.

If our Master, the Lord Jesus Christ, was not exempt from suffering it would be ludicrous for us to assume we should be exempt (Jn.15:18-19).

Acts 9:16 I will show [Paul] how much he must suffer for my name.

2 Corinthians 1:8-9 We do not want you to be uninformed, brothers, about the hardships we suffered in the province of Asia. We were under great pressure, far beyond our ability to endure, so that we despaired even of life. 9 Indeed, in our hearts we felt the sentence of death. But this happened that we might not rely on ourselves but on God, who raises the dead.

Every parent knows what it is like to struggle with a toddler who does not want to be held. He desperately wants down—not understanding that there is busy traffic or some other threat from which he must be protected. The more the child struggles the more tightly his father has to grip him—causing even still more discomfort. If there is pain it is caused by his own resistance. If he would simply submit to his father and accept the fact that he must be held at this moment, he could be at rest in his father's arms. Very often it is our resisting and struggling and refusal to accept suffering that is the cause of much of our pain. So one way to strengthen a person who is experiencing the "mighty hand of God" (suffering) is to encourage him to simply stop resisting and accept it from God's hand.

1 Peter 5:6-7 Humble yourselves, therefore, under God's mighty hand, that he may lift you up in due time. 7 Cast all your anxiety on him because he cares for you.

Consider the Benefits of Suffering

When we suffer, Scripture calls us to count it all joy (Jas.1:2), rejoice (Ro.5:3), and leap for joy (Lk.6:23) because of all the amazing benefits that we receive through suffering. For the believer, suffering is always good (Ps.119:75). Unbelievers suffer in ways that do not benefit them, but all our suffering as believers is beneficial in at least twenty-three ways (no doubt there are others I have not thought of). These benefits are enjoyed in greater or lesser degrees depending upon the person's response to the suffering, but the benefits are always available to believers when we suffer.

Since the benefits of suffering, in great measure, depend on having the right response to the suffering, help the counselee understand how to respond in ways to gain these benefits. For each of the following benefits, a description of the benefit will be followed by a brief statement on the right way to respond in order to gain that benefit.

1. Suffering Accomplishes God's Perfect Purposes

Romans 8:28 And we know that in all things God works for the good of those who love him, who have been called according to his purpose.

Deuteronomy 32:4 He is the Rock, his works are perfect, and all his ways are just. A faithful God who does no wrong, upright and just is he.

Everything God does, He does for a reason—an infinitely good reason. He does not waste His time and He does nothing arbitrarily. God only does good things (Dt.32:4). Oh, what a blessing it is to know that absolutely everything that ever happens to us—down to the smallest detail—is a purposeful, intentional, loving, wise, beneficial step in a grand, glorious design! Every moment of every day you are experiencing the unfolding of the great drama of God's perfect providential plan.

From an earthly perspective it is a frightening thing to be in the midst of the huge, massive powers that seem to determine what happens to us (like the weather, or the millions of people around us, or a hundred other threats that are beyond our control). The temptation is to feel like a mouse in the midst of some giant machinery, running around trying to avoid being crushed in the gears.

We are indeed inside a giant machine, but the machine is God's, and you are not a mouse, but a cog. The heavy, steel gears that are turning you are doing so by God's design and under His control. This truth alone should make all our suffering and everything else that happens to us exceedingly precious in our sight.

Respond to all suffering with the 1:5 principle. For every one thought about your hard circumstances, think five thoughts about God's purposes. Think about His purposes for as long as it takes for your heart to begin to rejoice in them.

2. God's Tool for the Advance of the Gospel

Philippians 1:12-14 Now I want you to know, brothers, that what has happened to me has really served to advance the gospel. 13 As a result, it has become clear throughout the whole palace guard and to everyone else that I am in chains for Christ. 14 Because of my chains, most of the brothers in the Lord have been encouraged to speak the word of God more courageously and fearlessly.

2 Timothy 1:8, 11-12... join with me in suffering for the gospel, by the power of God ... 11 of this gospel I was appointed a herald and an apostle and a teacher. 12 That is why I am suffering as I am.

In His wisdom, God has chosen suffering as one of the primary tools He uses for the effective spread of the gospel and the encouragement of the saints.

Gain this benefit by considering how much more important the work of the kingdom is than temporal comfort. And rejoice in God's ability to bring about eternal fruit through your suffering even when you cannot see how your suffering will accomplish anything.

3. Purification

Job 23:10 When he has tested me, I will come forth as gold.

Psalm 119:67 Before I was afflicted I went astray, but now I obey your word.

God uses suffering in countless different ways to increase our holiness and obedience. Even Jesus learned obedience through suffering (Heb.5:8). Some examples of godliness that can be gained from suffering are perseverance (Jas.1:2-3, Ro.5:3), character (Ro.5:3-4), hope (Ro.5:3-4), and humility (2 Cor.12:7). Suffering increases our sense of dependence on God and protects us from becoming puffed up with self-reliance, which is our greatest enemy. Our suffering is training from our Father in heaven. When it is chastisement for sin it teaches us to forsake sin. When it is not related to a particular sin, it trains us in other ways. Either way, it is training that results in "a harvest of righteousness" (Heb.12:7,11).

Respond to suffering by reminding your soul how weak, needy, and helpless it is, and strive to increase your sense of dependence on God.

Let your suffering humble you. The humbling is not automatic; so cooperate with it.

4. Increased Power from God

2 Corinthians 12:7-10 To keep me from becoming conceited because of these surpassingly great revelations, there was given me a thorn in my flesh, a messenger of Satan, to torment me. 8 Three times I pleaded with the Lord to take it away from me. 9 But he said to me, "My grace is sufficient for you, for my power is made perfect in weakness." Therefore I will boast all the more gladly about my weaknesses, so that Christ's power may rest on me. 10 That is why, for Christ's sake, I delight in weaknesses, in insults, in hardships, in persecutions, in difficulties. For when I am weak, then I am strong.

When we realize that our suffering opens up greater possibilities for God to demonstrate His power in our lives, we will delight in our sufferings. Lack of suffering tends toward self-reliance which reduces the level of divine power at work in your life.

The way Paul responded to his suffering so as to cause the power of Christ to rest upon him was by boasting all the more gladly in his weaknesses and sufferings. To boast means to regard them as a badge of honor and to think about them as being of great value.

5. Exposure of Faith and Unbelief

Luke 8:13 They believe for a while, but in the time of testing they fall away.

1 Peter 1:6-7 Now for a little while you may have had to suffer grief in all kinds of trials. 7 These have come so that your faith ... may be proved genuine

James 1:2-3 Consider it pure joy, my brothers, whenever you face trials of many kinds, 3 because you know that the testing of your faith develops perseverance.

All suffering is a test. Each trial exposes the genuineness or lack of genuineness of our faith. When a trial pushes a person away from God, that exposes the fact that faith, in that area, is not real. When suffering drives a person toward God, that exposes the fact that his faith is real. The prime example of this is Job. God sent intense and relentless suffering into Job's life for the purpose of demonstrating that Job's faith was indeed real.

Regardless of the outcome of the test, the test itself is a priceless gift. When suffering exposes a lack of faith, that alerts us to a very important reality (like discovering cancer in the early stages so it can be cured). When suffering exposes genuine faith, that glorifies God.

Gain this benefit from suffering by looking carefully at the test results. Did it drive you toward or away from God? Did you respond in a way consistent with faith? If so, rejoice! If not, be glad that the deadly disease was spotted in time, and strive to shore up that area of weak faith.

6. Ability to Glorify God through Faith

1 Peter 1:6-7 Now for a little while you may have had to <u>suffer</u> grief in all kinds of <u>trials</u>. 7 <u>These have come so that your faith</u> ... <u>may result in</u> praise, <u>glory and honor</u> when Jesus Christ is revealed.

The book of Job begins with a conversation between God and Satan in which the Devil questions the validity of Job's worship. He claims that Job only worships God because God has bought him off, and that if God took away the blessings, Job would curse God. In essence, Satan is saying that God is not really worthy to be worshipped apart from bribing that worship out of people. When Job lost everything and still worshipped God, that showed God to be worthy of worship and honored Him before Satan and all the angels and demons, as well as anyone who has ever read the book of Job.

The greater a person's suffering, the greater that person's ability to glorify God. The only way to please God is by faith (Heb.11:6), and faith is never so God-honoring as when it is in the midst of suffering. Anyone can say, "Praise the Lord" when there is blessing. But when a person remains devoted to the Lord even in severe pain—oh, how that honors God! When we suffer, we have a means of honoring God that the angels can never experience.

Furthermore, the more we suffer and remain faithful in this life, the more honor and glory Jesus will receive from our lives on the Day He returns (1 Pet. 1:7).

Gain this benefit simply by continuing to be faithful to God— especially in those times when the suffering seems so baffling, and in your wildest imagination you cannot see a good purpose for it. Memorize Job's responses:

Job 1:20-22 Then he fell to the ground in worship 21 and said: "Naked I came from my mother's womb, and naked I will depart. The Lord gave and the Lord has taken away; may the name of the Lord be praised." 22 In all this, Job did not sin by charging God with wrongdoing.

Job 2:10 "Shall we accept good from God, and not trouble?"

Respond that way and then sit back and enjoy God's smile on your faith.

7. Greater Ability TO Experience Various Attributes of God

1 Peter 4:13 Rejoice that you participate in the sufferings of Christ, so that you may be overjoyed when his glory is revealed.

Note carefully, it is not our suffering that results in being overjoyed at the Second Coming—it is our rejoicing in that suffering. Those who have rejoiced in their suffering for Christ more in this life will have greater joy on that Day. Those who have rejoiced less in their suffering for Christ will have lesser joy on that Day.

One of the reasons for our increased capacity for joy at the return of Christ is the fact that our suffering enables us to experience all the attributes of God that can only be experienced in the midst of pain. There is no greater thing than to have a favorable experience of an attribute of God. Experiencing what God is like is the greatest thing in the universe. The angels in heaven get to experience many of the aspects of God's glory firsthand. But think of how many attributes of God they can never experience. No angel will ever experience what it is like to be forgiven. None of them will ever feel God's compassion or pity or mercy. Those attributes of God cannot be experienced apart from suffering. The fact that we are subjected to sin and suffering places us in a position to experience God's tenderness, restoration, refreshment, guidance, companionship in the midst of loneliness, rescue from danger, peace in the midst of turmoil, and so many other marvelous facets of His glory.

One example of this is God's compassion and pity. Think of a child who gets a scrape and runs into the house crying, and then stops crying and goes on his merry way after mom gives it a kiss. What happened? Is there less physical pain? No. The pain is exactly the same after the kiss. The reason he ran in crying, and the reason he stops crying after the kiss is because compassion is such a delightful thing to experience. And as sweet as it is to receive it from mom, it is far more wonderful to receive it from God. In fact, it is better to suffer and receive God's pity than to never have suffered at all. Oh how important it is that we learn to enjoy God's compassion and pity when we suffer.

Gain this benefit by seeking God as your refuge, comforter, healer, guide, counselor, redeemer, restorer, shield, fortress, and rock.

8. *Increased Understanding of the Goodness of the Presence of God*

Psalms 13:1 How long, O Lord? Will you forget me forever? How long will you hide your face from me?

One of our greatest problems is our inability to appreciate what is so wonderful about the presence of God. We can read about it in Scripture, but often our emotions and desires do not get on board with what we know intellectually. But when we suffer, and we say to our soul, "See, the presence of God is so good; this is a sample of what it's like to be a little further from that presence"—that trains the soul to appreciate (with mind and heart) how wonderful the presence of God is.

9. *Increased Thirst for God's Presence*

In Psalm 63 David was going through horrible suffering. The person he probably loved most in the world, Absalom, had turned against him. His own son had rebelled against him, taken his throne by force, and was hunting David down to kill him. David was in unbelievable agony over this. He had been the greatest king of the world, and now he was in the desert running for his life from his son. The physical suffering of being out there in the desert combined with the emotional agony, felt unbearable.

He wrote about it in Psalm 63 while he was in the desert.

Psalm 63:1 O God, you are my God, earnestly I seek _____; my soul thirsts for _____, my body longs for _____, in a dry and weary land where there is no water.

I left a few words out. Ask the counselee, "What would you naturally expect a person in David's position (and yours) to put in those spaces?" "My soul thirsts for…my son to come to his senses"? "My soul longs for…restoration of my family and vindication and the return to my throne"? "Earnestly I seek…to recover what was lost"? That is what most people would say because most people think those are the things that would restore happiness. But that is not what David said. He had one desire:

Psalm 63:1 O God, you are my God, earnestly I seek you; my soul thirsts for you, my body longs for you, in a dry and weary land where there is no water.

Respond to agonizing pain by using that pain to increase your thirst for God's presence, because only His presence can restore joy. Suffering is of incalculable worth to us, because God said we will not experience His presence unless we seek Him with all our heart and all our soul (Jer. 29:13). Most people are unable to enjoy deep, rich, satisfying experiences of His presence because they never get thirsty enough to really seek with all that is in them. But one thing intense suffering can do (if it is interpreted properly) is increase our thirst to a level that we ARE motivated to seek God with all our heart and soul. Always use suffering and pain to increase your thirst for God. Look at the pain and interpret that pain as thirst for the presence of God.

10. Drives us to God, Intensifies Prayer

Luke 22:44 And being in anguish, he prayed more earnestly.

We have all experienced the calamity of having a dry, dull heart toward God that results in passionless, weak prayer. In some cases, when we were passionate in our prayers without suffering, there is no need for God to send suffering. But where passion is lacking, it is worth suffering some pain if it restores our zeal in seeking God. Passionate prayer is of infinite worth, but it is hard to come by. Praise be to God for supplying the suffering we need to drive us to pray with passion! Gain this benefit by pouring out your heart in passionate, earnest prayer when you suffer.

11. Makes us Long for Heaven

2 Corinthians 5:8 We are confident, I say, and would prefer to be away from the body and at home with the Lord.

The greater our hope for heaven the more we honor God. Suffering increases that hope. Respond to suffering by thinking more about heaven.

12. Increased Hope for the Second Coming

Revelation 21:4 He will wipe every tear from their eyes. There will be no more death or mourning or crying or pain, for the old order of things has passed away.

Oh, the glory Jesus will receive on that Day that He puts a permanent end to all suffering. The shouts of the angels on that Day will be one thing, but nothing compared to the praises of those who have endured suffering and death. Let suffering turn your thinking to that glorious Day.

13. Snaps Us Out of the Fog of Trivia

Psalm 102:4 My heart is blighted and withered like grass; I forget to eat my food.

Suffering—especially severe suffering, has a way of awakening us to what is truly important. We get so caught up in the trivia of life that little things get us worked up, then some major trial comes along and opens our eyes to how meaningless all those little things are compared to eternal realities.

When suffering is extreme, take advantage of it by seizing on the prime opportunity to preach to your soul about what is important and what is not.

14. Teaches Us to Understand God's Word

Psalm 119:71 It was good for me to be afflicted so that I might learn your decrees.

Very often the key to understanding God's Word comes only through suffering. A painful ordeal breaks into your life, and the agony of it drives you to seek a solution from Scripture with an intensity you would not otherwise have. When you listen to sermons your ears are alert to principles that would address your problem. And when they come, you hear what no one else hears, and you have insights into how to apply that Scripture that no one else picks up on because they are not going through what you are going through.

Gain this benefit by seeking answers from God's Word when you are suffering. And do not give up until you find them![42]

15. Teaches Us the Horror of Sin

Romans 8:19-22 The creation waits in eager expectation for the sons of God to be revealed. 20 For the creation was subjected to frustration, not by its own choice, but by the will of the one who subjected it, in hope 21 that the creation itself will be liberated from its bondage to decay and brought into the glorious freedom of the children of God. 22 We know that the whole creation has been groaning as in the pains of childbirth right up to the present time.

Not all of your suffering is due to sin in your life. But all your suffering is due to sin. It is sin that caused the Fall and the curse. All pain exists because of sin, and is designed to teach us how horrible sin really is. None of us hate sin enough, but suffering, if we use it right, can train us to hate sin more. Let all your distress over suffering feed your hatred for sin and increase your love for righteousness.

16. The Privilege of Participation in the Sufferings of Christ

1 Peter 4:12-13 Dear friends, do not be surprised at the painful trial you are suffering, as though something strange were happening to you. 13 But rejoice that you participate in the sufferings of Christ.

Philippians 3:10 I want to know Christ and the power of his resurrection and the fellowship of sharing in his sufferings, becoming like him in his death.

---

[42] By "answers" I do not mean answers to questions God doesn't address, like "Why did God let this happen at this time?" I'm referring to answers to the question, "What does God's Word say about this?"

Acts 5:41 The apostles left the Sanhedrin, rejoicing because they had been counted worthy of suffering disgrace for the Name.

Philippians 1:29 For it has been granted to you on behalf of Christ ... to suffer for him.

When an employee in the United States is injured on the job, it is the employer's responsibility to cover the medical bills. And in a similar way, when a Christian suffers any hardship while on the clock for Jesus, that is considered suffering for Jesus. An example of this is Epaphroditus, who was to be honored because he almost died for Christ (Php.2:30). What happened? Was he scourged like Paul? Beaten by an angry mob for preaching the gospel? Threatened by government officials? No. He got sick while traveling to deliver a financial gift to Paul (Php.2:27). Somewhere along the line he inhaled a germ and became ill, and God considered that suffering for Christ because it happened while on the job for Christ. If your spouse or boss mistreats you, if you are in that job or marriage because you are seeking to follow God's will for your life, then ALL suffering in that job or marriage counts as suffering while on the job for Christ.

Gain this benefit first by making sure your suffering is for Christ's sake, and not because of unrepentant sin or folly on your part. We can rejoice over suffering that is the consequence of sin (see #3), but if the sin or foolishness is currently ongoing, put a stop to it.

Secondly, spend time thinking about the grand honor of suffering for His name.

17. Reward

Luke 6:22-23 Blessed are you when men hate you, when they exclude you and insult you and reject your name as evil, because of the Son of Man. 23 "Rejoice in that day and leap for joy, because great is your reward in heaven.

Suffering for Christ is a grand and glorious privilege, and will be richly rewarded. No matter what you go through in following Christ, He will make it worth your while—times ten billion! Respond to suffering by thinking about the wealth and generosity of the One who is going to repay you for all that you have lost in His service.

18. Motivation to Change

Psalm 119:67 Before I was afflicted I went astray, but now I obey your word.

Psalm 119:71 It was good for me to be afflicted so that I might learn your decrees.

The reason lepers lose their limbs is not because the leprosy destroys them; it is because the lepers themselves destroy them. They lose the feeling in their skin, so grabbing something that is hot, or sharp, or having a rock in their shoe—things like that destroy their hands and feet because they feel no pain, so they do not know to stop doing what is causing harm. Pain is a gift. It motivates us to stop what we are doing and figure out what is wrong so we can avoid doing damage to ourselves.

Emotional pain is the same way. It is a gift from God that motivates us to take action to solve problems in the soul. When our pain is due to a pattern of wrong thinking or behavior or attitudes, when the pain becomes intense enough it drives us to find answers about the cause of that pain. If God had designed us in such a way that we could wander from Him and not suffer any pain as a result, that would be unloving. We would most certainly wander far from Him.

Use emotional pain to drive you to examine the complex inner workings of your heart (see Chapter 4). Utilize a wise counselor if need be.

19. Enables Compassion

Hebrews 2:18 Because he himself suffered when he was tempted, he is able to help those who are being tempted.

Compassion is a crucial component of Christ-likeness, but it is impossible apart from suffering. You cannot feel for someone who is suffering if you have no idea what it is like to suffer. And the closer your suffering is to that of the other person, the greater your ability to have compassion. So the greater the intensity and variety of your sufferings, the better!

And not only does suffering help you have compassion, but when you have suffered that also helps the other person to take comfort in the fact that you can empathize with what he is going through. In His omniscience, God the Son could have fully understood what our suffering was like without experiencing it Himself, but He went through it anyway in order to help us take comfort in the fact that He has felt the sting of what we are feeling and is therefore a compassionate High Priest. The more you suffer, the greater a commodity you are in the Church.

Gain this benefit by remembering your pain so you can bear the burden of others when they suffer.

20. Enables us to Help Others

2 Corinthians 1:3-4 Praise be to the God and Father of our Lord Jesus Christ, the Father of compassion and the God of all comfort, 4 who comforts us in all our troubles, so that we can comfort those in any trouble with the comfort we ourselves have received from God.

This verse does not say that you will automatically be able to comfort people just because you went through suffering. It only works if, in your suffering, you succeeded in finding comfort from God. But if you do suffer and find comfort from God, you now have the ability to show others how it is done.

21. Increased Glory

2 Corinthians 4:17 Our light and momentary troubles are achieving for us an eternal weight of glory.[43]

The promise is not simply that once our troubles are over we will receive glory. The promise is that the troubles themselves are accomplishing that glory. That is, the greater your suffering now, the greater the glory of heaven for you when Jesus comes.

22. Footsteps of Jesus

Philippians 3:10 I want to know Christ and the power of his resurrection and the fellowship of sharing in his sufferings, becoming like him in his death.

---

[43] Author's translation.

Hebrews 2:10-11 In bringing many sons to glory, it was fitting that God, for whom and through whom everything exists, should make the author of their salvation perfect through suffering. 11 Both the one who makes men holy and those who are made holy are of the same family. So Jesus is not ashamed to call them brothers.

1 Peter 2:19, 21 For it is commendable if a man bears up under the pain of unjust suffering because he is conscious of God. ... 21 To this you were called, because Christ suffered for you, leaving you an example, that you should follow in his steps.

We exist to be conformed to the image of Christ. That is the goal of our predestination (Ro.8:29). So every time we suffer and respond like Jesus responded, we are following in His glorious steps. When warning the Disciples about the suffering they would experience Jesus said, "A servant is not greater than his master" (Mt.10:24). If our Master was not exempt from suffering; we certainly should not expect to be exempt. Gain this benefit by following Jesus' example in the way He embraced and responded to suffering.

23. Enables Sacrificial Giving and Deeper Expressions of Love

2 Corinthians 1:6 If we are distressed, it is for your comfort,

1 John 4:9 This is how God showed his love among us: He sent his one and only Son into the world that we might live through him.

Something about love compels the lover to give sacrificially to the beloved. Like David, who refused to offer God that which cost him nothing (2 Sam. 24:24), we all desire to give something valuable— something that costs us a lot, to those we love. Giving in a way that causes us suffering is the most costly gift we can give. That is the way God gave to us. Suffering enables us to give precious, priceless gifts even when we are penniless.

Gain this benefit by giving generously—and by rejoicing whenever a gift costs you something.

Resources for Helping Someone Who is Suffering

Sermons by John Piper:[44]
- "Called to Suffer and Rejoice" on 2 Cor.4:7-18.
- "Suffering and the Second Coming" on 2 Thes.1:1-10.
- "Called to Suffer and Rejoice" on Col.1:24-29.
- "Spiritual Depression in the Psalms" on Ps.42.
- "The Sacrifice of Suffering" on Hebrews 13:13-14.
- "Called to Suffer and Rejoice" on Php.3:1-14.
- "I Will Sing of Thy Might and Mercy" on Ps.59:16-17.
- "Strengthened to Suffer" on 1 Pe.3:18-22.
- "Arming Yourself with the Purpose to Suffer" on 1 Pe.4:1-6.
- "Why We Can Rejoice in Suffering" on 1 Pe.4:12-19.
- "Called to Suffer and Rejoice" on 1 Pe.5:1-8.
- "Children, Heirs, and Fellow Sufferers" on Ro.8:14-18.
- "Thanksgiving in Suffering" on Heb.4:14-16.
- "Today's Mercies for Today's Troubles" on Mt.6:34.
- "The Price and the Preciousness of Spiritual Power" on Acts 5:17-21.
- For other John Piper sermons on the topic of suffering simply type "Suffering" in the search box in the DesiringGod.org Resource library.[45]

Sermons by Darrell Ferguson:[46]
- "Comfort for the Brokenhearted" from the series "Beatitudes."
- "The Approval of God" from the series "Favorite Psalms (part 3).

---

[44] Each of these sermons by John Piper is available at DesiringGod.org in the Resource Library in "Resource Categories by Scripture" (/resource-library/sermons/by-scripture).
[45] http://www.desiringgod.org/searches/suffering%20?utf8=%E2%9C%93
[46] FoodForYourSoul.net. The sermon series are listed in alphabetical order on the "Series Alphabetically" link.

- "God vs. Wind" from the series "Favorite Psalms (part 4).
- "How to take Refuge in God" from the series "Favorite Psalms (part 7).
- "Enjoying God's Love" from the series "Favorite Psalms (part 8).
- "Enjoying God's Gracious Memory" from the series "Favorite Psalms (part 9).
- "Enjoying God's Guidance" from the series "Favorite Psalms (part 10).
- "Enjoying God's Guidance" from the series "Favorite Psalms (part 11).
- "The Shade at Your Right Hand" from the series "Favorite Psalms (part 12).

Book: *A Place of Healing: Wrestling with the Mysteries of Suffering, Pain, and God's Sovereignty* by Joni Eareckson Tada. Note: this book is available as an audio book read by the author herself. Sometimes during severe suffering reading a book is more than a person can handle. In that case, the audio book may be a good option.

Devotionals from the book, *What's So Great About God?*:[47]

Meditations #**7-10**, **38**, **46-49**, **58-61**, **64-68**, **76-79**, 89, 106, 112, 139, 142, **156**, 164, **179**

---

[47] Bold numbers represent the meditations that are especially relevant.

CHAPTER FOUR:
HOW TO
DIAGNOSE A PROBLEM

The first step to solving any problem is, of course, identifying what the problem is. This is one of the most difficult and most important aspects of counseling and must be given careful attention. Failure to understand the real problem will lead to frustration for both the counselor and the counselee.

Labels

The label one uses to describe a problem is more important than one might naturally assume. Accurate names point to proper solutions. When a person has a dangerously low body temperature we call it hypothermia (*hypo*—"low" *thermia*—"temperature"). The label makes the solution obvious (raise the person's temperature). Applying an accurate label to the problem provides insight into the solution.

One of the most damaging effects of Freudian psychological jargon is the fact that most of the labels cloud, rather than clarify both the nature of the problem and the solution. Sigmund Freud wanted people to think of their non-physical problems as diseases of the unconscious mind, so the labels he invented were calculated to sound scientific and clinical. And that approach to labeling the struggles of the soul has caught on in modern psychology.

Even our secular culture has begun to realize how unhelpful many of these terms are (note the popularity of the term "psychobabble"). Nevertheless, psychological terminology has had a profound effect on the way our culture tends to think about spiritual problems. Those who have been diagnosed with a psychological "disease" will often identify themselves with the label they have been given to the degree that they feel it is part of who they are. As a result, any attempt to apply biblical terms to the particular issues at hand is considered simplistic or shallow, because it ignores the scientific-sounding disorder or "disease."

The biblical terminology, however, is anything but shallow. It reflects divine truth and sheds light on the nature of the problem. When a person's struggle can be stated in biblical terms, discovering the solution becomes much easier. In fact, in many cases the person will be able to find the solution by himself once a wise counselor has helped pinpoint the correct biblical terminology. The world's labels obscure; God's labels enlighten.

There are at least two important ways the psychological terminology tends to obscure:

1) **Euphemism**—Exchanging vocabulary that indicates evil, sin, or culpability for vocabulary that recasts sin in medical-sounding terms.

2) **Category Confusion**—Mixing unrelated categories together under one label.

Euphemisms for Sin

In Chapter two (under the heading "Destruction of the Conscience") we found that psychological jargon is calculated to eliminate guilt. An important step in diagnosis is to translate the problem back into biblical categories.

- Grumbling, not *venting*
- Lack of self-control or being controlled by the flesh, not *compulsive*
- Worry, fretting, and anxiety, not *stressed*
- Cowardice or fear, not *insecurity*
- Discontent, not *coping*
- Selfishness or pride, not *self-esteem*
- Enslavement, not *addiction*
- Fornicating, not *living together*

- Prideful, arrogant self-centered hard-heartedness against God, not *independent* or *self-reliant*
- Lacking conviction, not *moderate* or *open-minded*
- Bitter, angry, resentful, or self-pitying; not *wounded*
- Won't, not *can't*
- Hard-heartedness, not *emotional issues*
- Covetousness or greed, not *emotional needs*
- Fear of man, not *codependence*
- Selfish demands, not *rights*
- Revenge, not *defense mechanisms*
- Prideful self-absorption, not *inferiority complex*
- Drunkenness, not *alcoholism*
- Sin, not *disease*
- Ignorantly, not *subconsciously*
- Unrepentant or hard-hearted, not *in denial*
- Double-mindedness, not *rapid cycling*

Category Confusion

Another way psychological jargon obscures the truth is by mixing unrelated characteristics—some good, some bad—together in one label. For example, consider the following list of characteristics of codependency.[48]

- My good feelings about who I am stem from receiving approval from you.
- My mental attention is focused on manipulating you to do it my way.
- My fear of rejection determines what I say or do.
- My fear of your anger determines what I say or do.
- I put my values aside in order to connect with you.
- Your struggle affects my serenity.

---

[48] Taken from http://www.mental-health-today.com/articles/codepen.htm.

- My mental attention is focused on solving your problems or relieving your pain.
- My mental attention is focused on you.
- My mental attention is focused on protecting you.
- My own hobbies or interests are put aside.

The first five are symptoms of selfishness, pride, and fear of man; and the solution is humility, love, and fear of God. The last five are symptoms of godly, selfless love and they do not need a solution.

One person labeled "bipolar" may have a problem with an unwillingness to accept suffering from God, which leads to depression. Another person with that same label may have made an idol out of pleasure. Two very different problems with different solutions—both given the same label by the world.

Setting the problem in biblical terms can be a great encouragement to the counselee because it shows him that his problem is not a mental disease, but rather a list of traits, some of which may actually be virtues. For example, an anorexic must have extraordinary self-discipline to make herself exercise and resist food. Sometimes even biblical counselors will insist that is a bad thing in the case of anorexia. It is not. Self-control is part of the fruit of the Spirit and should be encouraged. The sin is not her self-control; it is her self-destruction (and the attitudes and affections that drive that self-destruction). Where there are wrong desires, motives, thoughts, or affections behind the behavior, those sins must be corrected. But the self-control itself is a virtue that should be encouraged.

In fact, that virtue could be a key to the solution. In some cases the anorexic's primary problem is lack of self-control over her thought life. When she applies the same discipline to developing a godly thought life that she does to controlling her physical body, so that she rejects unbiblical thoughts with the same vigor with which she shuns unhealthy food, her attitudes will change. Knowing that self-control is a godly trait that can be used for her recovery can be wonderfully motivating for her. It is worldly thinking to lump her self-discipline in with the rest of her problem.

Another example is mania. Manic behavior is a blend of sinful and non-sinful aspects:

- Feeling invincible, euphoric, or optimistic. Getting up early in the morning. Being extremely energetic.

- Selfishness, boasting, unbridled pursuit of pleasure, unfaithfulness, self-centeredness, irresponsibility, irritability, refusing to listen to wise counsel, rejecting wisdom.

Nothing in the first group is sinful and everything in the second group is sinful. Lumping them all together in the useless term "mania" does nothing to assist in the solution. But casting the issues in biblical terms makes the solution clear.

Using biblical terminology, then, is an essential first step in diagnosing a problem. Many Christians who would feel unqualified to help a person who says "I have codependency" would have no trouble at all counseling a person who says, "My behavior is driven by anger and a fear of rejection, and I'm so wrapped up in a relationship that I have been forsaking the assembly."

Dig Deep

Biblical counselors are often accused of oversimplifying people's problems, and in some cases this criticism is justified. It is not an oversimplification to use biblical terminology and apply biblical remedies, however, there is a tendency for some biblical counselors to fail to appreciate the complexity of a problem.

Not everyone with the same list of symptoms suffers from the same disease. Just as a runny nose may be caused by a variety of different illnesses, so a spiritual problem can have a variety of causes. One anorexic might be consumed with her looks, while another holds being in control as an idol. One person's temper problem may be a result of a wrong view of suffering, while another person is angry because of materialism, pride, or discontent.

People are complex, and their problems are complex. People do what they do because of an intricate mix of desires, values, beliefs, attitudes, cravings, goals, emotions, thoughts, impulses, perspectives, and affections. If the problem were simple they would not need counsel. Making assumptions about what is behind a problem tends toward shallow, misguided counsel that is usually both condescending and unhelpful. And when those shallow solutions do not work, it undermines the person's confidence in God's Word.

It is important to dig deep. Note carefully, however, the difference between biblical and psychological conceptions of "digging deep." In psychotherapy it means probing into the person's past and attempting to gain access to the unconscious. The biblical counseling approach is to delve deeply into the heart. And that is done by speaking with the person about his *conscious* mind—what he thinks, how he feels, what his motives are, etc.

Discovering what happened in the past that initiated the behavior is rarely important. What is important is discovering why the behavior is ongoing. There may be a woman, for example, who fell into a certain pattern of behavior as a teenager because she wanted to get the attention of the opposite sex. Now that behavior is persisting, not because she is still trying to attract men but simply because it has become a habit and she has not learned how to overcome habitual impulses. If a driver is traveling east when she should be going west, it does not matter what first started her on her eastward orientation; it only matters that she turn around and begin traveling west.

The reason psychotherapy focuses so much on the past is the Freudian doctrine that behavior arises from the unconscious, which was shaped by damaging past experiences. How hopeless would be our condition if that were true! No matter how many past traumas a therapist digs up one would have no way of knowing if there were still some unknown event that could cause trouble the rest of his life. The wonderful news of Scripture is that whatever happened in one's past, God has power to redeem and restore the heart right now—without undoing anything in the past.

Identity: Your Past or Your Future?

If there were no God and people were the product of accidental, evolutionary processes then one's identity would be nothing more than his past. A person would be nothing more than the product of all his past experiences. If he was abused as a child, that would define who he is. The Bible, however, gives us a very different picture. We are the product of a wise, purposeful God who has a plan for our existence. One's identity, then, is defined not by his past but by his future—what he is becoming. Past experiences and decisions do not define what a person is—only *where* he is.

The Bible describes this life as a walk. We are always stepping in some direction. Each person got where he is now through a series of steps. If he is in a bad place, then, the good news is that since he got there through a series of steps, he can get out through a series of steps. The things that happened to him did not put him in the place he is. It was the steps he took—decisions he made. That is why one abused child turns into a mess, and another is abused and grows up fine. Some people respond to abuse with wrong steps and others respond with right steps. The abuse itself does not cause spiritual damage—only the wrong steps that may result. And when there have been some wrong steps, the solution is not to retrace those steps backwards, but to simply make a course correction. If you get a phone call from a person who is trying to get to your house but is lost, you do not need to find out how he got lost or which turns he took. You simply give him directions from wherever he is to your house.

A man is what he is—not what he was. And even more significant is what he will be. Consider the biblical descriptions of a believer. His past—a condemned enemy of God. His future—righteousness and glorification. And when God speaks of a believer's identity it is in terms of his future, not his past.

George Washington is known as our first president, even though he became president at age 57 and died at age 67. For 85 percent of his life he was neither President nor a former president. But when we look back from our perspective in time we can see the big picture of who he was. He was our first president, because that is what he ended up *becoming*. When God looks at a person's life He sees the big picture—the eternal picture. George Washington was our first president; you are a saint—a holy one. God can see what you are becoming—what you were created to be and will be for all eternity. The fact that you have not yet reached your full maturity is incidental. In fact, that is where the George Washington illustration breaks down. He was a non-president throughout most of his life, but a saint will be holy for all eternity and is sinful only during this short life. A better illustration would be a fertilized egg compared to a fully developed human body. No one sees a crowded room and says, "Look at all these highly developed zygotes." One's identity is determined by what he is becoming.

This is one of the most glorious truths of the gospel. The believer's future is glorious beyond imagination, and his past is no problem! Grew up without any parents around like Samuel? No problem. Picked on, mistreated, and neglected by parents and older siblings like David? No problem. Used to be a fornicator, adulterer, homosexual, thief, or drunk like the people in 1 Corinthians 6:11? No problem. Maybe even a murderer like Paul? No problem. Denied Christ publicly three times like Peter? No problem. Your past is no problem because God specializes in redemption. This is the great news for every person we counsel!

Dig deeply—into the heart, not the past.

What Lies Beneath: Diagnosing the Inner Man

A common mistake in assessing one's spiritual condition is to focus mainly on actions and words. Words and actions are like fruit on a tree. They are produced by unseen processes within the trunk, branches, and root system of the inner man. All sin originates in the heart, (Mt.12:34, 15:18, Mk.7:21-22) so no sin problem can be corrected without addressing the part of the inner man that is the source of that problem. Assessing spiritual health by focusing only on one's actions is like a doctor who examines only the skin. It is the error of the Pharisees, who were repeatedly rebuked by Jesus for neglecting the matters of the heart.

Human pride takes a "head in the sand" approach to the sins of the inner man. A harsh or bitter word comes out of the mouth and we say, "I didn't mean that." Or "I don't know where these actions are coming from—I'm just not myself lately." We imagine that our sinful actions have some other source—or no source at all, and we are therefore absolved. There is no problem in the heart that must be addressed. Just a quick apology, an assurance that it did not come from the inside, and all is well. That is a fantasy. Sins do not come out of nowhere. Jesus was very clear:

Matthew 12:34 Out of the overflow of the heart the mouth speaks.

Mark 7:21-22 From within, out of men's hearts, come evil thoughts, sexual immorality, theft, murder, adultery, 22 greed, malice, deceit, lewdness, envy, slander, arrogance and folly.

There is much more to human sinfulness than simply carrying out wrong actions. To properly diagnose a problem one must discover which components of the inner man are not as they should be. No sin problem can be corrected without correcting the problems in the inner man that generated that sin.

The Components of the Inner Man

When Jesus pointed to the heart as the source of all our sin He used the word *heart* in a way that includes all the various functions of the inner man, including the thought life ("evil thoughts"), desires ("greed"), motives ("deceit"), and attitudes ("envy, arrogance, folly").

Great care must be taken at this point, however, because no counselor is able to see into someone else's heart. Assuming a person has a particular sin on the inside is the sinful kind of judging (Mt.7:1). For example, if a person is struggling with the sin of obscene language the counselor must never *assume* he knows the internal cause. It can only be discovered by the sinner himself. The counselor's role is simply to instruct the person in how to examine his own heart. This is done by pointing out from the Bible what God requires in the inner man and asking questions about the person's inner man.

There are at least six categories of the inner man that must be examined. A person carries out a sinful action or speaks sinful words because of at least one of the following:

1) A sinful will (wrong motives and decisions)
2) Ungodly attitudes
3) Evil desires
4) Wrong feelings/emotions

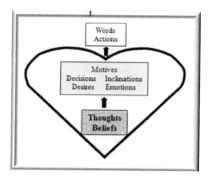

And all four of those are all the product of wrong 5) <u>thoughts</u> and 6) <u>beliefs</u>.

The inner man is complex. In fact, even the diagram above is an oversimplification. We know that all our actions are produced by the heart (inner man), and Scripture often speaks of beliefs and thoughts as

being the root cause underneath emotions, attitudes, desires, and will; however, it is also true that the emotions, attitudes, desires, and will have an effect on thoughts and beliefs. All the various parts of man interact with one another and affect one another in complex ways. This model is offered simply to make the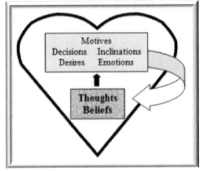
point that each of the various aspects of the inner man must be examined when diagnosing a problem. Every sin arises from the inner man and involves some combination of the various parts of the heart.

Psychologists also speak of the inner man being complex and deep, but in a much different way. One of Freud's most influential successes was his ability to convince modern culture of his ideas about the unconscious (or subconscious). He taught that thoughts, emotions, attitudes, etc. all rise up out of the unconscious. And beliefs, rather than being at the root, are merely a product of the unconscious like everything else.

Another key difference between psychology and Scripture is the location of the inner man. Because of the influence of naturalism on modern psychology, the tendency is to think of human nature in mainly mechanistic, physical terms. Jesus pointed to the heart (a spiritual entity) as the source of behavior (Mk.7:22-23); psychologists and psychiatrists point to the brain (a physical organ).

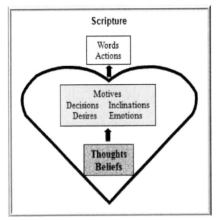

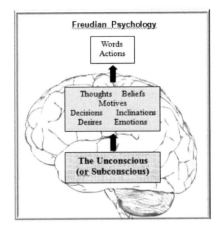

This is one reason there is such a propensity within psychology to understate responsibility and culpability for things that go wrong within a person. The way a person feels and thinks is supposedly caused by the subconscious mind, which is a product of one's past and is outside of one's control. And since actions are a product of attitudes, thoughts, and feelings, some take this model to its logical conclusion and say that not even one's bad actions are necessarily his fault. People decide to get drunk or commit crimes because of mental disease caused by incidents in the past that were outside the person's control.

Jesus' death on the cross, however, purchased every part of our being—heart, mind, soul, and strength; and no part of our humanity is outside the bounds of His requirement of righteousness. Every part has been damaged by sin, and every part is in need of redemption.

The Standard of Health

To diagnose a malady one must first know what health is. A dysfunctional liver is diagnosed by comparing it to the way a healthy liver is supposed to function. For a counselor to diagnose a problem in the inner man, then, it is essential to understand what God commands regarding the inner man. What is the standard for health with regard to the heart?

For the world, health is defined by that which is normal. If a person is behaving or feeling abnormally he goes to a psychotherapist or psychiatrist with the goal of getting back to normal. But normal is not the standard for children of God. In fact, for believers the norms of this world are the *problem*, not the solution.

1 Corinthians 3:3-4 You are still worldly. For since there is jealousy and quarreling among you, are you not worldly? Are you not walking according to man? 4 For when one says, "I follow Paul," and another, "I follow Apollos," are you not mere men?[49]

Paul wrote the book of 1 Corinthians to rebuke the church in Corinth for being normal. This is yet another reason why the Bible and the doctrines of psychotherapy are utterly incompatible and cannot be integrated. They have opposite goals. Psychotherapy seeks to make the counselee a normal, worldly person; but according to Scripture being a normal,

---

[49] Author's translation.

worldly person is the disease that needs a cure. Spiritual health is defined not by normality but by what God commands. The goal in diagnoses, then, is to discover actions, words, motives, emotions, attitudes, decisions, desires, thoughts, and beliefs that are not in line with what God commands in His Word.

Diagnosing the Thoughts

Every part of the inner man is very closely connected to the thoughts, so diagnosing the thought life is a crucial part of getting to the root of a problem. The following is a list of ways the thoughts typically depart from what God has commanded.

Regarding Truth...

1) All thoughts about God that are untrue are sinful (Mt.9:4).
2) Thoughts are sinful if they are a rejection of God's Word (Heb.12:25).
3) Thoughts are sinful if they are an evaluation of a concept or idea according to human wisdom rather than God's Word (1 Cor.1:18-2:5).

Regarding Attitudes...

4) Thoughts arising out of pride are sinful (Lk.1:51).
5) Thoughts that reveal a lack of love are sinful (Jas.2:4, Mt.5:22).

Regarding Desire...

6) Thoughts are sinful if they are fantasies about actions that would be sinful (Ro.13:14, Pr.14:22, Mt.5:28). Rule of thumb: if it would be wrong to do, it is wrong to fantasize about. (Sins in the thought life are not virtual sins—they are as real as adultery or murder.)
7) The thoughts of the flesh are sinful (greed, discontent, materialism, covetousness, or any other sinful desire—Eph.2:3).
8) Thoughts are sinful if they move in the direction of discontent (Heb.13:5).

Regarding the Future...

9) Thoughts about the future are sinful if they nurture worry, fretting, or lack of trust (Ps.37:8, Mt.6:25-34).

Regarding the Present...

10) Thoughts are sinful if they come from a temporal point of view (Col.3:1-2).

Regarding the Past...

11) Thoughts are sinful if they remove responsibility from past decision-making (Lk.16:15).
12) Thoughts are sinful if past events are not seen as intentional good acts of a sovereign and loving God (Ps.143:5).

Where any of these kinds of sinful thoughts exist, they will cause problems, and any attempt at solving those problems without addressing the sins in the thought life will be fruitless.

Diagnosing the Decisions

Decisions are not driven in a mechanistic way by chemicals in the brain or impulses from the subconscious. God commands us concerning the choices we make, which means the will is within our control. Any decision to choose something that does not please the Father falls short of Jesus' example (Jn.8:29) and must be corrected.

Diagnosing the Motives

In Matthew 6 Jesus condemned the Pharisees for giving to the poor, prayer, and fasting, because they had a sinful motive (self-glorification). He selected three actions that are generally regarded as righteous in order to drive home the point that *anything*, if done with wrong motives, is sin.

If the counselee's struggle is with a particular behavior, begin by exploring motives. Ask the counselee to think through whether he has a particular goal in mind when he does this behavior. What is he trying to accomplish? If the goal of an action is anything prohibited by God's Word, the motive itself is sin and must be repented of. One of the most common sinful motives is the desire to bring honor to oneself (Mt.6:1-6,16-18).

Very often the answer at this point is, "I don't know why I do it. I just do it without thinking." In this case a few suggestions from a humble counselor may provide insight. If a mother is mystified over why she always yells at her children, the counselor might ask, "Is it possible that your motive is revenge—a response of the flesh to strike back at them for irritating you? Or could it be that you do it in order to get them to obey, because the only way to get them to listen is to raise your voice? Or is part of your motive to make sure your husband hears what's going on, so he realizes the children are disobeying?" Sometimes when various possible motives are suggested the counselee will be able to identify one or more of them as the cause in her particular case.

Discerning wrong motives in oneself can be extremely difficult. We convince ourselves that we are carrying out tough love when in reality our motive is to exact some revenge. We insist we are innocently flipping through the channels on TV just to see what is on or innocently clicking on something online out of curiosity, when in reality we are hoping to "inadvertently" stumble across something to feed our lusts. A prayer request for someone becomes a cover for the desire to gossip. The way a story is told is disguised boasting. Under the pretense of helping our spouse make spiritual progress, the hidden motive is to get him or her to treat us better. The human heart can be so deceitful that some sinful motives can go undetected even when we search for them.

1 Corinthians 4:4-5 My conscience is clear, but that does not make me innocent. It is the Lord who judges me. 5 Therefore judge nothing before the appointed time; wait till the Lord comes. He will bring to light what is hidden in darkness and will expose the motives of men's hearts.

Tread carefully when diagnosing motives. We must never rely on our suspicions about the person's motives. No matter how good or bad a person's motives may *seem* to be, we are not God and we do not have the ability to see into the heart.[50] If you suspect a bad motive, simply ask

---

[50] One of the evidences that proved Jesus to be God was His ability to see what was in people's hearts.

the person if that motive exists. Or suggest to the person that it may possibly exist and urge him to give it some consideration. But once he has considered it, always accept what he tells you regarding what is in his heart. Make sure your suggestions are not veiled accusations. They must be genuine questions, and you much accept whatever the counselee tells you about his motives. Do remind the counselee, however, that there is a possibility that there could be a wrong motive that has gone undetected.

Diagnosing the Emotions

The emotions (or affections) are another example of where biblical counseling and secular psychology have dramatically different goals. For the world, the goal is to feel better (less internal suffering). For believers the goal is to feel *rightly*, which in some cases may actually increase suffering.

There is a great deal of resistance, outside and inside the Church, to the idea that we are responsible for how we feel and that it is possible to feel wrongly. Most people have been persuaded by modern psychology of a non-cognitive view of emotions. This is the view that suggests that emotions are simply something that happen to you and are outside of your control. [51] In the non-cognitive view, emotions can never be appropriate or inappropriate, right or wrong, moral or immoral. They are simply names of various sensations. Feeling angry or happy or hopeful or depressed in your soul is no more moral or immoral than feeling hot or cold in your body.[52]

This view decreases the sense of responsibility for actions that are related to feelings. One study, for example, showed that when subjects were given a placebo and told it would make them more emotional they were more likely to cheat on a test. [53] Sinful behaviors are seen as

---

[51] The most thorough study on emotions in the New Testament is currently Matthew Elliott's very helpful book, *Faithful Feelings: Emotions in the New Testament*. I am indebted to him for much of the material in this section.

[52] Elliott suggests that the foundation upon which modern non-cognitive theory has been built was laid by Darwin and Descartes. The philosophical framework proposed by Descartes then gave birth to modern psychological theories about emotion, which, in turn, have heavily influenced Bible commentators (pp.20-22).

[53] Elliott, *Feelings*, 51.

understandable if a drug or some other factor is making the person "emotional."

The cognitive view of emotions, on the other hand, holds that "emotions are not names of feelings, but rather the results of the interpretations of objects and situations."[54] Objects and situations are evaluated by the mind, weighed against the norms in one's belief system, and found to be desirable or undesirable; and the response to that assessment is emotion. According to this view there are indeed right and wrong emotions because there can be correct or incorrect assessments of objects and situations (assessments that do or do not correspond with reality), and there can be responses that are appropriate or inappropriate for the circumstances at hand. For example, suppose a person felt delight in response to an unjust attack on a helpless person. That would reflect a heart that prizes evil and would therefore be an evil emotion.

This is not to imply that all emotional responses are the result of detailed, conscious reasoning. Some emotional responses are seemingly instantaneous. Even those responses, however, are based on some kind of cognitive evaluation. Discerning that a charging lion is a threat, or that a plate of one's favorite food is delightful, are determinations that take place almost instantly; yet they are cognitive evaluations nonetheless. It is the intellect that is able to discern that the lion is not a rock and that the food is not garbage.

Because of belief systems and thought patterns, an observed object or situation is regarded as good or bad, threatening or safe, beautiful or ugly, desirable or repulsive. A person who has developed a belief system in which personal comfort is highly valued may have a seemingly instantaneous response of anger when a person or circumstance interferes with his comfort. While seemingly instantaneous, however, the angry response does not occur until after he has assessed the situation as a threat to his comfort at some level.

---

[54] Ibid, 29.

Biblical Argument for the Cognitive View of Emotions

Which view fits best with the approach that God's Word takes in discussing emotions? The following four observations point in the direction of the cognitive view:

1) Emotions are Portrayed in Scripture as Resulting from Evaluations of Circumstances.

Revelation 12:10-13 Now have come the salvation and the power and the kingdom of our God ... <u>Therefore</u> rejoice...

2 Samuel 3:8 Abner was very angry <u>because</u> of what Ish-Bosheth said.

Lamentations 3:19-20 I remember my affliction ... 20 <u>and</u> my soul is downcast within me.

Lamentations 3:21 This I call to mind and <u>therefore</u> I have hope.

1 Peter 1:25-2:1 This is the word that was preached to you. 2:1 <u>Therefore</u>, rid yourselves of all ... envy.

Psalm 6:2-7 My bones are in agony. 3 My soul is in anguish. ... 6 I am worn out from groaning; all night long I flood my bed with weeping and drench my couch with tears. 7 My eyes grow weak with sorrow; they fail <u>because</u> of all my foes.

Revelation 19:7 Let us ... be glad ... <u>for</u> the wedding of the Lamb has come.

Reasons are given for emotions, and the reasons that are given are offered not only as explanations for the emotions but also as means of bringing about the needed changes in emotions. When an emotion is commanded or forbidden, and a reason is supplied, that reason is also very often the instrument by which one can succeed in obeying the command.

The problem of sinful fear or fretting, for example, can be overcome by focusing upon the promises of God's help or the transience of the wicked. "Do not be afraid, for I am with you."[55] "Do not fret because of evil men ... for like the grass..."[56] Emotions of turmoil and anxiety can give way to emotions of peacefulness of soul *by means of* realizing and

---

[55] Gen. 26:24.
[56] Ps. 37:1-2.

believing that hope comes from God. "Rest in God alone, my soul, for my hope comes from Him."[57]

It is sometimes taught that the way to generate godly emotions is to carry out obedient actions, and the emotions will automatically follow like the caboose on a train. Such a promise is not found in Scripture, however. The biblical approach to changing emotions is changing *beliefs*.[58] The fact that reasons are given for emotions demonstrates that the truths that are genuinely believed in the heart are the determiners of how one feels. Richard Baxter's articulation of this principle is worth quoting at length:

> Consideration, as it were, opens the door between the head and the heart. The understanding having received truths, lays them up in the memory, and consideration conveys them from thence to the affections. ... Consideration presents to the affections those things which are most important. The most delightful object does not entertain where it is not seen, nor the most joyful news affect him who does not hear it ... Are not Christ and glory affecting objects? Would they not work wonders upon the soul, if they were but clearly discovered, and our apprehensions of them in some measure corresponded to their worth? ... Consideration, also, presents the most important things in the most affecting way. ... [and] helps to deliver [the intellect] from its captivity to the senses, and sets it again on the throne of the soul. When reason is silent, it is usually subject; for when it is asleep, the senses domineer. But consideration awakens our reason, till, like Samson, it rouses up itself, and breaks the bonds of sensuality, and bears down the delusions of the flesh. ... Meditation holds reason and faith to their work, and blows the fire till it thoroughly burns. To run a few steps will not get a man heat, but walking an hour may; and though a sudden occasional thought of heaven will not raise our affections to any spiritual heat, yet meditation can

---

[57] Ps. 62:5.

[58] This is not to say that behavior has no impact at all on the affections. God calls his people to "taste and see that the Lord is good," (Ps.34:8) and Peter links that tasting with resultant craving (desire). "Crave pure spiritual milk ... now that you have tasted that the Lord is good" (1 Pe.2:2-3). If a person dislikes hiking it is not guaranteed that he will automatically learn to enjoy hiking simply by engaging in the activity. If he does so with an attitude that says, "This is miserable and I can't wait for it to be over," and he has no knowledge or understanding about what is wonderful about hiking, the more he does the action the more his dislike of hiking will grow. However, if his attitude is one of wanting to learn to enjoy hiking, and he learns what aspects of hiking are delightful, the action can indeed assist the change in affections.

continue our thoughts till our hearts grow warm. … It is by consideration that we … take those heavenly doctrines which we intend to make the subject of our meditation; such as promises of eternal life, descriptions of the saints' glory, the resurrection, etc. We then present them to our judgment, that it may deliberately view them and take an exact survey, and determine uprightly concerning the perfection of our celestial happiness, against all the dictates of flesh and sense, so as to magnify the Lord in our hearts, till we are filled with a holy admiration. But the principal thing is to exercise, not merely our judgment, but our faith in the truth of the promises, and of our own personal interest in them, and title to them. If we did really and firmly believe that there is such a glory, and that within a few days our eyes shall behold it, O what passion would it raise within us! What astonishing apprehensions of that life would it produce! What love, what longing would it excite within us! O how it would actuate every affection! How it would transport us with joy, upon the least assurance of our title! Never expect to have love and joy move, when faith stands still, which must lead the way. … Love is the first affection to be excited in heavenly contemplation; the object of it is goodness.[59]

2) Emotions Are Spoken of in Scripture as Appropriate or Inappropriate, True or False, Right or Wrong.

When Mary was weeping at Jesus' empty tomb the angels asked her for an explanation for her inappropriate emotions.[60] Sadness was the wrong response to Jesus' tomb being empty on the third day because the emptiness of the tomb was the fulfillment of Jesus' prophesied resurrection. Mary wept because of an incorrect assessment of the circumstances (she interpreted the empty tomb to mean someone had taken the body of Jesus).

Scripture speaks not only of emotions stemming from incorrect assessment of circumstances but also from wrong beliefs. Emotions result not merely from the assessment of circumstances, but from judging that assessment against the norms of one's belief system.[61] This is why as beliefs change emotions will also change even when

---

[59] Richard Baxter, The Saints' Everlasting Rest, [book on-line], (accessed 17 June 2008), available from http://www.ccel.org/ccel/baxter/saints_rest.txt, Internet.
[60] Jn.20:13.
[61] Elliot, Feelings, 31-36.

circumstances remain the same. If a person is fully convinced that a gift is of great worth, it will bring joy, whereas exactly the same gift, if it is believed to be given with ill-motives, may bring sadness or anger.

Jesus rebuked the disciples for having fear in the midst of the storm,[62] as that emotion was not fitting given the fact that Jesus was with them. Their assessment of the circumstances was correct (there was indeed a furious storm), but their beliefs about Jesus (that he did not care about their wellbeing or was not able to protect them) were incorrect resulting in an inappropriate emotion.

3) Emotions Are Portrayed in Scripture as Accurate Indicators of Righteousness or Unrighteousness.

Emotions always tell the truth about what is in the heart. Emotions cannot be trusted to teach truth about God or right and wrong, but they *can* be trusted to tell the truth about our own hearts. A person is only delighted by what is good if his heart is good, and he is only delighted by what is evil if his heart is evil. The righteous are those who *delight* in God's law, God's path, God's people, God's works, God's Sabbath, truth, the fear of the Lord, and the Lord himself.[63] The wicked are the ones who delight in lies, war, mockery, wrongdoing, abominations, and wickedness.[64]

While Scripture warns against carrying out seemingly righteous actions with sinful motives,[65] there are no warnings against having righteous emotions with sinful motives. It is possible to pray, give, or fast in a sinful manner, but it is not possible to delight in God in a sinful manner.

4) Emotions Are Commanded in Scripture

God directly commands delight, peace, joy, rest, compassion, patience, awe, fear, tender-heartedness, brotherly affection, sympathy, heart-felt

---

[62] Mt.8:26.
[63] Ps.1:2, 112:1, 119:16,24,47,70,77,92,143,174, Jer.15:16, Ro.7:22, Ps.119:35, Ps.16:3, Ps.111:2, Isa.58:13, 1 Cor.13:6, Isa.11:3, Ps.37:4, Ps.43:4, Isa.61:10.
[64] Ps.62:4, Ps.68:30, Pr.1:22, Pr.2:14, Isa.66:3, Hos.7:3.
[65] Mt.6:1-18.

love, hope, desire, contentment, confidence, and zeal.[66] Furthermore, God promised harsh punishment upon those who failed to obey with the emotions of joy and gladness, and upon priests who said "what a burden" while serving the Lord.[67]

Conclusion: The Bible Supports a Cognitive View of Emotions

The biblical view of emotions, then, is that they are responses to assessments of circumstances measured against one's beliefs and are therefore accurate indicators of what the heart truly believes. For this reason emotions are of prime importance and one is ultimately responsible for his emotional responses.

We do not have *immediate* control over our emotions, but we do have indirect influence. When an emotion is sinful we can discern which beliefs are wrong, which things are valued too highly or not highly enough, and which thought patterns are errant; and we can endeavor to make the needed corrections. As beliefs conform more closely to Scripture, emotions will become more aligned with God's emotions.

Diagnose the person's emotions, then, by comparing them with what is commanded in God's Word.

- Love God and His people, not the world (Mt.22:37, I Jn.2:15)
- Fear God, not men or circumstances (Isa.51:12, Mk.4:40)
- Have joy in the Lord (Php.4:4, Dt.28:47-48)
- Have no selfish anger (Eph.4:31)
- Do not worry or fret (Mt.6:25-34, Ps.37:1)
- Do not be anxious (Php.4:6)
- Do not envy (2 Pe.2:1)
- Hope in the Lord alone (1 Pe.1:13)
- Delight in the Lord (Ps.37:4)
- Enjoy peace in the Lord (Jn.14:1)
- Find rest in the Lord (Php.4:6, Mt.11:28)

---

[66] Ps.37:4, Jn.14:1, Php.4:4, Php.4:6, Heb.4:11, Col.3:12, Heb.12:28, Ecc.12:13, Eph.4:32, 1 Pe.3:8, 1 Pe.1:22, Ps.131:3, 1 Cor.12:31, Heb.13:5, 2 Tim.1:8, Ro.12:11.
[67] Dt.28:47-48, Mal.1:10-13.

- Have compassion for the suffering (Heb.3:12)
- Be in awe of God (Heb.12:28)
- Be tender-hearted (Eph.4:32)
- Have brotherly affection and sympathy (1 Pe.3:8)
- Be content (Heb.13:5)
- Have confidence in the Lord (2 Tim.1:8)
- Never be lacking in zeal (Ro.12:11)

Diagnosing the Desires

It is a revolutionary idea for some people to think that God makes demands on our desires. In fact, many people think the Christian life is a life of learning to say "no" to your strongest appetites and desires. That is not the Christian life. Believers are called not merely to resist evil desires, but to rid themselves of those desires (Col.3:5). The Christian life is a life of good desires—hunger and thirst for righteousness and for the presence of God.[68] It is a life of delighting in God and having the desires of the heart fulfilled.[69]

Appetite and Desire

It may be helpful to differentiate between desires and appetites. Appetites are general; desires are specific. Wanting food is an appetite. Wanting a hamburger is a desire. A person desires that which he believes will satisfy his appetite. The stomach becomes empty, there is a general appetite for food, and whichever specific food seems most likely to satisfy that appetite becomes the object of desire. Appetites are relatively similar among all people, while specific desires are very different from person to person. Two people have an empty stomach, but one believes a banana would be most satisfying while another looks to a steak as the solution.

Appetites and desires function the same way in the inner man. Everyone experiences similar spiritual appetites. All people experience

---

[68] **Matthew 5:6 Blessed are those who hunger and thirst for righteousness, for they will be filled.**
[69] **Psalm 37:4 Delight yourself in the Lord and he will give you the desires of your heart.**

times of feeling empty on the inside. Like a person tossing and turning in bed who cannot get comfortable, the soul becomes restless with unfulfilled longings, groanings, and dissatisfaction. That is a God-given appetite in the heart. Scripture refers to it as the thirst of the soul. And whatever a person thinks will cure that feeling of dissatisfaction will be the object of that person's desire.

IMPORTANT: Evil desire is when the soul believes some sinful thing will be the solution to the ache of the soul. Righteous desire is when the soul believes the nearness of God's presence is the only solution to the ache of the soul.[70]

Desire and Righteous Living

It should come as no surprise that God makes demands upon our desires because our lives are driven much more by our desires than by our commitments. We *commit* to all kinds of things, but we usually end up *doing* the things to which our cravings drive us. In a difficult decision between options A and B, if there is a strong desire in the soul for B, all the pros and cons will tend to be interpreted by the mind in a way that favors B. Our tests of God's will become self-fulfilling prophecies because even though we think our brain is fully in charge of decision-making, it is not. Behind the scenes, emotions and desires are driving the ship and dictating to the brain how to interpret the data.

And that is not bad. God designed our decisions to be driven by our desires. The goal is not to become totally unbiased and objective so that the mind is not influenced by the desires; the goal is to have good desires resulting in a strong bias toward what is good.

Diagnose the desires, then, by discovering what the counselee believes would be the solution to the emptiness and longings of his soul. If he is unhappy and is convinced there is something other than the presence and favor of God that would be required for him to be happy, his desires are defective. Only the presence of God can satisfy the hunger and thirst of the human soul, so when the desires become

---

[70] Ps.42:1-2, Ps.63:1, Isa.55:2.

distorted such that we crave things that will not satisfy, that is a disorder that will lead to death.

Suppose a person took a blow to the head one day resulting in a distortion of appetites so that every time his stomach was empty, instead of triggering feelings of hunger, it triggered a powerful desire to sleep. And every time he became dehydrated, instead of triggering feelings of thirst it triggered the desire to run. A person in that condition would soon die because he would never be able to remember to eat and drink enough to stay alive.

Craving things that cannot satisfy is a dire spiritual problem.

Isaiah 55:2 Why spend money on what is not bread, and your labor on what does not satisfy?

Why do we need a Bible verse to tell us not to eat and drink that which does not satisfy? God has to tell us that because sin has caused a terrible desire disorder in our souls such that we crave things that can never "hit the spot." Believing that something besides God can satisfy the thirst of the soul is a grave evil.

It is often an uphill battle persuading a person that the things that seem so delightful in this world are not really the source of delight. A person who loves music will tend to believe that music is actually a source of joy for him. If that were true, however, then music would *always* produce joy. But it does not—even for the most extreme music lover. There are times when the music lover is depressed, turns on some music, and remains depressed. The fact that music (or food, or skiing, or sex, or time off work, or a wonderful marriage, etc.) sometimes results in happiness and other times does not proves that *those things are not really the source of the happiness.* Only the presence of God produces joy. If there is happiness after listening to music it is because God granted an experience of His favor through that music. Only God's nearness can produce joy, and to remind us of that, God frequently allows our favorite things in this world to produce no joy at all. If God grants some grace—some access to His presence through earthly things, then they are satisfying. But when He doesn't, they aren't. Augustine's statement is true: "You have formed us for Yourself, and our hearts are restless until they find rest in You."

When this principle is understood, all desire can terminate on God.

> One thing I ask of the LORD, this is what I seek: that I may dwell in the house of the LORD all the days of my life, to gaze upon the beauty of the LORD and to seek him in his temple (Ps.27:4).

> Whom have I in heaven but you? And earth has nothing I desire besides you. My flesh and my heart may fail, but God is the strength of my heart and my portion forever (Ps.73:25-26).

> My soul finds rest in God alone ... Find rest, O my soul, in God alone (Ps.62:1,5).

> I said to the LORD, "You are my Lord; I have no good besides You (Ps.16:3 NAS).

Was it really true that Asaph did not have *one single* desire on earth other than God? Surely he must have desired a meal when he was hungry or a good night's sleep when he was exhausted or enjoyment of family and friends and material things. Evidently the normal, healthy desires of life were, for Asaph, desires for God.

Desire for earthly things, such as food, drink, shelter, relief from struggle, health, strength, wealth, or love from others; can be evil or good. It is evil if the desire terminates on those objects, but legitimate if they are desired only as expressions of God's presence. The only water that can satisfy the thirst of the soul is the presence of God. If anything in this world is treated as water, that is idolatry. However, if the good gifts of God are treated as drinking straws—means of enjoying the true water, that is acceptable. In fact more than acceptable—it is pleasing worship (because God is being enjoyed as the only true water).

One knows he has crossed the line into idolatry when he thinks he must have one particular drinking straw in order to be satisfied. If the pleasures of this world are truly straws, and we genuinely believe they are not sources of joy but only means of accessing the one true Source of joy, then any straw will do. If a person clings to some relationship or situation in life thinking he *must* have that in order to be happy, then he is not really looking at that relationship or situation as a straw, but as the water itself.

This is why it is not a contradiction for the psalmist to say "You are my Lord; apart from you I have <u>no</u> good thing," and in the very next line state that, "As for the saints who are in the land, they are the glorious ones in whom is <u>all</u> my delight" (Ps.16:3). God is the only good thing (the only water), but the psalmist delights in the saints as well because he sees enjoyment of the saints as a means of enjoying the true water. His delight in the saints does not terminate on them, but is an expression of his delight in God.

If one's delight in created things arises from the intended meaning behind those created things then such delight is pleasing to God, who created all things for the enjoyment of His people (1 Tim.6:17). If a man gives an engagement ring to the woman he loves and she delights in the ring *because of what it means,* then the more she delights in the ring the more she honors the man. However, if she delights in the ring only because she loves diamonds and has no thought at all about the meaning of the ring, the man will surely be grieved. In the same way God is honored when His creation is enjoyed *because of what it means* (a gesture of His love), but God is jealous when His creation is enjoyed without reference to Him.

The desirability of all good things comes from the goodness of God. Paul expressed the same principle in similar words. The Lord is called "Him who fills everything in every way" (Eph.1:23). That which has any fullness of any kind receives that fullness from the Lord. In order for enjoyment to exist there must be a spring of joy supplying that enjoyment. The natural assumption would be that the spring is the earthly things that one enjoys. The psalmist, however, points out that the spring of all his enjoyment was actually God.

There is a strong connection in Scripture between love for the world, idolatry, and spiritual adultery. Those who love the world are called adulteresses,[71] and those who are greedy are called idolaters.[72] The pleasures of the world are pictured both as rival gods and as rival husbands. This explains why adultery and idolatry are often used interchangeably in the prophets.[73] Desire is the foundation of all true

---

[71] Jas.4:4.

[72] Col.3:5, Eph.5:5.

[73] "Then in the nations where they have been carried captive, those who escape will remember me-- how I have been grieved by their <u>adulterous hearts</u>, which have turned away from me, and by their eyes, which have <u>lusted</u> after their <u>idols</u>" (Ezek.6:9). When a man or woman's heart prefers a created thing to God, that created thing is like a false god or another lover. When it is conceived in terms of how it is the object of worship, it is called idolatry. When it is conceived in terms of how it is the object of desire, it is called

worship. By desiring God the believer shows Him to be desirable, which glorifies Him. By desiring the world more than God a person tacitly declares the world to be more desirable than God. Looking to created things rather than God to satisfy desires, then, is idolatry. It lifts created things, rather than God, to the status of "most desirable."

Similarly, Israel's preference of their own "cisterns" (sources of satisfaction) over God's "spring of living water" constituted idolatry.

Jeremiah 2:11-13 'Has a nation ever changed its gods? (Yet they are not gods at all.) But my people have exchanged their Glory for worthless idols. Be appalled at this, O heavens, and shudder with great horror,' declares the LORD. 'My people have committed two sins: They have forsaken me, the spring of living water, and have dug their own cisterns, broken cisterns that cannot hold water.'

If a person's desire ever terminates upon a created thing rather than upon God, that person has fallen into idolatry. Lewis correctly notes that "In every wife, mother, child, and friend [Jesus] saw a possible rival to God."[74]

Diagnose desires by finding out from the person what he believes would be required in order for him to be happy. If it is something other than the nearness of God's presence, you have wonderful news for him. The thing he thinks he needs to be happy (most likely something he cannot have)—he does *not* need! And the thing that will satisfy the ache in his soul is available!

Diagnosing the Attitudes

The Greek word for attitude is *phroneo*. Like any word it can be used different ways, but generally it means *to be disposed or inclined, as having an attitude or frame of mind.* In most cases it either means to be inclined toward a certain viewpoint, or to be inclined toward a certain set of priorities. When Peter rebuked Jesus for talking about dying on the cross, Jesus reproved him for his attitude.

Matthew 16:23 Jesus turned and said to Peter, "Get behind me, Satan! You are a stumbling block to me; you are not thinking (*phroneo*) the things of God, but the things of men."

---

adultery. The comingling of the ideas shows the close connection between desire and worship.

[74] C.S. Lewis, The Four Loves, (New York: Harvest, 1960), 167.

The reference is not merely to Peter's thoughts, but to his frame of mind.[75]

Romans 12:15-16 Rejoice with those who rejoice; weep with those who weep, thinking (*phroneo*) the same toward one another...

"Thinking the same" means being inclined to weep over the same things and rejoice over the same things.[76]

Pride and humility fall into the category of attitudes. A few times we read that we are not to "think (*phroneo*) highly" regarding ourselves (Ro.11:20, 12:3,15-16). Instead, our attitude (*phroneo*) should be the same as that of Christ Jesus (Php.2:5).

Love also falls into the category of an attitude.

Philippians 1:7 It is right for me to feel (*phroneo*) this way about all of you.

Attitudes are particularly difficult to diagnose because they involve a complex of factors. In certain cases it may be appropriate to have a negative thought about a person, but not a negative attitude or disposition, and there is no objective point at which a series of thoughts crosses the line into being an attitude or disposition.

At the very least, however, the counselee should be instructed about God's requirements regarding attitudes. A frame of mind that is consistently or overly pessimistic, negative, harsh, condescending, selfish, or critical is sinful—even when negative thoughts are appropriate for certain specific elements. For example, if a church has a bent toward legalism or lack of compassion, it is appropriate for a person to humbly draw attention to that flaw in an effort to help solve the problem. But when there comes a point at which the person's critiques are always negative and he seems unable to appreciate anything positive that is an indication of a sinful attitude (In the letters to the churches in Revelation 2-3, even when churches were guilty of terrible sins, Jesus still did not overlook or minimize their areas of strength).

---

[75] See also Php.3:19, 4:2.for uses of the term *phroneo*.
[76] See also Ro.15:5, 2 Cor.13:11, Php.2:2, 3:15.

Diagnosing Beliefs

We have seen that words and actions arise from the heart. And the various sins in the heart (wrong attitudes, thoughts, motives, desires, decisions, and emotions) all rise out of wrong beliefs. The way to diagnose beliefs, then, is by observing the fruit they produce. A person who claims to believe the right thing even though his actions or feelings are not consistent with that belief is self-deceived.

James 2:18 ...I will show you my faith by what I do. ... 26 As the body without the spirit is dead, so faith without deeds is dead.

So wherever there is a sin in a person's life there will be a wrong belief at the heart of that sin. If a man views pornography it is because he believes, at the moment of temptation, that the pleasure he gets from that is to be preferred above the blessings of purity. A liar believes the benefits from the lie outweigh the benefits of telling the truth. There is always at least one wrong belief behind every sin, and the counselor's job is to help the person discover those wrong beliefs and assist him in persuading his soul of the truth.

Instill Hope! ! !

Taking a person through the process of diagnosis can result in a variety of responses. Some may be greatly encouraged, because what they thought was a hopeless mental disease turned out to be a problem for which Scripture offers solutions. Others, however, may become disheartened in this process as they discover that what they thought was a minor personality glitch actually stems from deeply rooted sins in the heart that are difficult to change.

An extremely important step in counseling is instilling hope in the counselee. Never simply expose problems and leave the person in despair until the next conversation. Despair results in paralysis and vulnerability to Satan. Reserve some time in the conversation to express optimism in the power of God's Word and the eagerness of the Lord to help the person. Counselees who expect God's Word to help them are much easier to counsel and have much better results than those who are discouraged.

CHAPTER FIVE:
ADDRESSING SIN

Whenever we discover a problem in the life of a brother or sister, God's command is that we restore the person.

Galatians 6:1 Brothers, if someone is caught by a sin, you who are spiritual should <u>restore</u> him gently. But watch yourself, or you also may be tempted.[77]

The word translated "restore" is *katarizo*, which means *to repair or make fit*. It was used in the Gospels of *mending* the fishing nets. In Luke 6:40, it refers to the process of training a disciple. It means to take someone from where he is to where he ought to be—repairing what is wrong, and bringing him to a point of spiritual fitness.

This command is revolutionary. Most people do not respond this way to sin in others. If our car breaks down, we spend time and money to get it repaired and back to proper working order. But when a brother or sister in Christ breaks down, how often is our response gossip, disdain, judgmentalism, ignoring the problem, or sweeping the person out to the fringes of our lives, rather than spending the time, energy, and resources necessary to restore the person? How often we are quicker to junk a servant of the living God than a broken-down car.

God commands restoration. And the first step in restoring a person who has been overtaken by a sin is to bring the person to repentance. If he is already repentant this step can be skipped, but if the person is continuing in unrepentant sin, Scripture gives the following instructions on how to stimulate a repentant heart.

"Show Him His Fault"

Matthew 18:15 If your brother sins against you, go and <u>show him his fault</u>.[78]

---

[77] Author's translation.

The counselee may be unaware of guilt because of ignorance of God's commands, self-deception, or lack of self-examination. Bringing such a person to realize his guilt involves two parts: exposing the wrongness of the action and persuading the person of guilt.

1) Expose the wrongness of an action

Ephesians 5:11,13 Have nothing to do with the fruitless deeds of darkness, but rather expose them. ... 13 everything exposed by the light becomes visible...

2) Persuade the person of his guilt

1 Corinthians 14:24 But if an unbeliever or someone who does not understand comes in while everybody is prophesying, he will be convinced by all that he is a sinner and will be judged by all....

Be Careful!

This is not a time for clumsiness or thoughtlessness. It is misguided to think that just because the person is in sin, it is OK to be rude, insensitive, or unnecessarily harsh. In many ways this is one of the most strategic moments in counseling. When you first present the person's fault to him, he can go one of two ways—humble repentance or defensiveness and denial. If something in your manner pushes him toward the latter, you have just made his condition much worse. Once he has denied the sin or begun making excuses for it, his heart has begun moving in the wrong direction. For him to be restored, that movement must be arrested and then reversed. Pushing a person toward a bad response by having a poorly thought-out approach is the height of cruelty. Use the Golden Rule. When someone sees a sin in your life, wouldn't you want that person to present it to you in a way that would make you open to receive correction, rather than pushing you in the direction of defensiveness?

---

[78] The Greek word here is *elegko*, and it is the same Greek word translated "expose" and "convinced that he is a sinner" in the texts above.

Rebuke

Once the sin is exposed, most Christians will respond with sorrow and repentance. If the person refuses to repent, however, it is time for rebuke.

Luke 17:3 "So watch yourselves. If your brother sins, rebuke him."

The Greek word here (epitimao) means *to rebuke, censure, warn, or punish.* This term is aimed at the will, not just the mind. It goes beyond persuading the person he has done wrong, and seeks to persuade the person to change. A rebuke is not a suggestion; it is a command that calls for action (Mt.8:26).

Admonish

The Greek word for *admonish* is *noutheteo*[79]. It means *to instruct or warn in an effort to correct behavior.*

1 Thessalonians 5:14 And we urge you, brothers, admonish those who are idle, encourage the timid, help the weak, be patient with everyone.[80]

2 Thessalonians 3:14,15 If anyone does not obey our instruction ... admonish him as a brother.[81]

Like every other step in the process, admonition must be done with God's Word. We must not use our own human wisdom to admonish one another.

Colossians 3:16 Let the word of Christ dwell in you richly as you teach and <u>admonish</u> one another with all wisdom....

Admonition gets its power from God's Word. Just pointing a finger and complaining about the person's behavior will not have divine power to bring about heart change. But showing a person his behavior and comparing it with what the Bible says infuses divine power and grace into the situation.

---

[79] This word is behind the phrase "Nouthetic Counseling." A nouthetic counselor is one who believes that people need biblical admonition, not psychological theories.
[80] Author's translation.
[81] Author's translation.

Admonition, Not Shaming

Admonishing is not the same as shaming—but it is similar enough that they can be easily confused. When Paul admonished the Corinthians, his words seemed so much like shaming that he had to clarify that what he was doing was admonition and not shaming.

1 Corinthians 4:14 I am not writing this to shame you, but to admonish you, as my dear children.[82]

The word translated *shame* means to cause someone to look down on himself. We are not to shame people (beat up on them and try to make them feel bad). The goal is to bring the person to the point of contrition—not despair. If there is not a skillful, loving approach the person may become discouraged and give up. Admonition tends to generate Godly sorrow driving the person to repentance; shaming tends toward worldly sorrow resulting in self-destruction (2 Cor.7:10) and self-condemnation.

Admonition, however, can look quite similar to shaming. Consider Paul's admonition:

1 Corinthians 4:7-8,10,13 For who makes you different from anyone else? What do you have that you did not receive? And ... why do you boast...? Already you have all you want! Already you have become rich! You have become kings—and that without us! ... We are fools for Christ, but you are so wise in Christ! We are weak, but you are strong! You are honored, we are dishonored! ... Up to this moment we have become the scum of the earth, the refuse of the world.

What sarcasm! No wonder he had to clarify that he was admonishing and not shaming. Sometimes admonition has to be harsh in order to be effective. But even if that kind of harshness is necessary it should break your heart, just as it did Paul's. Like a father welling up with compassion for the child he is disciplining, Paul finds himself unable to continue with the harshness any longer:

1 Corinthians 4:14,17 I am not writing this to shame you, but to admonish you, as my dear children.... I am sending to you Timothy, my son whom I love, who is faithful in the Lord. He will remind you of my way of life in Christ Jesus....

This is the heart of love. He would prefer to embrace them, but he knows there are times when strong words are needed:

---

[82] Author's translation.

1 Corinthians 4:18 Some of you have become arrogant....

People can become so desensitized to the convicting ministry of the Holy Spirit that gentle words simply do not get their attention. They need someone to love them enough to grab them by the lapel and shake them. The counselor must have the courage and strength to do that, and the wisdom and love to know the difference between admonishing and shaming.

Warning

When the sinning brother does not respond to admonition the temptation will be to give up. But there is still a powerful tool that must not be neglected—*warning*. Warn the person by alerting him to the consequences that will come if he does not repent. This can be tremendously helpful to the person in sin. Sin causes a loss of perspective and an inability to consider long-term consequences, and a loving, firm warning can bring him back to reality.

Some Categories of Biblical Warnings

Persistence in Sin

Deuteronomy 29:19-20 When such a person ... thinks, "I will be safe, even though I persist in going my own way." This will bring disaster ...20 The Lord will never be willing to forgive him; his wrath and zeal will burn against that man. All the curses written in this book will fall upon him.

Hebrews 10:26-27 If we deliberately keep on sinning after we have received the knowledge of the truth, no sacrifice for sins is left, 27 but only a fearful expectation of judgment and of raging fire that will consume the enemies of God.

Making Excuses

Proverbs 28:13 He who conceals his sins does not prosper, but whoever confesses and renounces them finds mercy.

Proverbs 10:9 The man of integrity walks securely, but he who takes crooked paths will be found out.

Dabbling with Sin

Proverbs 5:22 The evil deeds of a wicked man ensnare him; the cords of his sin hold him fast.

Ecclesiastes 7:26 I find more bitter than death the woman who is a snare, whose heart is a trap and whose hands are chains. The man who pleases God will escape her, but the sinner she will ensnare.

Forfeited Grace, Estrangement from God

Jonah 2:8 Those who cling to worthless idols forfeit the grace that could be theirs.

Proverbs 28:9 If anyone turns a deaf ear to the law, even his prayers are detestable.

Psalm 30:6-7 When I felt secure, I said, "I will never be shaken." 7 O Lord, when you favored me, you made my mountain stand firm; but when you hid your face, I was dismayed.

Proverbs 15:8 The Lord detests the sacrifice of the wicked, but the prayer of the upright pleases him.

Isaiah 57:12-13 I will expose your righteousness and your works, and they will not benefit you. 13 When you cry out for help, let your collection [of idols] save you! The wind will carry all of them off, a mere breath will blow them away. But the man who makes me his refuge will inherit the land and possess my holy mountain.

Ephesians 5:3-7 But among you there must not be even a hint of sexual immorality, or of any kind of impurity, or of greed, because these are improper for God's holy people. 4 Nor should there be obscenity, foolish talk or coarse joking, which are out of place, but rather thanksgiving. 5 For of this you can be sure: No immoral, impure or greedy person-- such a man is an idolater--has any inheritance in the kingdom of Christ and of God. 6 Let no one deceive you with empty words, for because of such things God's wrath comes on those who are disobedient. 7 Therefore do not be partners with them.

Exposure and Punishment

2 Corinthians 5:10 For we must all appear before the judgment seat of Christ, that each one may receive what is due him for the things done while in the body, whether good or bad.

Proverbs 15:10 Stern discipline awaits him who leaves the path; he who hates correction will die.

Hebrews 13:4 Marriage should be honored by all, and the marriage bed kept pure, for God will judge the adulterer and all the sexually immoral.

Destruction and Death

Hosea 9:10 ... they became as vile as the thing they loved.

Romans 6:21-22 What benefit did you reap at that time from the things you are now ashamed of? Those things result in death! 22 But now that you have been set free from sin and have become slaves to God, the benefit you reap leads to holiness, and the result is eternal life.

Job 31:1-4 I made a covenant with my eyes not to look lustfully at a girl. 2 For what is man's lot from God above, his heritage from the Almighty on high? 3 Is it not ruin for the wicked, disaster for those who do wrong? 4 Does he not see my ways and count my every step?

Proverbs 25:28 Like a city whose walls are broken down is a man who lacks self-control.

Proverbs 7:21-23 With persuasive words she led him astray; she seduced him with her smooth talk. 22 All at once he followed her like an ox going to the slaughter, like a deer stepping into a noose 23 till an arrow pierces his liver, like a bird darting into a snare, little knowing it will cost him his life.

When is the last time you warned someone of the consequences of sin? Warning is a neglected responsibility in our day, as it is unpleasant and requires careful thought and study. But it may very well be the key to rescuing a brother from destruction.

Provoke

Like the English word *provoke*, the Greek word *paroxusmos* is normally used negatively, such as in being provoked to anger (1 Cor.13:5, Acts 17:16). The writer of Hebrews, however, commands that we provoke others—not to anger, but to love and good deeds.

Hebrews 10:24-25 And let us consider how we may spur (lit., provoke) one another on toward love and good deeds. Let us not give up meeting together, as some are in the habit of doing, but let us encourage one another—and all the more as you see the Day approaching.

In addition to exposing the person's fault to him, rebuking him, admonishing him, and warning him, seek to *provoke* him to love and good deeds. Inflame the person—not to wrath, but to the Christian way of life. Give some extended thought to how to "push his buttons"—not buttons that activate sin, but buttons that stimulate righteousness. Learn what kinds of things motivate this particular person and make your appeal from that perspective. Strive to make the godly response seem attractive to him.

Repentance

The goal of exposing, admonishing, rebuking, warning, and provoking is repentance. Once the person has repented, all reproof and rebuke should cease and give way to forgiveness, encouragement, and comfort.

Life or Death

When Scripture summarizes the entire message of Jesus, one word emerges: "Repent."[83] The same goes for the ministry of John the Baptist and the apostles.[84] Where there is no repentance, there is no hope of forgiveness of sins, knowing God, or going to heaven.[85] It is possible for a true Christian to go for a time refusing to repent, but generally speaking, the unrepentant heart is the heart of an unbeliever.

Definition

Repentance is not simply sorrow or regret over sin. One can feel suicidal with guilt and regret and still not be repentant. Nor is repentance simply admitting to being imperfect and resolving to do better. Everyone does that.

In the Old Testament there are two components of repentance: sorrow and turning.[86] When a person finally admits the direction of his life is moving away from God and becomes contrite and broken, and then reverses the direction of his life toward God, that is repentance.

Repentance involves the whole person, including the inner man.

Isaiah 55:7 Let the wicked forsake his <u>way</u> and the evil man his <u>thoughts</u>. Let him turn to the Lord, and he will have mercy on him.

---

[83] **Matthew 4:17 From that time Jesus began to preach, "Repent, for the kingdom of heaven is near."**
Luke 5:32 "I have come to call ... sinners to repentance."
[84] Mt.3:12, Acts 2:14-41, Mk.6:12, Lk.24:46-47, Acts 17:30-31.
[85] Acts 2:38, 3:19, Lk.13:5, 2 Pe.3:9.
[86] The Greek word for "repentance" (*metanoeo*) translates both the Hebrew SHOOV (to turn or return) and NAHAM (to be sorrowful, to regret).

There is a reversal in both one's *thoughts* and his *way* (or path). It is a redirection of the will. It is not a mere resolution but a whole new path of life.

The Prodigal Son's Repentance

In Luke 15 Jesus describes the exuberant joy God experiences when a sinner repents. This chapter is particularly helpful for understanding what repentance is because Jesus actually describes the thought process of the prodigal as he repents.

He had taken his father's money, left home, and blown it all on wild living. Beginning in verse 17 Jesus describes the young man's repentance in several steps:

1. Waking up to Reality

When he came to his senses... (Luke 15:17a)

To come to one's senses[1] means to wake up to what is really going on. When we are in sin we are in denial—detached from reality in a fantasy world thinking, *I can keep going down this path and still be okay,* or *I'll be able to recover easily enough,* or *What I'm doing is not really sin.* The first step in repentance is to wake up to reality and acknowledge *I am walking away from God, and unless something drastic happens, I will only get further from Him.*

When a person comes to his senses it produces a powerful sense of urgency in repentance. A lackadaisical repentance ("Yeah, I guess what I did was wrong—sort of"), or a grudging repentance ("Alright already! I admit it—I was wrong. There—are you happy now?") are signs that the person really has not come to grips with reality yet. True repentance has a powerful earnestness. Another important passage in Scripture on the subject of repentance is 2 Corinthians 7:11, where the repentance of the Corinthian church is described. Notice how much Paul focuses on their passion and earnestness as markers of the genuineness of their repentance:

2 Corinthians 7:11 See what this godly sorrow has produced in you: what earnestness, what eagerness to clear yourselves, what indignation, what alarm, what longing, what concern, what readiness to see justice done. At every point you have proved yourselves to be innocent in this matter.

While I was studying this subject of godly sorrow, I received a call from a woman in our church who gently reproved me for lacking Christ-like compassion for people who suffer. At first I was a little defensive, but after listening for several minutes, I realized this was a valid rebuke.

When the conversation ended, I went right back to work. I did not want to let anything interrupt my study. After all, I don't have time to sit around and think about that sin in my life—I'm too busy preparing to teach the church how to be serious about repentance!

I had to study almost all of 2 Corinthians 7:11 before it finally sank in that I was ignoring the very truth I was attempting to learn. So I backed away from my desk and spent some time in prayer—confessing that I did not have the same attitude toward that sin that God had. I cried out to Him to conform my thinking to His, and to grant repentance. Then I spent some time thinking about how I could be energetic, zealous, and hasty about making changes in that area, and I began putting those ideas into action.

How easy it is for us to take our sin lightly! God is so patient, gracious, and forgiving that we can easily be deceived in thinking our sin is not really all that serious. But true repentance comes only when godly sorrow produces earnestness.

2. Realizing Consequences

... he said, 'How many of my father's hired men have food to spare, and here I am starving to death!" (Luke 15:17*b*)

The unrepentant person downplays the damage his sin has caused, but true brokenness involves coming to grips with the destructiveness of the sin.

3. Returning to the Father

I will set out and go back to my father. (Luke 15:18*a*)

This is the crux of the issue with repentance. He does not say, "Look at my budget; I've got to cut back on being so wild and promiscuous." The heart of the issue was not his spending or activities. *The real issue was that he had walked away from his father, and the solution was to go back to his father*. If one's repentance is nothing but reforming behavior, it is not true repentance. Repentance is not just turning from sin, but turning from sin *to God.*

In 2 Corinthians 7:10 Paul differentiates between worldly sorrow (which leads to death) and godly sorrow (which leads to repentance). Feeling bad about sin is not repentance. It is not even half the battle. It is none of the battle. Satan can use that sorrow over sin to destroy the person just as easily as he can use the sin itself. Sorrow over sin is only good when it drives a person back to the Father.

Part of returning to the Father is returning to His people. There is no fellowship with God without fellowship with the people of God.

1 John 1:7 But if we walk in the light, as he is in the light, we have fellowship with one another, and the blood of Jesus, his Son, purifies us from all sin.

One of the proofs of the genuine repentance of the Corinthians was their longing to be restored to fellowship not only with God but also with Paul (2 Cor.7:7). Unrepentant sinners generally do not desire the company of righteous people. The excuse may be that the Church is filled with hypocrites, or that they have been mistreated by Christians in the past, but the reality is that those who love the light love fellowship (1 Jn.1:7), and those who do not, generally have something to hide.

John 3:20 Everyone who does evil hates the light, and will not come into the light for fear that his deeds will be exposed.

True repentance brings a deep longing for nearness to godly people. When David repented of his sin with Bathsheba he said, "Men of a perverse heart will be far from me.... My eyes will be on the faithful in the land that they may dwell with me" (Ps.101:4,6).

4. Confession

I will ... say to him: "Father, I have sinned against heaven and against you." (Luke 15:18b)

Repentance requires admitting sinfulness—against both God and people. It is not enough simply to confess to God. Confession must also be made to those who were hurt by the sin. (Wisdom must be used here. If confessing the sin will do more harm than good, it may be wisest not to bring it up. For example, if a person has harbored angry, spiteful thoughts toward a brother, but that brother has no idea, it would be hurtful to confess the specifics of that sin to him. A better approach may be to simply say, "I have not loved you as I should").

5. Humility

I am no longer worthy to be called your son make me like one of your hired men. (Luke 15:19)

True repentance never says, "Okay God, I've jumped through your hoops, now it is time for you to restore me." It never demands anything. The repentant heart seeks restoration of the broken relationship on any terms, with a posture of lowliness and unworthiness. The person who balks at the idea of taking steps to prevent future temptation because he is afraid he may not be happy living that way gives indication that his repentance is not real.

Signs of True Repentance

Urge the counselee to honestly ask himself these questions:

1) Have I awakened from the spiritual stupor that got me here?
2) Have I confessed to those I hurt and to God?
3) Are those people satisfied that I have come to grips with how much damage my sin has done?
4) Am I merely turning away from the sin, or am I turning away from the sin *toward* the Father?
5) Do I have an insistent drive to be clean before God right now?
6) Is there a strong distaste for that sin?
7) Is there a healthy fear of God—taking His commands seriously?
8) Is there a longing for fellowship with godly people?
9) Is there a strong zeal for God's honor and glory?
10) Is there an unreserved, unqualified, unequivocal willingness to give up the sin by cutting off access to future temptation?

The last sentence of 2 Corinthians 7:11 is wonderful: "At every point you have proved yourselves to be innocent in this matter." How could they prove themselves innocent in the matter? Were they not guilty of the sin? Obviously they were—otherwise they would not have needed to repent. Clearly they were guilty, but now they are innocent. How? They are now innocent, because repentance brings forgiveness. Their guilt was transferred to Christ. Once a person has repented and turned back to the Lord, he does not have to live with oppressive feelings of regret and sorrow anymore. What a blessed truth!

In church "discipline,"[87] the process is to continue until the sinner repents, at which point the goal is reached and discipline is over. It is necessary, then, to understand what repentance looks like. We cannot see into people's hearts, yet it is our job to determine whether or not a person has repented (otherwise we cannot know whether to continue with the next step in the Matthew 18 restoration process).

Since we do not have the ability to see into another person's heart, Scripture teaches us to detect repentance by words and deeds. If a person claims to be repentant and is willing to take necessary steps toward preventing future temptation, we must regard him as truly repentant—even if there are repeated failures and stumbling.

Luke 17:4 If he sins against you seven times in a day, and seven times comes back to you and says, 'I repent,' forgive him."

Acts 26:20 I preached that they should repent and turn to God and prove their repentance by their deeds.

Seeking a Repentant Heart

In some cases, upon hearing what Scripture teaches about true repentance the person will say, "I wish I were truly repentant, but I do not see those qualities in my life. How do I become repentant?" Here are some steps:

1. Pray for It

Repentance is an act of the will, but it is also sovereignly granted by God. Ask God to break your heart over your sin and grant you repentance.

---

[87] "Church discipline" is not the best term to describe the process Jesus commanded in Matthew 18:15-20. The purpose is not punishment, but restoration. A better description would be "Church Restoration."

2 Timothy 2:25 Those who oppose him he must gently instruct, in the hope that God will grant them repentance leading them to a knowledge of the truth.

2. Use God's Chastisement to Generate Fear of Him

The pain of regret, the sense of distance from God's presence, Scripture becoming just print on a page rather than satisfying nourishment to the soul, prayers seemingly bouncing off the ceiling—all these can be expressions of God's displeasure. When we have sinned egregiously against God and have not repented, it is good to interpret those kinds of hardships as expressions of God's displeasure with us.

3. Consider God's Patience and Kindness

Romans 2:4 Do you show contempt for the riches of his kindness, tolerance and patience, not realizing that God's kindness leads you toward repentance?

Think about how much kindness and patience God has shown you even as you were sinning against Him. Thinking about His kindness in the face of our rebellion should break our hearts.

4. Immerse Yourself in God's Word with a Submissive Attitude

1 Corinthians 14:24-25 But if an unbeliever or someone who does not understand comes in while everybody is prophesying, he will be convinced by all that he is a sinner and will be thoroughly examined by all, and the deep things of his heart will be laid bare. So he will fall down and worship God, exclaiming, "God is really among you!"[88]

The prophecies have been preserved today in written form as the New Testament (2 Peter 1:19-21). God's Word has the power to convince a person that he is a sinner (v. 24). It puts both the sin and the person's guilt right out on the table in clear daylight.

Secondly, the person is "thoroughly examined" (v. 24), laying bare "the deep things of his heart" (v. 25). When repentance is shallow or halfhearted, it may be that the person is focusing on the actions only and

---

[88] Author's Translation.

has not considered the "deep things" (subtle motives, sinful attitudes, selfish biases, etc.).

When the deep things are exposed by the Word of God, the effect is to cause the person to "fall down and worship God" in humility and brokenness (v. 25).

5. Fast

In the Old Testament, people were judged not on the basis of their sinfulness, but according to whether they would humble themselves once confronted with their sinfulness.[89] One way of humbling our own hearts is by fasting.

Psalm 35:13 I put on sackcloth and humbled myself with fasting.

Going without food, in and of itself, means nothing. Going without food as an empty religious ritual is offensive to God. Going without food to punish yourself for your sin is a mockery of Jesus' work on the cross. Going without food for the purpose of humbling your heart, however, can pave the way for true repentance.

Assessing Repentance

Even with all the principles Scripture supplies describing repentance, assessing whether repentance is genuine is not always easy because our repentance, like any other act of righteousness, is never all that it should be. We fall short. Judging the genuineness of someone's repentance, then, is particularly difficult. Some of the marks of repentance are clear; others are questionable. If a person claims to be repentant but shows no fruit at all, that should not be regarded as true repentance. But how *much fruit* must be shown?

1. Set the Standard High for Yourself and Low for Others

Each person should err on the side of suspicion with his own repentance, and err on the side of grace with others.

---

[89] Ex.10:3; 2 Chrn.7:14, 30:11, 36:12; Jer.44:10; Dan.5:22, 2 Chrn.12:6-12, 33:11-13.

2. Make the Standard Clear

Very often when one person in the church is accusing another of unrepentance, there is no clear standard of what would be accepted as true repentance. The accuser must always be able to describe to the sinner exactly what would be accepted as repentance.

3. Focus on the Present

If the person's sin was in the distant past, and it is not ongoing now, and the person acknowledges that it was wrong, accept that as genuine repentance.

The most important marker of repentance is the actions of the person's life. It is difficult to assess those actions immediately after the sin, so the person's words of sorrow and resolve are the main indicators at the time of confession. When the sin is in the past, however, actions can be assessed, and the clear track record since is more significant than the apparent level of sorrow (since God does not want us to remain in a state of sorrow and brokenness indefinitely).

Self-Forgiveness?

Many times the problem seems to be just the opposite of unrepentance. The person has repented, but still feels condemned. The guilt feelings persist—even to the point of having a paralyzing effect on the person's walk with the Lord.

Some Christians attempt to use self-condemnation as a strategy for attaining greater success in the Christian life—attempting to punish themselves through intensifying feelings of guilt and failure. According to Scripture, however, self-condemnation is a problem that needs to be solved (1 Jn.3:21-22). Guilt feelings that drive a person to repentance and to seek nearness to God are good; but self-condemnation that paralyzes and causes the person to be reluctant to draw near to God with boldness and confidence is bad.[90] If all one's prayers are nothing but

---

[90] The New Testament is filled with passages that speak of the importance of having boldness and confidence in approaching God in prayer. Jesus devoted an entire parable to that point (Lk.11:1-13). See also...

self-deprecation, that does not lend itself to an intimate relationship. Once an offense has been fully forgiven, continual groveling harms rather than helps, the relationship.

Furthermore, self-condemnation is an effort to place one's self on God's throne as the ultimate Judge. It is a refusal to accept His verdict in favor of one's own verdict.

The solution secular psychology offers to the problem of self-condemnation is self-forgiveness. Many Christian counselors have accepted this unbiblical idea as well. "God has forgiven you; now you need to learn to forgive yourself." Nowhere does Scripture call us to forgive ourselves, because the very idea of self-forgiveness is nonsense. Forgiveness is the canceling of a debt and a willingness to absorb the loss. It is nonsense to speak of canceling a debt to oneself by absorbing that debt oneself!

Furthermore, urging the person to forgive himself only perpetuates the error that is causing the problem in the first place. The error is his belief that he, rather than God, is the ultimate Judge. Urging him to forgive himself only reinforces that false belief.

The solution to self-condemnation is found in 1 John 3.

1 John 3:19-20 This then is how we know that we belong to the truth, and how we set our hearts at rest in his presence 20 whenever our hearts condemn us. For God is greater than our hearts, and he knows everything.

When our hearts condemn us, the solution is to preach to our hearts and convince them that God is greater than our hearts. When our feelings say one thing and God's Word says something different, God's Word is right and our heart is wrong. God's assessment is that when we have repented the guilt is gone, and God's assessment trumps ours. Pointing to self-forgiveness as a solution implies that our own assessment is what matters, rather than God's.

---

1 John 5:14 This is the confidence we have in approaching God: that if we ask anything according to his will, he hears us.
2 Corinthians 3:4 We have such confidence through Christ before God.
Ephesians 3:12 In him and through faith in him we may approach God with freedom and confidence.
Hebrews 3:14 We have come to share in Christ if we hold firmly till the end the confidence we had at first.
Hebrews 4:16 Let us then approach the throne of grace with confidence.
Hebrews 10:19, 22, 35 Therefore, brothers, since we have confidence to enter the Most Holy Place by the blood of Jesus ... let us draw near ... 35 So do not throw away your confidence; it will be richly rewarded.

It is Satan who continues to accuse and condemn us after we have repented and have been forgiven. Self-condemnation is nothing less than joining the Accuser in his work. Satan's aim is to destroy the work of God in our lives, limit our intimacy with Him and boldness in prayer, and paralyze us in ministry. When we submit to Satan's efforts to condemn us, the solution is not self-forgiveness, but rather repentance of our failure to trust in the work of the Lord Jesus Christ on our behalf.

Many times when there is ongoing, crippling anxiety over past sin it is because the person does not trust God with regard to His perfect plan in the past. God could have prevented the sin, but He chose not to. He has a perfect purpose in all that He does and all that He allows. And while there may be bitter consequences from a past sin, we can trust God that He knew what He was doing when He chose not to prevent that particular sin, and as bitter as the consequences are, the good that God is accomplishing through that past action is so marvelous that it dwarfs the size of the evil.

When There is No Repentance

In the tragic case of hardened refusal to repent, the counselor must follow the Lord's command in Matthew 18:15-18 and 1 Corinthians 5:1-13. Bring one or two witnesses and try again to bring him to repentance with a humble, gentle attitude (Gal.6:1). If he still will not repent, take the matter to the church and allow the entire assembly to humbly call him to repentance. If he continues to persist in sin even then, put him out of the assembly.

CHAPTER SIX:
HEART SURGERY

Chapter 4 discussed diagnosis—discovering problems in the heart. The process of heart diagnosis exposes sins in the motives, decisions, will, attitudes, desires, emotions, thoughts, and beliefs. Step one in recovering from these sins is repentance (Chapter 5). Repentance, however, is not the only step in overcoming sin. Unless steps are taken to defeat sin in the heart, there will be a continued cycle of falling, repenting, then falling again. The purpose of this chapter is to explore ways to help a person once he has repented and is willing to change.

Don't Forget the Basics

Thinking through all the complexities of the heart can be a daunting task and can leave both counselor and counselee overwhelmed. When this happens, remember the basics—Scripture, prayer, and fellowship. These will solve a great number of problems even when those problems are beyond the understanding of the counselee—much like food strengthens the body whether or not the eater understands the nutritional properties and digestive processes.

Imagine a person going to a doctor because he is feeling weak and lethargic. The doctor asks, "Have you been eating any food?"

"No, I have not had food in several weeks, but that's not my problem. It goes much deeper than that. Can't you run some tests on my hormones and blood sugar levels or do a CAT scan or something?"

That doctor will put all his years of medical training to work and tell him, "Go have a sandwich." It is a simple solution, but it is not superficial. The way the nutrients in a sandwich are absorbed and used in the body are incredibly complex. A person could spend years of his life studying all the reasons he feels better after eating. But it is not necessary for him to understand those reasons. All that is necessary is for him to put some food in his mouth and chew it up and swallow. If he does that and still has a problem, then the doctor will examine the issue further.

A conversation like that with a doctor would sound ridiculous in the physical realm, but it happens all the time in the spiritual realm.

"I'm struggling in my Christian walk."

"Are you attending a solid, Bible-teaching church every week?"

"No."

"Are you involved in regular corporate prayer at church?"

"No."

"Are you a part of a small group during the week where people can get to know you and be involved in your life and know how to pray for you?"

"No."

"Do you spend time each day in God's Word and prayer, seeking spiritual nourishment?"

"No."

"Are you making any concerted effort to pursue deep Christian friendships outside of Sunday morning services?"

"No."

There is nothing superficial about urging a person like this to focus on the basics. Sustained, long-term spiritual nourishment will result in strengthening in every area of the heart. The solutions below and in the rest of this book can be helpful in areas of particular problems that persist even after the person has been faithful to feed his soul, but the basics of nutrition are always the starting place.

Correcting Wrong Motives

When the process of diagnosis reveals sinful motives, step one is repentance. Urge the counselee to confess and renounce wrong motives and to turn back to God in that area.

Sinful motives are the product of pride (the desire to gain glory for self) and selfishness (placing self ahead of the best interests of others). The solution to both is humility. Assist the counselee in seeking to learn this all-important virtue. (See below under "Correcting Wrong Attitudes.")

Like all sins in the heart, sinful motives spring from wrong beliefs. A second crucial factor in correcting sinful motives, then, is discovering what wrong beliefs underlie them. If a person has motives of self-glorification, it may come from the belief that honor from men is more valuable than honor from God. If the motive is revenge, the underlying belief may be that God's justice is not reliable. If the motive is relief from suffering at all cost, there may be a problem with believing what God has said in his Word about suffering.

Correcting Wrong Decisions

Walk by the Spirit

When a Christian is resolved to choose what is right but finds that he repeatedly chooses what is wrong at the moment of decision, it is because he is being controlled by what Paul calls "the flesh," and the solution is the walk by the Spirit.

Galatians 5:16 But I say, walk by the Spirit, and you will not gratify the desires of the flesh.[91]

The "flesh" is used figuratively by Paul for that part of a Christian that sins. The flesh wars against the believer and constantly pushes in the direction of sin. Fighting against the flesh will always be a losing battle if any method is used other than walking by the Holy Spirit. The Spirit uses Scripture to guide the believer moment by moment on where to take the next step. He uses conscience, emotional impulses, thoughts, particular insights, wise decisions—all informed and powered by Scripture to enable us to keep in step with Him as He leads us. As long as a person keeps in step with the Holy Spirit, that person will be able to resist the impulses of the flesh toward sin. Stepping away from the way the Spirit guides makes one vulnerable to the flesh.

For example, if the Spirit enables a person to know that the best decision on a particular evening would be to go to a Bible study, but the person chooses instead to stay home and do some chores, he is out of step with the Spirit, and when temptation strikes he will not succeed in

---

[91] ESV.

fighting it. If the Spirit makes it clear by means of biblical principles and wisdom that the best decision on a particular evening would be to stay home and not go to the Bible study, but the person goes to the Bible study anyway, again—he will be vulnerable to the power of the flesh when temptation comes. It is by keeping in step with the Spirit that we remain in the bubble of protection that enables us to conquer the flesh.

This is why Scripture so often warns of the danger of flirting with temptation.

Proverbs 5:8 Keep to a path far from her, do not go near the door of her house.

The fool thinks he can pass nearby temptation's door, give a few curious glances, even dabble just a bit, but still be able to resist. Prior to the onslaught of temptation it always seems as though resisting would be easy. Prior to being tempted, there is no strong desire for the sin, so there is a feeling of invincibility. Lack of temptation is mistaken for spiritual strength. No doubt Satan often goes out of his way to make sure we do not feel any tinges of temptation until he gets us lured in close enough to spring the trap. But as soon as the fool has wandered within reach, temptation reaches out her hands, and the moment those hands touch him he discovers that her hands are actually handcuffs.

Ecclesiastes 7:26 I find more bitter than death the woman who is a snare, whose heart is a trap and whose hands are chains. The man who pleases God will escape her, but the sinner she will ensnare.

The only escape is to walk in a way pleasing to the Lord (walk by the Spirit). The fool who wanders from the Spirit's guidance will be ensnared when the trap springs.

The question for the believer, then, is not, "Is what I'm doing right now OK?" or "Would God understand, given my circumstances?" or, "Is this hurting anyone?" but rather, "Is this what the Holy Spirit wants me to be doing right now?" If the answer is "no" then the person is in sin, he is out of step with the Spirit, and he is making himself a sitting duck for the enemy to tempt toward even more destructive sins.

Starve the Flesh

Colossians 3:5 Put to death, therefore, whatever belongs to your earthly nature: sexual immorality, impurity, lust, evil desires and greed, which is idolatry.

Even after receiving a new nature, still the Christian has sinful desires that are so much a part of him they are like body parts. Those evil desires must be put to death. The word translated "put to death" is a rare term that speaks of death by withering away. The idea is not so much to actively kill something as it is to neglect it to the point that it withers on the vine.

Imagine you are back in school and you are being terrorized by a bully by the name of Sarx. You complain to the principal, and he responds by giving you Sarx's meal ticket. So unless you feed him, he cannot eat. After a couple of weeks without eating, Sarx is no longer any problem. As long as you have that meal ticket, you can keep him as weak as you want.

Sarx is the Greek word for "flesh" (the part of the Christian that sins). The flesh will weaken if it is not fed. When it is fed, however, it becomes overwhelmingly powerful. The man who struggles with lust clicks on the television at night and sees things that are not necessarily pornographic but worldly enough that they feed the flesh, and soon temptation is out of control.

This principle holds *whenever* the flesh is fed—even if it seems to be in an unrelated area. A person who struggles with overeating might feed the flesh in the morning by giving in to laziness. "I'll sleep in an extra half hour." Then again a few hours later, "I don't feel like doing laundry right now. I'll catch up tomorrow." With each decision to give in to the impulses of the flesh, Sarx gets a little stronger. Then, in mid afternoon, the flesh makes his demands, "Indulge in this sin—NOW!" and the battle is no contest. Feeding the flesh 12 hours a day and feeding the spirit with the Word of God five minutes a day and then expecting spiritual victory is like sowing weeds throughout a field and expecting to harvest wheat.

Understand the Source of Satisfaction

Obviously there are countless factors that go into why a person decides one way or another. One of the most important is this: Where does he look for satisfaction of the appetites of his soul? If a person resolves to study Scripture, but at the moment of decision decides in favor of watching TV instead, it is because deep down his soul thinks that TV watching will be more satisfying. The allure of sin and the power of temptation will be overwhelming as long as the soul believes the "benefits" of that sin are needed to satisfy its appetites.

This calls for a two-part solution. First, instruct the counselee about the food-likeness of God—that God is the only source of joy and satisfaction of the soul, and looking to anything else is a desire disorder (like craving sawdust when one is thirsty) and idolatry (putting a created thing in the place of God). Once the counselee understands this principle,[92] step two is to retrain the desires.

To retrain the desires, the pleasures of sin must be eclipsed by greater delights. This is the only way to attain lasting victory. The man in Matthew 13:44 sold all his possessions. What motivation was powerful enough to enable him to make such a sacrifice? *Joy*!

Matthew 13:44 The kingdom of heaven is like treasure hidden in a field. When a man found it, he hid it again, and then in his joy went and sold all he had and bought that field.

The treasure in the field was worth so much more to him than his possessions that he could not make the trade fast enough. There was no sacrifice—only gain. Consistent victory over a besetting sin will come only when the gain of greater nearness to God is a treasure so supremely valuable to the heart that it dwarfs the pleasure of the sin.

Correcting Wrong Desires

The reason the pleasures of this life exist is to teach us what it is like to be in the presence of God. They are samples of heaven. Desires become corrupted when earthly delights are seen as the sources of joy and satisfaction, rather than as mere "straws" through which the water of God is enjoyed (for an explanation of this principle review the section titled "Desire and Righteous Living" in Chapter 4). To guard us from this mistake God sometimes allows the pleasures of this world to leave us dry and empty. He allows them to be a straw with no water on the

---

[92] For an explanation of this principle review the section titled "Desire and Righteous Living" in Chapter 4.

other end so we are reminded that the straw has no power in itself to quench the thirst of the soul and is not a joy-source.

Make Much of the World's Failures to Satisfy

Urge the counselee to take notice and preach to his soul whenever earthly things leave him empty: "Do you see that, soul? Nothing in this world can satisfy your hunger and thirst!" Of course there is temporary pleasure associated with earthly things, but apart from an experience of the presence of God it not only fails to satisfy the soul, but once the fleeting pleasure is gone it leaves an even greater sense of emptiness and craving than before.

Look beyond the straw

When the pleasures of this world do bring a sense of satisfaction and joy, the sermon to self becomes, *"Don't get confused, soul—this sense of satisfaction is not coming from the straw (the pleasurable activity, relationship, music, etc.). It is coming from the water itself (the presence of God). The only reason this activity is producing a sense of satisfaction and joy is that God is graciously granting that the end of the straw be dipped into the water of His presence."* Remind the counselee to never let a satisfying experience attract his soul to an earthly thing. Use all the delights of life to cause the soul to be attracted to the Source of the satisfaction that comes through those delights—the presence of God.

All satisfying experiences and all unsatisfying experiences, then, can be used to assist the person in repairing desire disorder.

Scriptures for changing desires: Isaiah 55:2, Jeremiah 2:13, Psalm 36:7-8, Psalm 63:5, Psalm 4:7, Jonah 2:8

Sermons on changing desires:
- "Loving God with All Your Heart" sermon series[93]

---

[93] FoodForYourSoul.net. The sermon series are listed in alphabetical order on the "Series Alphabetically" link.

- "Righteousness and Possessions" sermon series

Correcting Wrong Attitudes

The word "attitude" (Greek, *phroneo*) refers to one's outlook on something or someone. An attitude is sinful if it does not conform to God's, so the solution to sinful attitudes is to understand the beauty and goodness of God's attitude.

Again, step one is repentance. Very often the counselee will have repented of specific sinful words and actions, but not for his sinful attitude in general.

Negative Disposition Toward a Person

One of the most common attitude problems is a negative, unloving disposition toward a particular person. When the counselee notices everything that person does wrong, nothing that person does right, and tends to cast a negative light on everything about that person—that is an attitude that conflicts with God's way of looking at that person. Urge the counselee to spend time studying and thinking deeply about God's heart toward that person. Remind him of what was going through the mind of God toward that person when He sacrificed His own Son so he could be forgiven. A good exercise for reversing a negative attitude toward a person is to always think of that person whenever Scripture speaks of God's love. Normally when we hear sermons or read books about God's love we think in terms of His love for us. Urge the counselee to think instead of God's love toward that individual.

Pessimism

Another common attitude sin is pessimism. The pessimist assumes God will probably send the most painful, troublesome circumstance rather than a delightful one for no good reason. This reflects a distorted view of God's nature. Correct this attitude by helping open the counselee's eyes to the goodness of God. This is done by studying passages of Scripture that speak of His kindness and goodness and by pointing out examples of God's kindness in the person's life. Every person receives thousands of blessings from God every day. Teach the counselee to cultivate a lifestyle of gratitude toward God for past, current, and future blessings.

Aversion to Authority

A third common attitude problem is an aversion toward authority. When a person has a negative, ungrateful view of authority, teach him from Scripture about the blessedness of being led by God. It is a great privilege to be guided through this life and shown the right way to go. And God delegates His authority to human authorities (Ro.13:1-2). Even when those human authorities make foolish decisions, if what they are requiring is not sin then the person under authority can be assured that the mandates from that authority are the very will of God for him— even if they are unwise. Teach him to delight in knowing the will of God!

Pride and Selfishness

Two other common attitude problems are pride and selfishness. The solution to both is humility.

Resources for Learning Humility

Scriptures: Philippians 2:1-11, Luke 18:9-14, 1 Peter 5:5, Psalm 35:13

Sermons on humility by Darrell Ferguson:[94]
- "The Right Side of the Bus" (Mt.5:3)
- "The Sooners and the Soft" (Mt.5:5)
- "Fasting" parts 1-2 (Mt.6:16-18)
- "Logectomy" (Mt.7:3-5)

---

[94] FoodForYourSoul.net. Sermons on each text can be found by clicking "Sermons by Book/Chapter."

- "Learning Humility" parts 1,2 (Eph.4:2)
- "Humility" parts 1-16 (Php.2)
- "Ingredients of Joyful Worship" (2 Sam.6:13-23)

Book: The book "Humility" by C.J. Mahaney

Correcting Wrong Emotions

Sinful emotions are another area where repentance must be emphasized because the idea that emotions can be sinful is so foreign to our culture. Anything in a person's life that does not conform to the standards of God's Word must be repented of, including ungodly feelings. Repentance of wrong emotions, however, is more difficult because emotions are the result of assessments and beliefs. A situation is assessed by the mind, that assessment is weighed against the norms of the belief system, and the feeling that results is emotion.[95] Whenever an emotion violates Scripture it is either because the situation is being assessed incorrectly or the belief system is flawed. Some of the most common emotional problems are anger, fear, worry, apathy, fretting, discouragement, and depression. Each of these will be discussed in depth in Part Two of this book ("Mood Problems").

Correcting Wrong Thoughts

The most difficult aspect of self-control is discipline in the thought life. It is so much easier to think a thought than to carry out an action, that if there is any willingness to sin at all it will come out in the thought life.

Fighting Obsessive Thoughts

Very often counselees will suffer from a thought pattern that relentlessly dominates the thinking. A person prone to depression might obsessively think along hopeless lines until he falls into a downward spiral. The addict becomes preoccupied with thoughts about the object of his desire

---

[95] See Chapter 4 for a fuller explanation.

until the flesh finally overwhelms him. The person crippled by worry or fear becomes preoccupied with painful possibilities until the negative emotions become too strong to fight. People with eating problems have out-of-control thoughts about food or body shape. Most self-control problems have at the root a lack of self-control in the thought life, which is why transformation comes, in large part, through the renewing of the *mind.*

Romans 12:2 Be transformed by the renewing of your mind.

Techniques for behavioral change that do not enable greater self-control in the thought life will be temporary fixes, if they do anything at all.

Steps in the Wrong Direction

The overall direction of one's life is dictated by the direction of the various steps he takes, and thoughts are steps. How does a woman go from being a faithful, loyal wife to committing adultery and leaving her husband? It is the culmination of a series of steps in the direction of unfaithfulness. She faces the normal struggles of all married people (her husband displays his areas of weakness and inadequacy as a husband— hurting her and sinning against her), and the temptation to focus on his faults begins to arise in her heart, resulting in an increasing bitterness and resentment. She is taking steps in the wrong direction.

From time to time some attractive person comes along or some enticing fantasy comes into her head. In years past she has simply pushed such thoughts out as soon as they arose. But one day she decides to entertain them a little bit—she does not dwell on them or obsess about them—she just allows herself to daydream about it for a few seconds. Then she pushes it out of her mind and gets on with her life. More steps. It seems like such a minor thing, she forgets it even happened. As far as she is concerned, she is just as committed to her husband as ever.

The next time a tempting thought like that comes along she indulges herself for several seconds—maybe a full minute—then puts it out of her mind. Sixty more steps. Over the course of a year or two the process continues, until she is entertaining tempting thoughts for several minutes at a time, several times a day.

Up to this point she has not taken a single external action that would indicate anything other than total faithfulness to her husband, but with her thoughts she has been taking steps away from the Lord and toward sin, and those steps have carried her far from the right path.

Eventually the temptation she has invited to come inside the door of her heart rises up. She allows a friendship with a man at work to go a little too far. He has never touched her, they have not talked about anything inappropriate in any way, but she becomes closer friends with him than with her husband. From there the friendship progresses to something else.

At some point she finds she is obsessed with thinking about another man and says, "Wait a minute—this is sin. I need to stop this." But she can't. Thoughts of him bombard her mind. No matter how hard she tries to push them away, they persist. To her it seems these thoughts are coming completely out of the blue—but that is not true. They are the result of a long process of undisciplined thinking. Finally she finds temptation too hard to fight and simply gives in to it.

A similar process of wrong thinking can be seen at the heart of virtually any of the problems for which people seek counseling. It is what lies behind overeating, depression, anxiety, addiction, and many other problems that involve thinking obsessions. There will be no success in changing wrong behavior without getting control of the thought life.

Guard the Door

Since ungodly thoughts are so difficult to escape once they find a home in the mind, the most important strategy in striving for a righteous thought life is in guarding the mind so wrong thoughts do not enter in the first place. It is impossible to keep all sinful thoughts out, but much can be done to reduce the volume of incoming sinful thoughts.

- Cut back on sources of sinful thoughts—Urge the counselee to think through what influences tend to get their wrong thoughts started. Television? Movies? A magazine? Secular music? A particular friend or group of friends? To whatever degree possible, slam closed the doors through which the evil thoughts are entering.

- Listen to Christian music—The lyrics of secular music, even if they are not overtly evil, are worldly. Listening to good Christian music for ten minutes can introduce many dozens of biblical thoughts and ideas into the mind. The likelihood of having that many biblical thoughts arising while listening to secular music for ten minutes is far smaller.

- Memorize Scripture—Memorization requires such a high level of concentration that it is far less likely that sinful thoughts will be able to enter the mind while reviewing memorized passages of Scripture. And even in moments when one is not directly thinking about those passages, they tend to lie in the background of the thoughts and are available for the Holy Spirit to call to mind at any moment. And it is remarkable how often the Spirit does just that!

- Listen to good sermons—Websites such as DesiringGod.org, GTY.org, and FoodForYourSoul.net offer expository sermon mp3's that can be searched by topic or Scripture passage, and can be downloaded free. A person desiring to gain control of the thought life can pick a topic or passage of interest, load several sermons onto an mp3 player or cell phone, and listen to them while doing household chores, commuting, etc.

Steps in the Right Direction

What about the sinful thoughts that make it through the defenses and find a place in the person's thinking? How does one rid himself of wrong thoughts?

For the next five seconds try not to picture an elephant in your mind. How did you do? Impossible! The surest way to get yourself to think about something is to try not to think about it. The mind runs continuously, so the only way to successfully push something out of your mind is to replace it with something else. Let's try again—for the next five seconds, instead of thinking about elephants, think about a fire truck. A little easier this time? Like the demons in Luke 11:24-26, evil thoughts that are expelled will return with a vengeance if they are not crowded out of the mind altogether with good thoughts.

Philippians 4:8 Finally, brothers, whatever is true, whatever is noble, whatever is right, whatever is pure, whatever is lovely, whatever is admirable--if anything is excellent or praiseworthy--think about such things.

When sinful thoughts arise in the mind (lustful images, thoughts of revenge, self-pity, pride, worry, etc.) they must be crowded out by godly thoughts. Arm the counselee with passages of God's Word that address the area of concern.

Eternal Perspective

Colossians 3:1-2 Since, then, you have been raised with Christ, set your hearts on things above, where Christ is seated at the right hand of God. 2 Set your minds on things above, not on earthly things.

The more one thinks about everything in life from a biblical point of view, the more attractive God's way appears. Righteousness becomes more appealing and sin becomes repulsive. In the words of John Piper, "When you begin to be lazy and allow your thoughts to become earthly, at first it doesn't seem like any damage is done, but in the weeks to come you pay the price: Your life sinks into shallowness, powerlessness, vulnerability to sin, preoccupation with trifling little things, superficial relationships, and a frightening loss of interest in worship and the things of God."[96]

Why is it that a temptation can be so overpowering on a Friday night or Monday afternoon, but that same temptation on a Sunday morning at church has no pull at all? It is because on Sunday morning the attention is set on things above. Spending an hour or two thinking about things from an eternal perspective enables the heart to see things as they really are. When spiritual vision is clear, righteousness is beautiful and desirable, and sin is ugly and repulsive. After spending several hours (or days) thinking about things from an earthly, temporal, worldly perspective, spiritual vision becomes distorted. Sin becomes

---

[96] John Piper, *Godward Life* (Sisters, Ore.: Multnomah Publishers, 2001), 104.

attractive and righteousness begins to appear boring, stuffy, and unappealing; and when that happens temptation will feel irresistible.

Imagine yourself seated at a table salivating over a plate of your favorite food at dinner time. Your desire for this food is so compelling that it is all you can do to wait until the family is seated to begin eating. Powerful desires. Would it be possible at that moment to change those desires? Erase them altogether? Is there something a counselor could say that would turn them off like a switch?

Yes! Imagine that just before you place the first bite into your mouth you hear your wife say, "Uh oh—I just realized—I grabbed the wrong box. Instead of seasoning I put rat poison into the food." At that moment you realize that if you put that bite of food in your mouth it will result in violent illness and possibly death. At that moment you see the truth about the food, and suddenly all desire for it is gone! When poison is seen for what it is, desire for it evaporates.

Satan takes sin, which is like the disgusting, sickening sludge scraped off the bottom of a garbage dumpster, and disguises it to look like a wonderful plate of food. Spending the day thinking about things from a biblical, eternal perspective enables one to see sin for what it really is, and it loses its appeal.

For most people this requires making some changes. If a person fills his day with television, secular reading, secular music, secular talk shows, secular conversation, etc., he will be unable to view life from an eternal perspective. Thinking on things above requires significant effort. Turning away from the attractions of the world and focusing on Scripture memorization, meditation, listening to Christian music, spiritual conversation, etc., is crucial.

Correcting Wrong Beliefs

Galatians 2:20 The life I live in the body, I live by faith in the Son of God.

Nothing is more central to living the Christian life than faith—trusting the Lord Jesus Christ. Everyone's life is based on confidence in *something*—either confidence in something God has said (faith) or confidence in something God has not said (presumption). Living by faith in God, then, means trusting in what God has promised, and that trusting is what enables escape from the corruption of the world.

2 Peter 1:4 Through (his glory and goodness) <u>he has given us</u> his very great and precious <u>promises,</u> so that <u>through them</u> <u>you may</u> participate in the divine nature and <u>escape the corruption in the world</u> caused by evil desires.

It is through faith in His promises that we escape the corruption caused by evil desires. God has promised that His way will always be more beneficial to us than sin—no exceptions. If we choose sin, then, it is because we do not believe that promise. His promises of provision rule out worry; His promises of justice rule out revenge; His promises of reward rule out laziness; His promises of forgiveness rule out self-condemnation; His promises of glory rule out discouragement.

The Lord desires not only that we conquer sin, but that we do so by means of trusting in His great and precious promises. If we conquer sin any other way it shows us to be impressive and says little about Him. But if we defeat sin by trusting in His promises, it points to Him as trustworthy, generous, powerful, desirable, and good.

It is crucial that every possible step be taken to persuade the counselee of the fact that an experience of God's presence really would be more satisfying than the pleasure of the sin. As long as there is a sense that the person is "missing out" by saying no to temptation, victory will not last long. If resisting a sin feels to the soul like a loss rather than gain, resolve will soon falter. The only long-term way to resist pleasure is with a greater pleasure.

How, then, can beliefs be changed? A man can tell himself a million times that God's presence is more satisfying than pornography, but if he continues to prefer immorality at the moment of temptation, clearly his soul is not convinced. So how does he persuade his soul to believe the truth?

Through Scripture

Romans 10:17 faith comes from hearing the message, and the message is heard through the word of Christ.

Faith comes through hearing the Word of God. When a person discovers an area of unbelief or weak faith, the solution is saturation with all that God's Word says in that area. "Hearing" the Word occurs through reading, studying, biblical conversation, listening to recordings of Scripture, meditation, memorization, and, most of all, faithful, accurate, passionate, expository preaching. In the Gospels and Acts we see that preaching is the primary method God has ordained for penetrating the hearts of people with His Word.

Teach the person to seek God with an attitude of expectance, like David, when his soul was dry in Psalm 63.

Psalm 63:1,5 O God, you are my God, earnestly I seek you; my soul thirsts for you, my body longs for you, in a dry and weary land where there is no water. ... 5 My soul will be satisfied as with the richest of foods.

To the degree that one has fellowship with God that person's soul *will be* satisfied. Psalm 34:8 does not say, "Taste and see *if* the Lord is good," but "Taste and see *that* the LORD is good."[97]

God is everywhere present all the time and yet the Christian is not full and satisfied all the time. This is because even though the Christian has access to God perpetually, he is not always *drinking and eating* (that is, experiencing the food-likeness) of God. When the prophets wrote of their hunger and thirst for God, they were describing their desire to have an experience of fellowship with God in which their souls enjoyed and were nourished, strengthened, refreshed, sustained, and satisfied by direct involvement with one or more of God's attributes.

When a particular sin has dominating, overwhelming power over a person, it is because that person believes the cravings of his soul cannot be satisfied any other way. Saying "no" to that sin means saying "no" to being happy—or at least to having the longing of his soul satisfied. Helping the person understand the amazing fact of the food-likeness of God is not all there is to winning the battle, but it is a crucial first step because it breaks the power of the temptation by opening his eyes to the fact that great satisfaction is available apart from that sin.

In most cases it takes more than a single conversation to bring a person to truly believe and trust in the doctrine of the food-likeness of God. One way to help the person you are counseling is to urge him to go

---

[97] Calvin observes, "The words literally rendered are, Taste and see, for the Lord is good; but the particle כי, *ki*, for, is taken exegetically. David's meaning, therefore, is, that there is nothing on the part of God to prevent the godly, to whom he particularly speaks in this place, from arriving at the knowledge of his goodness by actual experience." John Calvin, *Psalms*.

through the first twenty devotionals in the book, *What's So Great about God?*.[98]

Through Experience

Beliefs are also formed through experiences. If the man's experiences with pornography have always been pleasurable and his experiences with prayer and Scripture have usually been boring and unsatisfying, his soul will never buy it when he tries to say, "Resist this temptation because the presence of God will be more satisfying than this sin." For that argument to be compelling to the soul there must be a track record of delightful experiences with the presence of God. Teach the counselee to develop a habit of interpreting all the times of joy and fullness in life as illustrations of what it is like to be in God's presence, and to interpret all periods of emptiness and dryness as illustrations of what it is like to be distanced from His presence.

Displacing Sin

After sin has been dealt with in each of the various aspects of the heart, it is essential to remember that if that sin is not replaced by virtue, it will return.

Matthew 12:43-45 When an evil spirit comes out of a man, it goes through arid places seeking rest and does not find it. 44 Then it says, 'I will return to the house I left.' When it arrives, it finds the house unoccupied, swept clean and put in order. 45 Then it goes and takes with it seven other spirits more wicked than itself, and they go in and live there. And the final condition of that man is worse than the first. That is how it will be with this wicked generation.

The fact that Jesus applies the principle to the entire generation shows that it is a principle that applies generally to evil. Eliminating a sin from the heart is like digging a hole in water. The moment one shovel full of water is removed, more water rushes right back in to that place. Keeping the water out of that space requires the placement of some other object

---

[98] The book is available for free download from the Resource Library at TreasuringGod.com (click on "articles"). Resources are listed in alphabetical order. Scroll down to "W" for "What's So Great about God?").

in that space that will displace the water. Each sin that is pushed out in the process described above must be replaced by the opposing virtue or it will return. The fourth chapter of Ephesians instructs us on how to free ourselves from sin, and this displacement principle is repeated throughout:

- put off your old self ... put on the new self (vv.23-24)
- put off falsehood ... speak truthfully (v.25)
- steal no longer ... share with those in need (v.28)
- get rid of unwholesome talk ... say only what is helpful for building others up (v.29)
- get rid of all bitterness ... be kind and compassionate (vv.31-32)

Whenever a sin is discovered in the heart ask the question, "What virtue is missing?" and strive to obtain that virtue, and let that virtue crowd sin out of the heart.

Resources for Addressing Some Common Problems in the Inner Man

Devotionals from the book, *What's So Great About God?*:[99]

Coveteousness – **1-20**, 23, **31, 36, 50, 87**
Guilt – 46, **51-54**, 78, 79, **86, 104, 152**
Ingratitude – **31, 61-63**, 68, **69, 73, 77, 81, 83-87, 92, 94-95, 102, 106, 107, 112, 118**, 143, 144, 155, 162
Lack of awe/fear of God – **22-30, 57, 60, 76**, 103
Lack of brokenness over sin – **18-19, 52, 54-56, 57, 59, 79**
Lack of desire for Scripture – **1-20, 65, 73-76, 124-128**, 132
Lack of hope – **5**, 12, **17-20**
Lack of motivation – **4, 9**, 35, **70**, 73-75, 90, 163

---

[99] Bold numbers represent the meditations that are especially relevant.

PART 2 MOOD PROBLEMS

CHAPTER SEVEN:
MOOD MEDICATIONS

The "Chemical Imbalance" Theory

Over the past two decades, there has been a dramatic shift in the way our culture thinks about mood problems, such as depression, anxiety, and fear. The trend is to regard them as treatable, medical conditions caused by chemical imbalances in the brain that are easily corrected with medication. Drug companies have increased sales exponentially by marketing antidepressants directly to consumers, claiming that mood problems are caused by an imbalance of chemicals in the brain that can be "evened out" with drugs.

The chemical imbalance theory, however, is far from enjoying any scientific consensus. Elliot Valenstein Ph.D., Professor Emeritus of psychology and neuroscience at University of Michigan, states emphatically, "Contrary to what is often claimed, no biochemical, anatomical or functional signs have been found that reliably distinguish the brains of mental patients."[100] In other words, there is no discernable physical difference between the brain of a mental patient and the brain of a healthy person. It is not currently possible to measure serotonin levels or absorption rates inside the brain.[101] It can be measured in

---

[100] Elliot Valenstein, *Blaming the Brain*, 125. Cited by Chris Kresser
http://thehealthyskeptic.org/the-chemical-imbalance-myth.
[101] "Estimates of brain neurotransmitters can only be inferred by measuring the biogenic amine breakdown products (metabolites) in the urine and cerebrospinal fluid. The assumption underlying this measurement is that the level of biogenic amine metabolites in the urine and cerebrospinal fluid reflects the amount of neurotransmitters in the brain. However, less than one-half of the serotonin and norepinephrine metabolites in the urine or cerebrospinal fluid come from the brain. The other half come from various organs in

various bodily fluids, but the levels in those fluids may not reflect levels in the brain. In a psychopathology textbook for second-year medical students, the authors state, "Psychiatry is the only medical specialty that ... treats disorders without clearly known causes."[102]

The only things we know for sure about these drugs are (1) they do something to the brain and (2) they affect the way a person feels.

Do Antidepressants Work?

In 2005, Joanna Moncrieff and Irving Kirsch published a review in the British Medical Journal of the data from studies done by the National Institute for Clinical Excellence (NICE). They point out that the NICE data reveals the following:

- SSRI's[103] have no clinically meaningful advantage over placebo.
- Claims that antidepressants are more effective in more severe conditions have little evidence to support them.
- Antidepressants have not been convincingly shown to affect the long-term outcome of depression or suicide rates.[104]

NICE continues to recommend that antidepressants should be first line treatment for moderate or severe depression, despite the evidence from its own research data.

The Placebo Effect

These findings are remarkable, particularly in light of the fact that it is impossible to know how much influence the "placebo effect" has in the

---

the body. Thus, there are serious problems with what is actually being measured." (http://thehealthyskeptic.org/the-chemical-imbalance-myth)

[102] Maxmen and Ward, Essential Psychopathology and Its Treatment, 1995, p.57. Cited by John D. Street, "The Failing Attempt of Integration Psychology," lecture, Shepherds' Conference, 2004.

[103] Selective Serotonin Reuptake Inhibitors.

[104] Joanna Moncrieff and Irving Kirsch (http://talkingcure.co.uk/articles/bmj-331-moncrieffkirsch.pdf)

studies. [105] The placebo effect refers to the fact that there are very powerful influences at work in the body in response to the belief that a medicine will work.

It is not unusual for doctors to prescribe placebos when no medical problem can be discovered, and research has demonstrated that this practice can be remarkably effective. The pharmacist fills a bottle with sugar pills, affixes a fictional label such as, "Reniphin, for severe pain," and very often the patient experiences relief.

This does not mean the ailment was imaginary. The body has remarkable ability to heal itself when there is a high level of confidence in a remedy. Double-blind crossover studies have shown that placebos have worked well for a variety of ailments, including:

- severe pain (35 percent of those studied said a placebo had the same effect as an injection of morphine)
- stomach ulcers (the placebo was found to be 50 percent to 75 percent effective in stopping the bleeding, even though there was no active ingredient)
- incontinence (74 percent of the people with this problem improved with a placebo)
- arthritis
- high blood pressure (85 percent of those affected experienced a significant drop in blood pressure with a placebo). [106]

If placebos are that effective for physical problems, it would be no surprise to discover they can be even more effective for mood problems.

---

[105] Even double-blind studies are not truly blind because the subjects who receive the antidepressant rather than placebo experience the side effects of the antidepressant, so they know they got the real thing.

[106] Lecture by Carey Hardy, "A Prescription for Sanctification," Shepherd's Conference, 2001. In the studies placebo was more effective when the following factors were present:
- an enthusiastic doctor
- white lab coat
- hospital machines in the room
- capsules rather than tablets
- bad taste
- exact dosages
- warning labels

And the placebo effect in mood medications is decidedly greater due to the fact that they take so long to take effect. A patient feels depressed, is given an antidepressant, and is told to watch for a change in the next couple weeks. It is normal to have emotional ups and downs over a period of weeks, and if a person has begun taking a medication, the natural "ups" will be attributed to the drug rather than to the countless other factors that may have caused them.

It Isn't Working

The use of SSRI's has increased 1300 percent since 1990,[107] but the percentage of the population suffering from depression has not seen a corresponding decrease. In fact, studies have shown no decrease at all in the occurrence of depression over the past ten years.[108]

There are some who report feeling better after taking certain antidepressants, but the reason remains unknown. There is a possibility that the drugs actually have a positive effect on the mood of certain people. However, there are other possible explanations:

- The placebo effect.
- The general deadening effect antidepressants often have on the emotions. Taking an antidepressant does not cause a person to feel refreshed, energetic, happy, and full of motivation. Even those who are helped the most by antidepressants usually report not joy or happiness, but rather feeling slightly less depressed.
- Other medications. Sedatives are often given along with the antidepressant to alleviate side effects. Because of the calming effect of the sedative, the person may feel that his depression is less severe.

There are studies that point to antidepressants having slightly better short-term results than placebo. Care must be taken, however, in examining the credibility of the various studies. Particularly relevant is the question of who funded the study. Antidepressants are a $12 billion-

---

[107] Kresser, http://thehealthyskeptic.org/the-heart-of-depression.
[108] http://www.pophealthmetrics.com/content/2/1/9.

146

a-year industry. It would be naïve to assume there is no bias in studies funded by those who stand to gain billions of dollars by increased use of antidepressants. Drug companies are under no legal obligation to publish unfavorable study results, and an estimated 23 percent of their studies on mood medications have not been published.[109] They are required, however, to report them to the FDA. Using the Freedom of Information Act, Irving Kirsch gained access to the unpublished studies and found that those studies showed antidepressants as actually being *less* effective than placebo. This means a person taking a sugar pill would be more likely to recover from depression than a person taking an antidepressant. Kirsch argues that the preponderance of the evidence shows that antidepressants do not have a clinically meaningful advantage over placebo,[110] and his findings have been almost universally accepted within the scientific community.[111]

The Dark Side of Antidepressants

It is common for doctors to understate the side effects of mood medications. Drug companies market their products not only to consumers, but also to doctors. Physicians receive a sales pitch from drug company representatives, and the doctor who wants to know the negative effects or other drawbacks has to research those on his own.

With the newer medications, many of those effects are still unknown. As time goes by, however, more is coming to light about the negative effects of antidepressants.

Physical Side Effects

Side effects of SSRI's include nausea, insomnia, anxiety, diarrhea, headache, drowsiness, and loss of appetite. For cyclic antidepressants, add to the list dry mouth, constipation, difficulty with urination, blood pressure problems, nervousness, irritability, palpitation, rapid heartbeat, tremors, sweating, weight gain, indigestion, swelling, stiffness, slowness, restlessness, and rash.

---

[109] Kresser, http://thehealthyskeptic.org/a-closer-look-at-antidepressants.
[110] Irving Kirsh, The Emperor's New Drugs.
[111] Ibid.

More serious effects include movement disorders, agitation, sexual dysfunction, improper bone development, improper brain development, and gastrointestinal bleeding, which can become a life-threatening condition. Improper bone development in children is a serious problem that can lead to increased skeletal problems and frequent bone fractures as they age. Most studies examine the effect after six weeks, but the most significant harm appears only after months or years of use and therefore does not become evident in the short-term studies.

Antidepressants have been shown to produce long-term, and in some cases, irreversible chemical and structural changes to the body and brain. The administration of Prozac and Paxil raises cortisol levels in human subjects. [112] Given the fact that elevated cortisol levels are associated with depression, weight gain, immune dysfunction, and memory problems; the possibility that antidepressants may contribute to prolonged elevations in cortisol is alarming to say the least.

Psychological Side Effects

- #### *Deadening of Positive Emotions*

Since the primary effect of antidepressants is to deaden all the emotions, they function as a double-edged sword. They mitigate the intensity of the pain of depression, but at the same time they deaden sensations of happiness, joy, and hope. Perhaps this explains why the long-term recovery rate is so abysmal for those treated with antidepressants.

A growing body of research supports the hypothesis that often the long-term effect of antidepressants is to cause depression to become more chronic,[113] and more severe.[114] Most episodes of depression, when left untreated, end after three to six months. However, almost half of all

---

[112] Grace Jackson, MD, Rethinking Psychiatric Drugs: A Guide for Informed Consent, Bloomington, IN, AuthorHouse: 2005, 90.

[113] Weel-Baumgarten 2000 http://www.ncbi.nlm.nih.gov/pubmed/10771465.

[114] Moncrieff and Kirsch 2006 http://www.bmj.com/content/331/7509/155.full see also www.blackwell-synergy.com/doi/abs/10.1111/j.1600-0447.1992.tb03218.x?journalCode=acp, http://bjp.rcpsych.org/cgi/content/abstract/171/5/427).

Americans treated with antidepressants have remained on medication for more than a year.[115]

Many people on antidepressants have noticed a decrease in their ability to love. Rutgers University anthropologist Helen Fisher has suggested that beyond the well-known problem of sexual dysfunction caused by antidepressants, there is also a decrease in one's feelings of love for others.[116] This is a tremendous problem in recovering from depression because loving others is the most important avenue for receiving fullness of joy in Christ (Jn.15:10-12).

Other psychological side effects include the following:

- *Amotivational Syndrome*

This is a condition with symptoms that are clinically similar to those that develop when the frontal lobes of the brain are damaged. The syndrome is characterized by apathy, disinhibited behavior, demotivation, and a personality change similar to the effects of lobotomy.[117] All antidepressants are known to blunt emotional responses to some extent.

- *Agitation*

Studies by Eli Lilly employees found that between 21 and 28 percent of patients taking Prozac experienced insomnia, agitation, anxiety, nervousness, and restlessness, with the highest rates among people taking the highest doses.[118] Agitation is such a common side effect with SSRIs that the drug companies have consistently sought to hide it during clinical trials by prescribing a tranquilizer or sedative along with the antidepressant.

---

[115] David O. Antonuccio, David D. Burns, and William G. Danton, Antidepressants: A Triumph of Marketing Over Science? 2004 http://www.antidepressantsfacts.com/2002-07-15-Antonuccio-therapy-vs-med.htm.

[116] http://www.psychologytoday.com/articles/200704/sex-love-and-ssris.

[117] Marangell et al. 2001, p.1059. Cited by Troy Centazzo (http://www.mblwellness.com/community/shining-a-light-on-the-dark-side.htm).

[118] Beasley et al. 2001.Cited by Chris Kresser (http://thehealthyskeptic.org/the-dark-side-of-antidepressants).

- *Movement Disorders
  (restlessness, shaking, etc.)*

- *Suicide*

The risk of suicide in children on SSRI's increases 300 percent[119]—an alarming statistic given the fact that the fastest growing segment of the non-adult population being prescribed SSRI's is children ages five and under. [120] Children as young as four have attempted suicide while influenced by such drugs, and five-year-olds have committed suicide. Between 1995 and 1999, antidepressant use increased 580 percent in the under-6 population and 151 percent in the 7-12 age group. [121] Even among adults SSRIs have consistently revealed a risk of suicide (completed or attempted) that is two to four times higher than placebo.[122]

Combining Side Effects

Antidepressants typically cause nervousness, so physicians often prescribe a sedative to enable sleep. Many people then need a third drug to help them wake up. And doctors are starting to prescribe acid-inhibiting drugs such as Nexium to prevent the gastrointestinal bleeding caused by antidepressants. It is not uncommon for a person who takes an antidepressant to also have to take several other drugs to help him cope with the side effects. Very little is known about the long-term effects of the various combinations of these drugs. Author Ed Welch tells about a man experiencing periodic confusion and intellectual decline who was treated with medication and diagnosed with Alzheimer's disease at age 52. His situation had deteriorated to the point that he was put in a nursing home, where he stayed for nine years. After almost a decade, when he was 61, the family's resources were depleted

---

[119] David Healy, Antidepressant Drug Use and the Risk of Suicide, 2005.
http://www.ncbi.nlm.nih.gov/pubmed/16194787
[120] http://www.fightforkids.org/facts.php.
[121] Ibid.
[122] Healy, Antidepressant Drug Use and the Risk of Suicide, 2005.
http://www.ncbi.nlm.nih.gov/pubmed/16194787 There are volumes of published research and many books which present this information with much more detail on long-term negative effects, including Peter Breggin's landmark "Brain Disabling Treatments in Psychiatry" and Grace Jackson's "Rethinking Psychiatric Drugs."

and his wife took him out of the hospital and discontinued his medications. After going through withdrawal symptoms he improved dramatically and went on to teach college math.[123]

Withdrawal

Once a person has begun taking a mood medication, getting off that medication can be agony. Typical withdrawal symptoms include dizziness, lightheadedness, irritability, fatigue, and nausea. Benzodiazepines (tranquilizers) are one of only two kinds of drugs that can result in fatality if discontinued too abruptly.[124]

Chemical Sanctification?

Even in cases where a medication does seem to help, it does not follow that the problem was caused by a chemical imbalance. When aspirin takes away a headache we do not assume the headache was caused by an aspirin imbalance in the brain. A spiritual problem can have physical effects, and reducing those effects with drugs does nothing to address the spiritual problem.

For example, if a person robs a bank and is plagued with debilitating guilt, then he drinks an entire bottle of wine and then feels much better, the fact that the wine seemed to "help" with his guilt problem does not mean it was a purely physical issue with no spiritual component. If a man brutally beats his wife when he gets mad, and then he takes some lithium and stops beating her, does that prove he was without sin while he was beating her? Not at all. It does point to a physical *component* to his problem, but not a physical *cause*. If a married man routinely commits adultery, then begins taking a drug that drastically reduces his sex drive so he no longer commits adultery, does that mean his adultery was caused by a chemical imbalance and was therefore not a spiritual issue? If a slothful person becomes more motivated after taking speed,

---

[123] Edward T. Welch, Blame it on the Brain? (Phillipsburg, N.J.: P&R Publishing, 1998), 72-73. Whenever I have taught this material people have come up to me afterward and related very similar stories in their own lives.

[124] The other is alcohol.

does that mean his sloth was not a spiritual issue after all—only a "speed" deficiency in the bloodstream?

The intensity of a temptation can be dramatically affected by physical factors, but the *decision* to sin is always a matter of the heart. Is it possible for a person to have some physical defect in the brain that makes a particular temptation harder to resist? Yes. Any kind of physical weakness can contribute to spiritual weakness. Most people tend to be more selfish and irritable after two nights without sleep than when they are well rested. But it is not the sleeplessness that causes the sin. Sin is in the heart already, and when a person is physically strong that sin can be resisted (or hidden) more effectively than when the body is weak. This is why sin tends to increase with physical weakness—whether it be a brain injury, old age, fatigue, or illness. But the decision to sin is always a spiritual decision made by one's spirit and merely carried out by his body.

What about the effect of hormones? How is it that a woman may have a tremendous struggle with irritability, sadness, or some other form of moodiness like clockwork during her period each month, but not other times in the month? There are a couple of possibilities. One is that the effect of the hormones is to weaken her, so it is more difficult for her to resist wrong beliefs, since physical weakness contributes to spiritual weakness.

Another possibility is that the chemical imbalance theories of our culture have taken a toll on the woman's attitude toward her level of responsibility for her mood. Just as the test subjects in Chapter 4 tended to be more likely to cheat on a test when they were told they had taken a drug that would make them more emotional, so a woman who feels more emotional due to hormones may have a reduced sense of culpability for wrong attitudes during that time, so she does not restrain them with the same urgency she normally has.

Of course the body has an effect on the spirit. That is why Paul worked so hard to keep his body under control (1 Cor.9:27). But for the Christian, there is never a moment when the flesh is so dominant that there is no choice but to sin. Psychiatry has replaced "the devil made me do it" with "chemicals made me do it," but neither excuse holds in light of God's promise never to allow us to be tempted beyond our ability (1Cor.10:13).

Whatever the connection between hormones and the spiritual struggle, it must be remembered that sanctification is not accomplished by means of chemicals. Part of the fruit of the Spirit is joy (Gal.5:22). The Holy Spirit dwells within the believer, acts upon the soul, and the fruit—the result—is joy. What happens, then, when the Spirit encounters a chemical imbalance in the brain? Is He rendered incapable of producing His normal fruit? Not at all! The Holy Spirit is not handcuffed by chemicals.

The person who claims that his lack of joy is a purely physical issue and not a spiritual one is no different from a person who claims he is not responsible for his drunkenness because he has a predisposition to weakness in that area. The close connection between the body and soul does not mean that spiritual conditions have a physical cause. Anything Scripture speaks of as a spiritual issue, including joy and hope, is a spiritual issue.

It is not God's design for us to be dependent on drugs for the basic functions of life. When a person is using prescription medications to calm down, wake up, go to work, relax, improve the appetite, etc., it is difficult to see the difference between him and the addict who uses just one drug to do all those things. Ephesians 5:18 tells us, "Do not get drunk with wine ... but be filled by the Spirit." The implication is that we should not look to chemicals to provide what we should be getting from the Holy Spirit. What is the difference between a person who looks to antidepressants for his joy (or caffeine for his strength[125]) and the person who says, "I just seem to handle life better after I've had a few beers"?

Spiritual goals cannot be achieved by chemical means. There is no drug in the world that will ever be able to solve the following problems:

- Lack of love
- Unwillingness to accept suffering from the hand of God
- Ungodly thoughts
- Ingratitude

---

[125] It is not necessarily sin to ingest caffeine, but when a person becomes dependent upon that drug to function in life, he has violated the principle of Ephesians 5:18.

- Selfishness
- Unfaithfulness
- Pride
- Disrespect
- Disobedience
- Joylessness
- Discontent
- Lack of faith in God

Confidence in God's Word (Taking Advantage of the Placebo Effect)

I believe the placebo effect is a God-given mechanism for our healing. The placebo effect is not restricted to drugs with no active ingredient. It is present whenever there is a high level of confidence in a remedy. For example, if a person takes an aspirin for a headache, pain is reduced by the aspirin, but the effect is even greater if the person has a high level of confidence that the aspirin will work. This underscores the importance of working with the counselee to increase his confidence in the power of God's Word.

Conversely, it may also be helpful to reduce the counselee's level of confidence in antidepressants. When the counselee believes the problem is mainly a chemical one, and drugs are the primary hope of recovery, any improvements will be attributed to the drugs rather than to the true source. In one study, for example, depressed individuals who were given an exercise program without antidepressants were less likely to relapse into depression than those who used both exercise and medication.[126] Those who recovered by means of exercise had a sense of accomplishment, which is a great help in fighting depression. Those who were treated with medication and exercise tended to attribute the

---

[126] Kresser, http://thehealthyskeptic.org/treating-depression-without-drugs-part-i. In a study published in Psychosomatic Medicine in 2000, another important advantage of exercise over antidepressants was revealed. Participants in the exercise group were less likely to relapse than participants in the two groups receiving medication. Other studies have confirmed this effect, demonstrating that aerobic exercise is especially helpful in the prevention of relapse and recurrence of depression.

recovery to the drugs, so instead of thinking, "It wasn't easy, but I worked hard and licked it," it was, "I have a disease and took a pill and felt better."

This is not to say the power of God's Word is dependent upon the level of one's faith. The Word of God is living and active, and it has divine power. However, the way one experiences that power can vary according to attitude. Where there is a low level of confidence, the healing power of God's Word will be hindered. Where there is a high level of confidence it will go unhindered and have its full effect. The sad reality is that many Christians place more confidence in a psychiatrist's medical degree or the properties of a drug than in the Word of God.

Curing the Disease

Physical pain is a very important gift from God. Without it we would destroy ourselves. If the brain received a signal saying, "There is a rock in my shoe," but that signal did not involve pain, laziness might win, the rock would remain, and damage would be done to the foot. So to overcome our laziness, God gave us a signaling system that cannot be ignored: pain. Ongoing pain insists that we remove whatever is causing the problem. Emotional pain functions the same way. It shouts to us, "There is a spiritual problem that is causing damage. Fix it!"

Treating painful emotions such as depression, fear, or anxiety with mood medications is like treating a compound fracture with morphine. Morphine can do wonders to relieve the intensity of the suffering, but it does nothing to set the broken bone. Imagine an emergency room where morphine was always prescribed, no matter what problem a patient presented, and no other treatment was given. That is the way many psychiatrists work. Someone comes in complaining of emotional pain, and they prescribe something to deaden that pain. Very few psychiatrists understand spiritual causes. For example, I knew a woman who mentioned to her doctor that she was getting ready to go on a trip and was not looking forward to being with the people she was going to be staying with. Her doctor immediately suggested that she take tranquilizers! There was no concern or even awareness that the ability to deal with unpleasant social situations is a spiritual issue.

Even when antidepressants bring a measure of relief, they do nothing to address the spiritual problem that is creating the emotional pain. And if they reduce the suffering enough to enable the person to get by, the urgency of finding a cure for the actual problem diminishes. It is not necessarily wrong to use a painkiller, but it is foolish to use a painkiller *instead* of treating the real problem. Treating depression or anxiety or distraction with drugs alone is like taking care of a red warning light on the dashboard of your car by disconnecting it. If a drug alleviates the pain just enough to rob the person of the urgency needed to find a solution to the real problem, then it is doing more harm than good.

Addiction

The addictive nature of these drugs, especially benzodiazepines (Xanax, Librium, Valium, etc.), should not be minimized. The fact that a person with a medical degree authorizes taking them seems to legitimize it, but the reality is, taking anti-anxiety drugs is essentially the same as having a couple of shots of Scotch each day.

Any kind of addiction is sin, even if it is a substance prescribed by someone in a lab coat. Part of the fruit of the Spirit is self-control (Gal.5:23), and we are not to be mastered or controlled by anything (1 Cor.6:12, 2 Pe.2:19).

Ritalin

I recently asked a secular psychologist which of the commonly prescribed psychotropic drugs is creating the worst problem with addiction, and her response surprised me: "Ritalin—by far." Ritalin is a drug commonly given to children diagnosed with attention deficit disorder (ADD) or attention deficit and hyperactivity disorder (ADHD).

According to the U.S. Department of Justice Drug Enforcement Agency (DEA), "Ritalin is a Schedule II stimulant, structurally and pharmacologically similar to amphetamines and cocaine, and has the same dependency profile of cocaine and other stimulants. Ritalin produces amphetamine and cocaine-like reinforcing effects including increased rate of euphoria and drug liking.[127] Treatment with Ritalin in childhood predisposes takers to cocaine's reinforcing effects. ... Ritalin produces behavioral, physiological, and reinforcing effects similar to amphetamines.[128]

Side-effects of Ritalin include increased blood pressure, heart rate, respirations, and temperature; appetite suppression, weight loss, growth retardation; facial tics, muscle twitching, central nervous system stimulation, nervousness, irritability, agitation, psychotic episodes, violent behavior, paranoid delusions, hallucinations, bizarre behaviors, heart arrhythmias and palpitations, tolerance, addiction, and even death.[129]

Like other mood medications, it is not known how Ritalin works or what it does to the brain. Nor has any physical abnormality been discovered in the brains of ADD or ADHD patients. Ritalin is a stimulant, and its effects are experienced by anyone who takes it. We could all focus better if we were on speed, but the "cure" would do far more harm than the "disease."

ADD and ADHD

It is not a disorder for a seven-year-old boy to have a hard time sitting still for seven hours a day at school. God designed young children—especially boys—to run! Drugging them may make it easier for teachers to control the classroom, but there are better methods.

1) Discipline

If a child is unruly, teach the parents to bring his behavior under control through consistent, firm discipline. Disobedience is not a mental disease; it is the folly of the heart that must be driven out with loving, consistent use of the rod (Pr.22:15).

Whatever a person believes about ADD, one thing is certain—all sinful behavior comes from the child's heart, not from a brain disorder.

---

[127] That is, increased desire for other drugs.
[128] http://drbate.com/Ref/DEA.html.
[129] Ibid.

If a child is disrespectful, lazy, disobedient, or undisciplined; these are spiritual problems and should not be overlooked simply because the world diagnoses him with a mental disease.

2) Activity

My son had an extremely difficult time sitting still in school (or anywhere else). In the years we home schooled him, when we saw that he was unable to focus we would send him out to the backyard to jump on the trampoline for ten minutes, or run around the block. He would come back in the house huffing and puffing and much more able to concentrate. It worked wonders!

3) Nutrition

In some cases, feeding the child a healthy, high protein, low-carbohydrate breakfast can make a difference in his ability to focus through the day.

These solutions are healthy, free, and have none of the dangers of Ritalin. If you counsel someone with a child who is doing poorly in school, urge him to be very slow to start his child on a drug. Our children face enough struggles without becoming subject to addiction and chemical dependence by their own parents.

And even if other remedies do not seem to work, we should ask ourselves, "How important is academic excellence in the third grade in comparison with spiritual issues, anyway?" Many Christians put far too great an emphasis on performance in school, even though performance in school—especially elementary school—has not been shown to be related to success in life. A student who gets D's in school and is drug free will generally do far better in life than a child who gets A's and is dependent upon stimulants from an early age.

Marijuana

As more and more states legalize "medical" marijuana, the use of this drug is becoming a significant problem in the Church. With the legal prohibition removed, many Christians see no problem with the use of this drug. After all, doesn't Genesis 1:29 clearly say that God has given us every herb for our use? Before using marijuana the believer should consider the following ten factors.

1) Misuse

If smoking marijuana is justified on the basis of Genesis 1:29, cocaine use would also be permissible, as it comes from the coca plant. All plants are indeed given for our use, but none of them are given for our *misuse*. The mere fact that God placed a particular plant in this world does not mean He intended for us to smoke it. In fact, Genesis 1:29 specifies that the various plants are given to us "for food," not for smoking. This does not mean every plant is to be ingested. Indeed, many plants are lethal if eaten. Therefore, Genesis 1:29 is speaking only about food-producing plants.

2) *"Pharmaceia"*

The Greek word *pharmaceia* (from which we get our word *pharmacy*) appears in lists of sins in Gal.5:20, Rev.9:21, 18:23, 21:8, and 22:15. It is usually translated "magic," but it refers to the use of drugs—especially hallucinogens like marijuana. Drug use in ancient times was closely connected to magic—as well as to false religion. In the mystery religions, drugs were often used to get closer to God through a chemically altered state. The word *pharmaceia* itself, however, points to drug use. Each of the passages that include *pharmaceia* in a list of sins, then, condemns the use of mind altering drugs for their mind altering properties.

3) Ephesians 5:18 and Drunkenness

Proponents of marijuana use often point to alcohol as being a more harmful drug. If alcohol is permissible for a believer, it is argued, why not pot?

When alcohol is used in a harmful way, however, it is not permissible for a believer. Drinking to the point of falling under the influence of the alcohol is forbidden in Ephesians 5:18—"Do not get drunk with wine, but be filled by the Spirit."

At exactly what point does one cross the line from being sober to violating the principle of that verse? Is it the end point (being so plastered you cannot even stand up)? Or the beginning point, when the alcohol first begins to have any effect at all? In other areas we understand that sin is to be cut off at the beginning point. Lust must be resisted not only at the end point of sleeping with someone outside of marriage, but at the point of a lustful look. If the sin of drunkenness is to be treated the same way, then the line is crossed the moment the alcohol begins to have an effect on the brain (not an easy thing for the drinker to detect—which is why drinking calls for a great deal of carefulness). The same principle applies to marijuana use. As soon as there is a chemical effect, the line into sin has been crossed.

The juxtaposition of drunkenness with the filling by the Spirit in Ephesians 5:18 implies that we are not to look to wine (or any other substance) for those things we should be seeking from the Holy Spirit, (such as peace, hope, or joy). Inability to sufficiently relax is a spiritual issue that should be addressed spiritually, not chemically.

4) Clarity of Thought

As Christians we are always on the clock. At any moment you might be in a position to present the gospel to someone, or help a brother or sister who is struggling and in need of counsel, or you might be faced with an especially difficult decision. It is crucial that we keep our minds as lucid as possible. Even those who claim marijuana does no harm to the clarity of their thinking, if they were going to have open-heart surgery tomorrow, would probably prefer a sober surgeon over one who had been smoking marijuana on a daily basis.

5) Weaker Brothers

Suppose there is someone who was saved out of a lifestyle that involved all kinds of immorality, and pot was a big part of that lifestyle. As a new Christian he might not be able to make distinctions between the pot itself and that whole sinful lifestyle. For him it is one big package.

When a person like that sees a mature believer using marijuana he is likely to think, "It must be OK to dabble in that *lifestyle*," so he does, and is then caught up in the whole immoral scene he used to be a part of.

6) Addiction

Like alcohol and other drugs, some people seem to be easily addicted and others are not. But unnecessary, long-term exposure to anything that is likely to be addictive is foolish if it can be avoided.

7) Marijuana Culture

Smoking marijuana brings a person into a culture that is never a good influence. Association with that culture is a step in the wrong direction.

8) Gateway to Stronger Drugs

It is very rare that a person who has never been high or drunk decides one day to go out and try methamphetamines or heroin. They work their way up to it. And since pot is so socially acceptable, it is an easy first step to take. Once a person gets used to the idea of getting stoned, getting stoned on something a little stronger is not such a big step.

9) Stewardship

Pot is not a harmless drug. The only sources that claim otherwise tend to be sources with a pro-pot political agenda. Neutral sources consistently agree that there are harmful effects, which brings up issues that have to do with stewardship. It is poor stewardship to do unnecessary harm to one's body, because doing so limits the ability to serve God's people and carry out one's calling.

Medicine?

Paul urged Timothy to use wine in a medicinal way (1 Tim.5:23), so why not use marijuana as medicine? In instances where the drug can do more good than harm, it would be fine to use it as medicine. However, those instances are rare. The pill form of the active chemical in marijuana (dronabinal) can be helpful for the nausea caused by chemotherapy, but it is not as effective as other nausea medicines. Research is being done on the use of marijuana for chronic pain, but while research has pointed to limited clinical value in one compound of the FDA-approved form, the same benefit is not attained in its smoked or raw form. Smoking is an ineffective and illogical way to deliver medicine—dosage cannot be regulated, and tar and other harmful compounds are delivered directly to the lungs along with any helpful cannabinoids. In fact, Dr. Robert DuPont, former director of National Institute on Drug Abuse (NIDA), says, "There is no acceptable role in modern medicine for using burning leaves as a drug delivery system because smoke is inherently unhealthy."[130] Other delivery methods are also problematic. Vaporizing does not filter cancer-causing tar or other chemicals, and eating delivers the same damaging compounds as well as the insecticides and fungi found in unmonitored crops.

Most sources agree that in the short-term pot causes distorted perception (sights, sounds, time, touch), problems with memory and learning, loss of coordination, trouble with thinking and problem-solving, increased heart rate, reduced blood pressure, and in many cases, anxiety, fear, distrust, or panic.

When I have counseled people after they have smoked pot and are still under the influence, they are incoherent, distracted, irrational, and either remember nothing I said or remember it in such distorted fashion that it's not what I said at all. These people tend to think that they are perfectly lucid and can think clearly—even more clearly than normal. It is obvious to everyone around them, however, that they are in a fog. And being in a fog is a very dangerous place to be spiritually. It makes a person easily influenced by Satan.

Brain researchers tell us that while pot can help with pain due to the fact that there are cannabinoid receptors in the portions of the brain that process sensations of pain and pleasure, there are also many cannabinoid receptors in the parts of the brain that influence memory,

---

[130] http://www.dfaf.org/questions-answers/marijuana.

thought, concentration, sensory and time perception, and coordinated movement.

When high doses of marijuana are used it can result in hallucinations, delusions, disorientation, and adverse effects on the heart. Within a few minutes after smoking marijuana, the heart begins beating more rapidly and the blood pressure drops. Marijuana can cause the heart beat to increase by 20 to 50 beats per minute, and can increase even more if other drugs are used at the same time. Because of the lower blood pressure and higher heart rate, researchers found that users' risk for a heart attack is four times higher within the first hour after smoking marijuana, compared to their general risk of heart attack when not smoking.

Additionally, even occasional use of marijuana can result in many of the same respiratory problems as tobacco smoking. And marijuana contains more carcinogenic hydrocarbons than tobacco smoke, and because marijuana smokers typically inhale deeper and hold the smoke in their lungs longer than tobacco smokers, their lungs are exposed to those carcinogenic properties longer than when smoking tobacco.

Research indicates that THC (the main chemical psychoactive compound in marijuana) impairs the body's immune system from fighting disease, which can cause a wide variety of health problems. One study found that marijuana actually inhibited the disease-preventing actions of key immune cells. Another study found that THC increased the risk of developing bacterial infections and tumors.

If marijuana were a real medicine, it would be treated like any other medicine. Can you imagine buying Amoxicillin for your child with an ear infection at a dilapidated "Medical Antibiotic Clinic" that is unregulated, and the antibiotic is produced in someone's basement? If marijuana were a legitimate medicine, prescriptions would be filled at a pharmacy just like any other prescription. Medical marijuana is thinly-veiled effort to get around the current marijuana possession laws. One clinic in Denver is even named "The 420 Medical Marijuana Clinic." "420" is slang for "Let's go get stoned."

10) Stunted Spiritual Growth

Marijuana has a freezing effect on the maturing process. A young person becomes overwhelmed with his problems, begins smoking marijuana, and escapes from caring about the rent being late, or a relationship falling apart. His problems pile up, so he smokes even more, resulting in more problems, and a decade can slip by as he plays video games. A young person who begins smoking pot at 16 years old and continues until he is 25 will basically be a 16-year-old in a 25-year-old body.

Most people who smoke marijuana do so for the purpose of reducing stress and anxiety. Marijuana accomplishes this quite effectively, but it does so by creating feelings of apathy. A person who is high on pot does not care about anything. I believe this to be the most damaging effect of marijuana use. Apathy is one of the greatest enemies of the Christian soul. God has promised that we will find Him only when we seek Him with all our heart and soul (Dt.4:29), and He will not demean His greatness by allowing Himself to be found by halfhearted seekers. This means no one who is apathetic can find God.

The Christian life is a constant struggle against apathy. Caring too little about important things derails everything in the believer's walk with God. For prayer to be effective it must be earnest (Jas.5:16). Our love for God and hatred of evil must be passionate (Ro.12:9). The Christian life requires brokenness over sin (Isa.57:15) and compassion for others (1 Pe.3:8)—both of which are a kind of anxiety. We are to care so deeply for others that their weeping makes us cry, and their joy makes us laugh (Ro.12:15). Apathy destroys all of these things. Why would a true child of God intentionally take a drug that would *increase* the lethal spiritual disease of apathy?

Many proponents of legalizing pot will make the argument that pot is less harmful than alcohol because no one ever smoked pot and then beat his wife. That may be true. But a pot smoker can watch his wife pack her bags and walk out the door with their children and respond with a giggle, saying, "Oh well, she was hassling me all the time anyway. Where is another joint?" Beating your wife is a horrible thing, but not caring about important things and being unable to cope with life's problems any other way than being stoned are also horrible and destructive.

Electroshock Therapy

Electroshock Therapy (ECT) is a procedure in which an electrical current is sent through the brain causing a grand-mal seizure for 20 seconds. The patient generally wakes up about 30 minutes after the procedure confused, unaware of what has happened or where he is, and often with an aching jaw, sore limbs, and severe headache. The most common side effect of ECT is memory loss. Patients report memory loss for events that occurred during the day, weeks, and months preceding ECT.

Proponents of the procedure claim an 80 percent success rate in treating depression. These "successes," however, are short-lived. There is no evidence that ECT remains effective for more than four weeks.[131] The relapse rate is close to 100 percent. Nothing is known about why it helps in the short-term or exactly what it does to the brain. One possibility is that the shock damages the brain, causing memory loss and disorientation that creates a temporary illusion that problems are gone. Psychiatrist Peter Breggin warns, "Taking a chance at electroshock is like playing Russian roulette with your brain." He explains that what looks like "relief" is really just the "slap-happy" effect of a head trauma. "For a time, people become silly, shallow and giggly, like a teenager who has sniffed glue—or a person who has just had shock treatment."[132]

If a counselee is considering electroshock therapy, alert him to the risks and the lack of evidence for any long-term effectiveness.

---

[131] Andrew Weil, MD, http://www.drweil.com/drw/u/id/QAA400268.

[132] http://www.electroboy.com/electroshocktherapy.htm. For more information see Peter Breggin, Brain-Disabling Treatments in Psychiatry: Drugs, Electroshock and the Psychopharmaceutical Complex, Second Edition (2008).

CHAPTER EIGHT:
DEPRESSION

The pain of depression is difficult to describe. Depressed people simultaneously feel deep pain and emotional numbness. In a letter to J. T. Stewart, Abraham Lincoln said, "I am now the most miserable man living. If what I feel were equally distributed to the whole human family, there would not be one cheerful face on the earth. Whether I shall ever be better, I cannot tell; I awfully forebode I shall not. To remain as I am is impossible. I must die or be better, it appears to me."[133] A friend who was depressed wrote this: "I have no energy or reason to fight. I am numb and have tried all the things I know to try. I know that I will not be able to function like this much longer. There is no one to talk to. I'm suffocating. I can think the best thoughts all day and I still feel like this. No one knows how badly I want to die. My thoughts are obsessive and will not stop. They keep saying, 'I want to die.'" Depression can be one of the most agonizing kinds of suffering. If we have the heart of Christ, we will show compassion to those who suffer in this way.

Given the 1300 percent increase in the use of SSRI antidepressants over the past two decades,[134] one would expect a dramatic drop in the occurrences of depression. Studies have shown, however, no decrease at all in the occurrence of depression over the past ten years.[135] In fact, doctor visits for depression have skyrocketed over that period.[136] The world's solutions are not working.

Sometimes counselors feel unqualified to help a deeply depressed person because the counselor has never experienced such extreme joylessness and feels he could never relate to their suffering. Jeremiah, however, *could* relate. He lived through the horrors of the devastation of

---

[133] Cited by Henry Steele, Hendron's Life of Lincoln, (Cambridge, N.Y.: Da Capo Press, 1983), 215.
[134] Kresser, http://thehealthyskeptic.org/the-heart-of-depression.
[135] http://www.pophealthmetrics.com/content/2/1/9.
[136] http://www.psychiatrist.com/pcc/pccpdf/v03n06/v03n0611.pdf.

Jerusalem in 586 B.C.[137] It is helpful to read the first twenty verses of Lamentations 3 to the counselee to show him that Jeremiah's was a case of the most extreme kind of depression. He suffered from all of the following:

- Utter despair: "He has made me dwell in darkness like those long dead" (Lam.3:6)
- Lethargy, fatigue, lack of energy: "He has weighed me down with chains" (Lam.3:7)
- Hopelessness: "He has walled me in so I cannot escape" (Lam.3:7)
- Isolation: "Even when I call out or cry for help, he shuts out my prayer" (Lam.3:8)
- Frustration: "He has barred my way with blocks of stone" (Lam.3:9)
- Feelings of worthlessness: "He pierced my heart with arrows from his quiver. I became the laughingstock of all my people; they mock me in song all day long. He has filled me with bitter herbs and sated me with gall. He has broken my teeth with gravel; he has trampled me in the dust. I have been deprived of peace; I have forgotten what prosperity is. So I say, 'My splendor is gone and all that I had hoped from the Lord.' … my soul is downcast within me" (Lam.3:13-20)
- A sense of helplessness and paralysis: "… he has made my paths crooked. Like a bear lying in wait, like a lion in hiding, he dragged me from the path and mangled me and left me without help. He drew his bow and made me the target for his arrows" (Lam.3:9-12).

How is it possible to comfort someone in such dire straits? Later in the chapter we will see how Jeremiah recovered from his depression. But first we must understand depression in biblical terms.

---

[137] It was worse than what happened to Sodom (Lam.4:6). People were slaughtered; women and girls were raped; people lay languishing in the streets, wishing they had been killed by the sword. Jeremiah saw babies so thirsty they could not swallow, their mothers sitting by so despondent they did not even try to help them. Some women cooked their own children and ate them! To make matters worse, the Israelites brought all this suffering on themselves because of their rebellion against God. It was their own fault.

What is Depression?

The biblical words for what we refer to as depression are, *losing heart, joylessness, despair,* and *discouragement/weariness.* Urge the counselee to use the biblical terms rather than the word "depression." This will produce three benefits. First, the biblical terminology is more precise. The term "depression" lumps several different problems together under one heading. The biblical terms allow a person to deal with the various different issues individually.

Second, when the problems are identified with biblical terms it is much easier for the person to discover what Scripture says about those problems.

Third, in our culture depression is very often thought of as being a physical, medical problem. This obscures the spiritual aspect. The biblical terms make it easier to think in terms of spiritual issues.

Biblical Terms for the Various Elements of Depression:

1) **Losing Heart** (lack of motivation, feelings of wanting to give up, apathy)
2) **Joylessness** (sadness, inability to enjoy present blessings)
3) **Despair** (lacking hope—no feelings of pleasure in upcoming blessings)
4) **Discouragement/Weariness** (no energy for or delight in the tasks God has given)

1) Losing Heart

The Greek word for losing heart (*egkakeo*) appears six times in the New Testament,[138] and it refers to becoming so discouraged that almost all motivation drains away, apathy takes over the heart, and the person feels like giving up.

God designed us to live with a tension of simultaneous joy and distress at all times. The evils of our sin and this fallen world should

---

[138] Lk.18:1, 2 Co.4:1,16, Gal.6:9, Eph.3:13, 2 Thes.3:13.

distress us and the goodness of God and expressions of His love should delight us. The anxiety needs to be there to motivate us to action. For example, we will never have the passion we should have to share the gospel until our hearts are compelled by compassion when we literally become emotionally upset thinking about people going to hell. We need to have a certain amount of distress in our hearts about evil and sin so we will be moved to take action and do something about it. In 2 Corinthians 11, Paul lists all his troubles and suffering, and then adds…

2 Corinthians 11:28-29 Besides everything else, I face daily the pressure of my concern for all the churches. 29 Who is weak, and I do not feel weak? Who is led into sin, and I do not inwardly burn?

That is anxiety. Inward burning. Daily pressure. Those are descriptions of decidedly unpleasant stresses. This is appropriate for the Christian and is not wrong.

However, that anxiety should not run rampant and unrestrained in our hearts so that it causes us to lose heart. And the thing that should hold it in check and keep it from getting out of control is our joy (enjoyment of present circumstances) and hope (enjoyment of future blessing). In 2 Corinthians 6:9, Paul describes himself as "sorrowful, yet always rejoicing." Sorrow and joy exist simultaneously in our hearts at all times, but it is crucial for the Christian that our joy always be greater than our sorrow.

2 Corinthians 4:8-9 We are hard pressed on every side, but not crushed; perplexed, but not in despair; 9 persecuted, but not abandoned; struck down, but not destroyed.

When the sorrow becomes greater than joy—that is when we lose heart.

2) Joylessness

Persistent, overwhelming feelings of deep sadness and a troubled, discouraged mood reflect an inability to enjoy the blessings of life. Even in the midst of suffering life is full of potential joys, but the soul is not always able to enjoy them.

Ecclesiastes 5:19 When God gives any man wealth and possessions, and enables him to enjoy them, to accept his lot and be happy in his work--this is a gift of God.

There are people who are so wealthy they can have as much of almost any earthly pleasure as they want, and still, in some cases, they become so despondent and unhappy that they commit suicide. Unless God grants both the gift and the ability to enjoy the gift, no joy is possible. When this happens there is a loss of interest in the pleasures of life.

Psalm 102:4 My heart is blighted and withered like grass; I forget to eat my food.

3) Despair

Despair is when sorrow eclipses hope. Hope is a feeling of happiness in the present because of some wonderful thing that is going to happen in the future. It is not merely believing something good is going to happen in the future, nor is it merely thinking about that good thing. Hope is a feeling of happiness and an elevated mood that results from being sure that good thing is coming. When a person feels there is nothing to look forward to, the soul succumbs to despair.

If something good is coming in the future, but it does not bring a feeling of happiness, it is because either the person does not fully believe the good thing will happen, or he does not fully believe that when it does happen it will be delightful and satisfying.

Hope is essential for recovering from a downcast soul. The word translated "downcast" in Psalms 42 and 43 is SHACHACH, and it refers to feelings of deep sadness and a troubled, discouraged mood, and is connected with lack of hope.

Psalm 42:5 Why are you downcast, O my soul? Why so disturbed within me? Put your hope in God.

Psalm 42:11 Why are you downcast, O my soul? Why so disturbed within me? Put your hope in God.

Psalm 43:5 Why are you downcast, O my soul? Why so disturbed within me? Put your hope in God.

Lamentations 3:20-21 I well remember them, and my soul is downcast[139] within me. 21 Yet this I call to mind and therefore I have hope.

In each case, the solution to being downcast is hope.

---

[139] Hebrew SHUCHA.

4) Discouragement/Weariness

Fatigue is part of the human condition, and there is nothing necessarily sinful in it. Jesus Himself became weary (Jn.4:6). There is a kind of weariness, however, that is forbidden.

Galatians 6:9 Let us not lose heart in doing good, for in due time we will reap if we <u>do not grow weary</u>.[140]

Hebrews 12:3 Consider him who endured such opposition from sinful men, so that you will <u>not grow weary</u> and lose heart.

Revelation 2:3 You have persevered and have endured hardships for my name, and have <u>not grown weary</u>.

All of us become tired, but we are not to become weary to the point of discouragement, so that we lose heart. When we come to the point where we have no energy for or delight in the tasks God has given, that is when we have crossed the line into discouragement (or weariness).

Causes of Depression

The suggestion that depression is caused by serotonin imbalance or absorption in the brain is a theory that has not been proven (see Chapter 7). No doctor could examine the body of a depressed person and discover depression. The only way he can know if depression is a problem is if the patient tells him. As far as medical science can tell, the body of a depressed person is working fine. And in studies that artificially lowered serotonin levels in the subjects, depression did not result. However, there are physical problems that can contribute to depression. Low thyroid, for example, tends to make people much more prone to depression.[141] Alcohol can also intensify depression.[142]

Whatever the connection between chemicals and depression, it should not be assumed that chemicals cause thoughts. A drug may

---

[140] NAS.

[141] Low thyroid is a fairly common problem, especially among women. It is a good idea for any depressed person to have thyroid levels checked.

[142] Alcohol is a depressant. In one study, subjects who normally consume one alcoholic drink per day abstained for three months. At the end of that time their scores on standard depression inventories improved.
(http://depression.about.com/od/drugsalcohol/a/alcoholanddep.htm).

hinder or enhance the ability of the brain to think, but chemicals do not create thoughts. Thoughts originate from an immaterial source (the heart—Mt.15:19).

The most basic cause of depression is a blockage of the inflow of joy into one's life. God designed our river of joy to be continually fed by three tributaries: His past goodness, His present goodness, and His future goodness. All three tributaries must be flowing in order for a person to have adequate joy.

So what is it that blocks the tributaries of joy?

1) Ingratitude

The tributary of joy from God's past goodness is blocked by ingratitude. Failure to notice God's past acts of kindness, or failure to appreciate them for what they are, or failure to remember them, or failure to spend adequate time thinking about them results in a lack of gratitude, and the flow of joy from past blessing is cut off.

2) Separation from the Presence of God

Since the only source of joy is the presence of God (Ps.16:2,11, 73:25), joylessness is a symptom of failing to experience the presence of God. This cuts off the flow of joy from present blessings.

3) Self-Pity (Grumbling)

Perhaps the most common cause of joylessness is self-pity, which is inward grumbling. When a person is distressed by circumstances and expresses his distress to others, that is complaining. When he expresses it to God, that is lament. But when he expresses it to himself, that is self-pity, and it is extremely destructive. Whenever the focus turns mostly inward, joy will always diminish. When suffering invades a person's life, and rather than seeing the big picture of God's sovereign purposes he turns his attention on himself and develops a "woe is me" perspective, the result is a tunnel vision that blocks out all cause for rejoicing and sees only those things that support his belief that he deserves pity. His heart is building a case for how hard he has it, and he becomes blind to all of God's blessings, which cuts off the stream of joy from present blessings.

It also cuts off the stream of joy from future blessings, which normally flows through hope. Hope is rejected by the soul that is consumed with self-pity. Self-pity always seeks to justify itself by proving that "everything" is going wrong. This causes the person to notice only negative things while being blind to blessings, even to the point where the soul actually refuses comfort. Like Jacob, who wept and "refused to be comforted" (Gn.37:35), the self-pitying soul rejects thoughts about the kindness that God is showing, has shown in the past, and will show in the future.

Psalms 77:2 When I was in distress, I sought the Lord; at night I stretched out untiring hands and my soul refused to be comforted.

This unwillingness of the soul to be comforted is paradoxical, because for most people who suffer from extreme joylessness, their greatest desire is to recover. More than anything else in life they long to feel joy again. Yet at the same time something inside them resists comfort.

Self-pity is actually a form of self-exaltation. Thinking the most important object of my thoughts is me and my troubles—that exalts me to the place of highest importance.

4) Lack of Hope

The flow of joy coming from the future is blocked by lack of hope. Hope is a feeling of happiness or elevated mood in the present because of some good thing that is coming in the future. When you are leaving for your dream vacation tomorrow, you find yourself in a great mood at work today. Why? You are still at work. You are not experiencing any of the pleasures of the vacation yet, so why do you feel happy? That feeling of happiness is what the Bible means by the word "hope." God designed us to be able to enjoy future blessings in the present, and that enjoyment is a key tributary to a person's river of joy. It is blocked when a person either does not believe that future blessing will happen, or does not believe it will be delightful and satisfying.

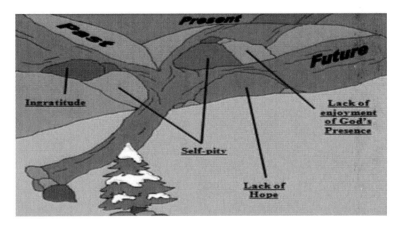

When any one of those three becomes blocked, the river of joy will drop to a level that is too low to flow over the dams of sorrow and hardship in life.

Steps to Recovery

Diagnose the Problem

After explaining the various components of depression in biblical terms, ask the counselee to diagnose himself. Give him the following list and ask him to check which apply to his situation, and what role he sees that aspect playing (Is it a cause or a symptom?). Feel free to photocopy the following form.

Actors that Apply in Your Situation   Role (cause or symptom)

☐ **Losing Heart** (lack of motivation, feelings of wanting to give up, apathy about most anything other than feeling better)

    ☐ Cause
    ☐ Symptom

☐ **Despair** (lacking hope—no feelings of pleasure in upcoming blessings)

    ☐ Cause
    ☐ Symptom

☐ **Joylessness** (sadness, inability to enjoy present blessings)

    ☐ Cause
    ☐ Symptom

☐ **Weariness, Discouragement** (no energy for or delight in the tasks God has given)

    ☐ Cause
    ☐ Symptom

☐ **Self-Pity**

    ☐ Cause
    ☐ Symptom

☐ **Inner Grumbling** (expressing your disapproval of circumstances)

    ☐ Cause
    ☐ Symptom

☐ **Obsessive Negative Thoughts**

    ☐ Cause
    ☐ Symptom

☐ **The heart clinging to sorrow and refusing to be comforted**

    ☐ Cause
    ☐ Symptom

☐ **Lack of Appreciation for God's Expressions of Love**

    ☐ Cause
    ☐ Symptom

Help the counselee discern which aspects of his condition are sinful and which are not. It is not wrong to experience a measure of distress in suffering. Jesus was greatly distressed the night before the crucifixion. Paul, the psalmists, and other godly examples experienced tremendous anxiety. Anxiety becomes sinful when it eclipses joy in the long-term (see the section "Fear of Pain" in Chapter 9).

Anxiety and sorrow are also sinful when they arise out of sinful attitudes. Saul, for example, became depressed because of jealousy (1 Sam.18:8-9). Ahab was despondent when he coveted Naboth's vineyard and couldn't have it (1 Ki.21:4). Judas was so depressed after betraying Jesus that he killed himself (Mt.27:5). Cain was rebuked for being downcast after God rejected his half-hearted, faithless worship (Gn.4:5).

Make sure the counselee understands that not all sorrow and sadness is sin. But it is important to discern which parts are sinful so repentance can lead to restored joy. Once the sinful aspects are determined, help the counselee discern where his thinking begins to leave the biblical path. It is at that point of departure that the remedy must come. The depressed man quoted above said he could think the best thoughts all day long and it would not help. But how does he know that? No one but Christ has ever thought the best thoughts all day long. No matter how good a person's thought life has been in the past, it can always be better, and better thinking will most certainly help.

Accept Suffering

Joylessness, despair, discouragement, and losing heart usually begin with an attitude of rejection toward suffering. God sends suffering into a person's life, and rather than accepting and submitting to it as a gift from God, the person rejects it as an intolerable intrusion into his life. As long as suffering is thought of as an intolerable intrusion, the person will always be discouraged because there will always be suffering.

Remind the counselee that God promises to only send suffering that will do us good (Ro.5:3, Jas.1:2-4, Ro.8:28, Jer.29:11, Heb.12:7-11, 1 Pe.4:1). When we experience the mighty hand of God in suffering, instead of arrogantly resisting, we must humbly submit (see Chapter 3 under "Strengthening").

The desire to feel better, when it becomes a person's highest goal, can actually become one of the greatest hindrances to reaching that goal. Abraham Lincoln said, "To remain as I am is impossible. I must die or be better." That attitude actually increases feelings of despair. If the highest, most important goal is to feel better, and feeling better seems out of reach, then the most important goal of the person's life is impossible to achieve, and that will intensify the despair.

It is fine to have joy as a goal, but it must never be the highest priority. Our highest goal must always be the glory of God, and that goal is never out of our reach regardless of how we are feeling. We must follow Jesus, who did pray, "Let this cup pass from me" but also said, "Nevertheless your will, not mine, be done" (Mt.26:39). The will of God must always be more precious to us than relief from suffering. Urge the counselee to give up the *priority* of feeling better, and say to his soul, "It's OK for me to suffer for now—for however long God decides to allow it to continue." That can relieve the pressure of *having* to feel better, which will alleviate much of the despair. Once people come to a point of willingness to suffer, very often within days they are no longer depressed (or at least they feel *significantly* better).

God requires suffering from some people. Immediately after the apostle Paul was converted, God appeared to Ananias and told him to go to Paul (then Saul) with these words:

Acts 9:15-16 "This man is my chosen instrument ... 16 I will show him how much he must suffer for my name."

And did he suffer! Time after time he was whipped, imprisoned, beaten with rods. People stoned him, tortured him, persecuted him … that was how it was for Paul right up to his appointed time to enter the presence of the Lord. Paul's life, all told, turned out well. He was possibly the most successful Christian who ever lived. Did he accomplish incredibly great things? Yes. Did he advance the kingdom of God around the world? Yes. Are there countless thousands in heaven because of God's work through the apostle Paul? Yes. Is he enjoying paradise right now? Yes. So what does it matter that, for the relatively short time he was on this earth, he suffered?

If someone suffers from depression, maybe God, on the day of that person's conversion, said to the angels, "I will show her how much she must suffer for My name. She will have to endure crippling emotions throughout her life." This would not prevent her from having a life like Paul's. *There is hope outside of feeling better!*

Be Willing to be Comforted

Help the counselee discover thought patterns that show a refusal to accept comfort from God, such as focusing on hardships while ignoring blessings. Help the counselee become willing to let go of the blanket of sorrow with which they have wrapped themselves.

Consider God's Past Goodness

Unclog the tributary of joy from past blessings by considering carefully God's past goodness. This was the solution for the depression of the writer of Psalm 77, whose soul was refusing to be comforted to the point of causing insomnia.

Psalm 77:2-12 In the day of my trouble I sought the Lord; In the night my hand was stretched out without weariness; My soul refused to be comforted. ... 4 You have held my eyelids *open;* I am so troubled that I cannot speak. ... 11 I shall remember the deeds of the Lord; Surely I will remember Your wonders of old. 12 I will meditate on all Your work and muse on Your deeds. [143]

Urge the counselee to describe to you a list of God's past blessings—in the past days, then weeks, then months, then years, then all the way back to the creation. Help the person establish a routine of consideration of God's past goodness. For instance, begin a routine of kneeling on the floor each night before bed and thanking God for each of His acts of kindness over the past twenty-four hours—intentionally taking delight in each of them.

Control Your Words

In Psalm 73 Asaph could feel himself slipping into despair. When he saw the prosperity of the wicked and then considered all his suffering and hardship, he started to stumble into thoughts of self-pity, which is always marked by exaggeration.

---

[143] New American Standard (NAU).

Psalm 73:3,13-14 For I envied the arrogant when I saw the prosperity of the wicked. 4 They have no struggles ... 13 Surely in vain have I kept my heart pure; in vain have I washed my hands in innocence. 14 All day long I have been plagued; I have been punished every morning.

The wicked have NO struggles whatsoever, while poor Asaph has gained zero benefit from serving God. Both are ridiculous exaggerations, and Asaph knew it—so he kept his mouth shut.

15 If I had said, "I will speak thus," I would have betrayed your children.

He resisted the temptation to verbalize these thoughts. He knew that to do so would be a betrayal of the people of God, because complaining harms all who hear it—even if the only one who hears it is you!

Inner Grumbling

The verbs in verse 21 of Psalm 73 are in a grammatical form that is reflexive[144] (action acted upon oneself), so a literal translation would be, "My heart embittered itself and my insides pierced themselves." Inner turmoil and anxiety is something the heart inflicts upon itself. Runaway thoughts of complaint, self-pity, and ingratitude are like the heart taking a knife and repeatedly stabbing itself. If a person repeatedly bludgeons his heart with a hammer, he should not be surprised when afterward his heart is in great pain.

When we grumble to ourselves we do spiritual damage. Reassure the counselee that it is appropriate to pour out his distress to God in prayer. But urge him, when he has finished praying, to be done with his complaint. Suggest that he resolve to never dwell on his suffering or troubles unless he is speaking to God about it (unless it is something that requires him to think about it because he must take some action). This will help with the problem of exaggeration, as we are not as quick to overstate things when we are talking to the One who knows everything.

This, of course, is easier said than done. The flesh, when it has a complaint, will insist on being heard. There are times when your flesh (the part of you that is prone to sin) talks to you, and there are other times when you talk to it. Scripture speaks of this inner dialogue.

---

[144] Both verbs are in the hithpael form.

Psalm 14:1 The fool says in his heart, "There is no God."

Psalm 10:6 [the wicked man] says in his heart, "I shall not be moved; throughout all generations I shall not meet adversity."[145]

Psalm 10:11 He says in his heart, "God has forgotten, he has hidden his face, he will never see it."[146]

The way to silence the flesh is by preaching to it. Shout it down. When the psalmist fell into despair, instead of listening to the grumblings of his soul, he preached to his soul.

Psalm 42:5 Why are you downcast, O my soul? Why so disturbed within me? Put your hope in God. For I shall yet praise Him, my Savior and my God.[147]

Martyn Lloyd-Jones has helpful insights on this text:

> The first thing we have to learn is what the Psalmist learned—we must learn to take ourselves in hand. This man was not content just to lie down and commiserate with himself. … he talks to himself. This man turns to himself and says: 'Why art thou cast down O my soul, why art thou disquieted within me?' He is talking to himself, he is addressing himself.…
>
> We must talk to ourselves instead of allowing 'ourselves' to talk to us! Do you realize what that means? I suggest that the main trouble in this whole matter of spiritual depression in a sense is this, that we allow our self to talk to us instead of talking to our self. … Have you realized that most of your unhappiness in life is due to the fact that you are listening to yourself instead of talking to yourself? Take those thoughts that come to you the moment you wake up in the morning. You have not originated them, but they start talking to you, they bring back the problems of yesterday, etc. Somebody is talking. Who is talking to you? Your self is talking to you. Now this man's [solution] was this; instead of allowing this self to talk to him, he starts talking to himself. 'Why art thou cast down, O my soul?' he asks. His soul had been depressing him, crushing him. So he stands up and says: 'Self, listen for a moment, I will speak to you'. … You have to take yourself in hand … preach to yourself, question yourself. You must say to your soul: 'Why art thou cast down' — what business have you to be disquieted? … And then you must go on to remind yourself of God, Who God is, and what God is and what God has

---

[145] ESV.
[146] ESV.
[147] The writer does this again in verse 11, and again in Ps.43:5.

done, and what God has pledged Himself to do. Then having done that, end on this note: defy yourself, and defy other people, and defy the devil and the whole world, and say with this man: ["For I shall yet praise Him, my Savior and my God"].[148]

Demand an accounting from your soul. Require an explanation for its grumbling. But don't be content just to rebuke yourself. Beating up on yourself will only perpetuate the problem of the self-focus. Preach to yourself not about you, but about God. That is what the psalmist did— he pointed his soul to God. The solution to self-pity is to turn attention from self to God. Teach the counselee the 5-to-1 principle: resolve to have five delightful thoughts about God for every one thought about self. So if a discouraging thought comes to mind, respond by thinking, "OK, what are five wonderful truths about God? 1) God is patient (followed by a few moments of thinking about God's patience) 2) God is faithful (then a few moments pondering why His faithfulness is such a great thing) 3) God is kind..." Do this exercise out loud with the counselee to give him a feel for it.

Enjoy God's Presence

Asaph recovered from his near-miss with despair first by backing up to consider the long-term, big picture of eternity (Ps.73:16-20), then by focusing his attention on appreciating the incredible benefits of the presence of God (vv.23-28). Learning to enjoy the presence of God is the most important key to unclogging the tributary of present joy.

Psalm 73:23-28 Yet I am always with you; you hold me by my right hand. 24 You guide me with your counsel, and afterward you will take me into glory. 25 Whom have I in heaven but you? And earth has nothing I desire besides you. 26 My flesh and my heart may fail, but God is the strength of my heart and my portion forever. 27 Those who are far from you will perish; you destroy all who are unfaithful to you. 28 But as for me, the nearness of God is my good. I have made the Lord Yahweh my refuge; I will tell of all your deeds.[149]

Joy is always available to the believer through enjoyment of the presence of God. On rare occasions God may withdraw His presence in

---

[148] Martyn Lloyd-Jones, *Spiritual Depression*, 20-21.
[149] Author's Translation.

temporary discipline, but most of the time when a believer is not gaining joy from the presence of God it is because of a failure to take advantage of the experience of God's presence that is available.

Here are some possible causes of inability to enjoy God's presence:

1) Hanging on to a sin or some cherished idol in the heart
2) Failure to interpret the countless blessings you experience each day as direct expressions of His love for you—ignoring His gestures of love
3) Failure to understand that all glimmers of joy and ability to enjoy life are experiences of His presence
4) Lack of wholeheartedness in seeking His presence
5) Lack of willingness to believe what He says about forgiveness and His delight in His people
6) Distraction from God because of a focus on self (self-pity)
7) Listening to yourself instead of preaching to yourself—letting the flesh dictate all your thoughts
8) Dwelling on hardship
9) Preferring some other source of comfort rather than waiting for Him

Urge the counselee to have a planned statement to make to himself each time he begins to have feelings of despair. Here is what I tell myself: "It is not necessary for me to feel discouraged right now. God is right here! And I have His favor. And if I seek Him, there is a great enough experience of His presence available to me right now to satisfy my soul enough so that I will have more joy than sorrow."

Anticipate Future Blessing

Help the counselee unclog the flow of joy from future blessing by teaching him how to hope in God. One of the most extreme examples of major depression in Scripture is Jeremiah in Lamentations (read Lam.3:1-20). But as depressed as Jeremiah was, he *did* recover. His despair gave way to hope in verse 21.

Lamentations 3:20-21 My soul is downcast within me. 21 Yet this I call to mind and therefore I have hope ...

Have you ever noticed that the effect trials have on you depends on your view of the future? If you are excited about what is coming tomorrow, the suffering of today has little impact. But if you have nothing to look forward to, even the smallest difficulty today can seem devastating. The day before getting married to the love of your life you can get a flat tire in the rain and laugh it off. But if tomorrow and next week and next year all seem to promise nothing but drudgery as far as the eye can see, something as small as stubbing your toe can make you want to give up.

Despair is not a chemical imbalance; it is a hope imbalance. It is not that your brain is leaking serotonin; it is that your spirit is leaking hope.

Yet even in the depths of his depression, Jeremiah found hope. How? What specific good thing did he think of that God might do? What light did he see at the end of his long, dark tunnel? And what about you? How can you find hope like he did?

If you *do* see light at the end of the tunnel, of course you will come out of your depression—that's easy. The problem is, what do you do when there is no light at the end of the tunnel? What do you do when even in your wildest dreams you cannot think of anything God might do to make the situation better? What do you do when all your hope is gone?

Here is where we learn an important lesson from Jeremiah. For Jeremiah there was no light at the end of the tunnel. There was no relief he could think of or could see on the horizon. What encouraged him and restored his hope was not something he could see coming, rather it was a specific piece of information: "Yet this I call to mind and therefore I have hope...."

This is important, because there are many who would say that when people are hurting, that is not the time to try to teach biblical principles. They would say you need to just be there for people and offer them a shoulder to cry on. A shoulder to cry on is a wonderful thing, and offering it is a great act of love. But by itself it is incomplete. Jeremiah was brought from a state of major depression to being filled with real hope not through someone's sympathy alone, but through a particular truth about God.

What was that truth?

Lamentations 3:21-22 Yet this I call to mind and therefore I have hope: 22 Because of the Lord's great love we are not consumed.

He called to mind something about the amazing character of God: His great love. Just thinking about God's love made Jeremiah realize that blessing *is* around the corner. You do not have to see a light at the end of the tunnel. All you need is to consider the nature of the God who is at the end of the tunnel.

Imagine a child who has two uncles that come visit every Christmas. One is great at picking out gifts and the other is not. The second uncle always gives some book the child will never read, or new tube socks, or some other lame gift. But the first uncle is the opposite. Every year his gift ends up being the child's favorite gift. And it is never something the child asked for. This uncle is so creative, he always thinks of something that is better than anything the child thought to put on his list. That first uncle is so good at picking out gifts—so generous and creative—that all that is required to fill the child's heart with joy is just the sound of his car pulling up in front of the house. The child does not need to have a glimpse of what is inside the box in order to be excited about it. It is recalling the character of the giver, not getting a glimpse of the gift, that brings hope.

And the more specific and detailed the understanding of God's character, the greater the hope. "God is loving" is too general. Jeremiah was more specific than that. What turned Jeremiah's despair into hope and joy was contemplating the fact that God is not only loving, but He is by nature *creative* in His love.

Lamentations 3:22-23 His compassions never fail. 23 They are new every morning; great is your faithfulness.

God's nature is such that He will think of a way to show you kindness and tenderness—a new way every single morning. This is one reason God made mornings. When God created the solar system, He divided time into days. That gives us all a new beginning every twenty-four hours. God is a God of new beginnings and fresh starts, and He even built that into the creation.

Zephaniah 3:5 The Lord ... is righteous; he does no wrong. Morning by morning he dispenses his justice, and every new day he does not fail.

Jeremiah called to mind the fact that God is creative in the ways He blesses His people. His eyes were opened to the fact that God had something in mind right around the corner that will be delightful and satisfying.

Jeremiah was not comforted by minimizing his suffering. He did not say, "Well, I have some hope because I realize things can't be as bad as they seem. At least this or that didn't happen…." Rather, he was comforted in the midst of great anguish by turning his attention away from his circumstances and to the character of God, from Whom flows an inexhaustible fountain of creative kindness.

Notice his response in verse 24: "I say to myself, 'The Lord is my portion; therefore I will wait for him.'" What does that mean? Portion of *what*?

The word *portion*, which means "amount or share," is a reference to Numbers 18:20. When God brought Israel into the promised-land, He divided it up eleven ways, but there were twelve tribes. When He got to the last tribe—Levi—nothing was left.

Numbers 18:20 The Lord said to Aaron, "You will have no inheritance in their land, nor will you have any share among them; I am your share and your inheritance among the Israelites."

So the priests were given no portion of the land. They owned nothing. Their list of assets was blank, yet they ended up being better off than everyone else. (Eleven tribes gave them a tenth, so they ended up with eleven tenths—one tenth more than any other tribe.)

That is what happens when the Lord is your portion. The only difference is, you can't see it and you don't know where it is coming from. God gave an inheritance to all twelve tribes. To eleven He gave an inheritance that could be seen; to the twelfth, the priests, He gave the same inheritance—in fact, bigger—but it could not be seen.

When God says, "I am your portion," think of it this way: Suppose a man brings a youth group into the mountains and gives them each a small survival kit. His young son says, "Dad, where is my survival kit?" and the man replies, "I am your survival kit—you stay with me."

Or imagine that the billionaire CEO of the company you work for is your best friend, and when he is setting salaries, he says, "This is your salary, this is yours, this is yours," etc. When he finally has gone through everyone but you, and you say, "What about me?" he says, "Don't worry—I'll take care of all your needs myself."

Jeremiah had lost everything. He was depressed and at the end of his rope. He could not even imagine what God might do to make things better. But then the depression lifted and he was filled with hope because he began to think about the nature of God, who is like that first uncle—creative in His love. Jeremiah's response was to say, "The Lord is my portion. I do not need or want anything other than what He is pleased to provide. I look around and can't see provision or blessing. I am like the tribe of Levi—all I have for a blessing is You. But I am confident I will end up with something wonderful—because I know what You are like."

Christians who struggle with depression should spend what little energy they have focusing on the goodness of God. Not only does God have infinite wisdom to guide them in life, infinite resources to provide for them, infinite knowledge to teach them, infinite mercy to care for them, infinite compassion to comfort them, infinite love to restore them, and infinite strength to protect them; He has also given future promises that are wonderful beyond imagination or comprehension.

> "Put your ear to the ground of God's word and listen to the rumble of His faithfulness coming."
>
> – John Piper

Enjoy Ministry

Twice in 2 Corinthians 4 Paul says that he does not get discouraged and lose heart even while being hard pressed on every side, perplexed, and struck down. How is that possible? Even in the midst of almost unbearable hardship Paul did not lose heart because of the joy he derived from his ministry.

2 Corinthians 4:16 Therefore, [given the undiminished, untarnished glory of the New Covenant][150] since through God's mercy we have this ministry [the ministry of the New Covenant, the Gospel] we do not lose heart.

---

[150] See the context 2 Cor.3:7-4:1.

The thing that kept Paul from losing heart was thinking about the nature of his ministry. If God called you to something that might turn out to be a failure, disgrace, or embarrassment, you would tend to lose heart when things started looking bad. But when your task is part of something that is guaranteed to be a glorious success, that is encouraging. Encouragement comes from ministry.

We are all called to various aspects of the same ministry—the Gospel of the Lord Jesus Christ. Your calling in the church represents your role in this ministry—in something truly great. The less a person thinks about life in terms of ministry and calling, the less encouraged he will be by the fact that those things are guaranteed to be a glorious success. But since God has promised grand success to every Christian, the more a person focuses on that, the more strength he will have to persevere. That is exactly the point of Galatians 6:9.

Galatians 6:9 Let us not become weary in doing good, for at the proper time we will reap a harvest if we do not give up.

This is the same point Paul is making in 2 Corinthians 4. It is the hope of the great harvest, the fruit of our ministry, that gives us the stamina to persevere. No matter how things look, the Gospel (and its bearers) will prove to be glorious, therefore we do not lose heart.

Someone may argue, "That's fine if you're Paul. But my discouragement comes from the fact that I botch the task so much. I am so weak and inept—my contribution probably does more harm than good." Paul also lamented his inadequacy for the task (2 Cor.2:16). But it is actually our very inadequacy that makes us just right for the task.

2 Corinthians 4:7 We have this treasure in jars of clay to show that this all-surpassing power is from God and not from us.

The glorious treasure of the work of the gospel has been placed in weak, fragile, breakable pots like us so that no one is ever confused about where the real glory is.

Help the counselee think through all the various aspects of his calling—ministries at church, his role in his family, his role in the world—and how those things are of breathtaking, eternal importance because of how God has promised to use them in His kingdom.

This will not only bring the joy that naturally comes from accomplishing important things, but it will also help the counselee become more outwardly focused, which will help in the fight against self-pity.

Persevere

Won't, Not Can't

Those who are losing heart are tempted to give up altogether (Gal.6:9). Giving up can mean turning away from the faith, or committing suicide, or just checking out of life and staying in bed most of the time. The severely discouraged person feels he has no choice but to give up. But that is never the case.

Philippians 4:13 I can do all things through him who strengthens me. [151]

1 Corinthians 10:13 No temptation has seized you except what is common to man. And God is faithful; he will not let you be tempted beyond what you can bear. But when you are tempted, he will also provide a way out so that you can stand up under it.

God always provides us with the ability to do what is right. It is essential that the depressed person understand that he can do everything God calls him to do. He can get out of bed when he needs to; he can serve his family; he can carry out his responsibilities. Failure to do what he should do is never justified under the excuse, "I just can't." It feels that way, but God's Word tells us otherwise.

The remedies suggested in this chapter may not provide immediate relief from the suffering of joylessness, and in the mean-time the darkness will remain. While it does, urge the counselee to persevere.

Restore Long-Term Thinking

Despair has a way of shortening one's perspective. The distant future means nothing. All that can be seen is the moment. But since so much of the flow of joy comes to us from thinking about future blessing, it is crucial to expand one's thinking into the long-term.

One of the reasons people fall into despair is they lose sight of the importance of everything they do, and they stop doing it. Then they are

---

[151] ESV.

not productive, and being unproductive makes them feel worthless, which saps their joy even more.

The important things, the truly great things, generally cannot be accomplished in an afternoon. They are done by tiny increments over a long period of time, and none of those increments seem all that significant. Since a depressed person tends to lose his long-term perspective, it becomes especially hard for him to do anything that does not have short-term results.

Discouraged people are often like the teenager who wants to look like a bodybuilder, so he goes to the gym and works out for two hours. Then he stands in front of the mirror and flexes, but he looks the same as he did before. To get big muscles, he would have to get into a routine of lifting weights every day for years. And each one of those days would hardly make a noticeable difference. He could even skip working out any one of those days and it would not matter (as long as he did not skip all the other days).

Some take a similar approach to spiritual things: They read the Bible every day for a week, and then look in the mirror and do not see any spiritual muscles. They start a new ministry and are enthusiastic for a month or two, but when they do not see any fruit, they lose interest.

Urge the counselee to establish a realistic, doable routine. Spiritual progress is a massive task, and progress is slow. Even after the best day of sanctification, a person goes to bed almost the same in his character as when he woke up. But just as faithfully working out every day will eventually result in larger muscles, or eating fewer calories than one burns each day will eventually result in weight loss, so it is with spiritual progress. Measuring success only by immediate results will result in discouragement.

For this reason, establishing a routine is crucial for a person who is losing heart, because it enables him to know what to do when it feels like nothing is worth doing. When a person loses heart, motivation disappears. He cannot find any reason to do anything. Having a routine helps keep the person moving even when he loses sight of the reason why those things are worth doing.

Laziness has a way of feeding on itself. The lazier a person is, the harder everything becomes—until he can hardly lift a fork from the plate to his mouth (Pr.15:19, 19:24). One of the best things for a depressed person, many times, is to sweat.

Focus on Heaven

Perseverance is the opposite of giving up. It is when we become more severe than our trial, and we press on even through suffering. Hebrews 12 teaches us how to persevere. The word "persevere" *(hupomeno)* appears three times in the first three verses (translated "perseverance" once and "endured" twice).

Hebrews 12:1-3 Let us run with <u>perseverance</u> the race marked out for us. 2 Let us fix our eyes on Jesus ... who ... <u>endured</u> the cross... 3 Consider him who <u>endured</u> such opposition from sinful men, so that you will not grow weary and lose heart.

The key to persevering is fixing our attention on Christ's example. He endured. Does that mean He never got tired or never felt sad or never felt like giving up? No. He experienced all those things in degrees we cannot begin to fathom. But He absolutely could not be derailed from His purpose. The enemy would repeatedly throw his full weight against Him, and Jesus would take blow after blow, but He *would not* be knocked off course. He could be reduced to tears because of how difficult it was for Him (Heb.5:7), but He could not be diverted from the path of God's purpose.

But didn't Jesus have an advantage? After all, He is God. It is true that Jesus is God, but it is not true that Jesus used His deity in a way that gave Him an advantage in the fight against discouragement. In His human nature Jesus subjected Himself to the same weaknesses to which we are subject (Heb.4:15). This means it was no easier for Him than it is for us.

So how did He do it? The answer is in verse 2. He persevered by means of the joy that was set before Him. He looked ahead to the final outcome of persevering. This is exactly the same way the faithful saints in Chapter 11 persevered through all kinds of horrible suffering. They were tortured and refused to be released, faced jeers and flogging, were chained and put in prison; they were stoned, sawed in two, and they were put to death by the sword. They went about in sheepskins and goatskins, destitute, persecuted, and mistreated. They wandered in deserts and mountains, and in caves and holes in the ground. And yet they persevered. They didn't give up. Why? Because they wanted to obtain a better resurrection (Heb.11:35). Moses chose to be mistreated along with the people of God rather than to enjoy the pleasures of sin for a short time because he regarded disgrace for the sake of Christ as of greater value than the treasures of Egypt, because he was looking ahead to his reward (Heb.11:25-26). The promise of heaven is our primary hope.

Help the counselee develop a habit of thinking about the glories of our heavenly reward. This can be done by reading a good book about heaven, or by listening to sermons on heaven, or by memorizing Scripture that speaks of heaven.

Put Your Suffering in Perspective

Hebrews 12:4 In your struggle against sin, you have not yet resisted to the point of shedding your blood.

Keep suffering in perspective by remembering the suffering of the saints in Hebrews 11, and the suffering of Christ on the cross. Most people who are depressed have not shed any blood in the ordeal. It is as if the writer were saying, "Why are you becoming discouraged? You aren't even bleeding. There is no crown of thorns on your head, no spear in your side. Are you being sawed in half, stoned, or flogged? I don't see any drops of blood on your forehead. I don't see any bodies lying around. You've hardly resisted anything yet." Considering the suffering of Christ helps the counselee fight the tendency to exaggerate his suffering.

Suicide

Depressed people often think about dying. Their thoughts revolve around a desire to end the pain so they no longer have to suffer. Those are not necessarily sinful thoughts. Paul had thoughts like that. Philippians is a thank-you letter from Paul to a church that had sent him a gift. The letter is primarily about joy and encouragement, yet Paul devotes a significant portion of the first chapter to his desire to die! That may sound like a rather morbid topic to include in a thank-you note, but it is actually quite uplifting.

Philippians 1:23 ... I desire to depart (die) and be with Christ, which is better by far;

It would be so much better to be with Christ than to be down here in prison, or on a sinking ship, or under a pile of rocks, or at the business end of a whip. All the suffering would be over, and the pain would end. It would be wonderful. There is nothing wrong with thinking like that. Paul wanted to die. But in the same verse he says, "I am torn."

"Why, Paul? Why are you torn? If being with Christ would be so wonderful, what could be appealing enough in this life that you would be torn about whether you want to live or die?" He was torn because for him, "to live is Christ" (Php.1:21). Paul realized that this life is our only opportunity to represent Christ and serve Him in this world. It is our only opportunity to bear on our bodies the marks of Christ and endure suffering for His name. Now is our opportunity to sacrificially serve God's people in their time of need (Paul *loved* being the flesh-and-bone delivery system of God's love to His people). This life is our only opportunity to fill up in our flesh what was lacking in Christ's suffering. We desire to die and be with Christ, which would be so much better, but it is more necessary for God's people that we remain in the body as long as God grants us breath.

From a selfish perspective, the question of whether to live or die is the easiest choice in the world—go for the relief! But when the kingdom of God is taken into account, it is not such an easy choice. Both options are extremely appealing—to go to be with Christ, or to stay on this earth to suffer on His behalf and bring Him great glory. Paul thinks it over, and then one of the two options emerges as being more appealing to him:

Philippians 1:25-26 Convinced of this, I know that I will remain, and I will continue with all of you for your progress and joy in the faith, so that through my being with you again your joy in Christ Jesus will overflow on account of me.

There is much joy to be found in bringing joy to others. Those who suffer from joylessness can become so focused on finding joy for themselves that they lose sight of the most effective method of finding joy, which is bringing joy to the hearts of others (Jn.15:10-12). When a person devotes himself to making others happy in Christ, it will take his focus off himself (eliminating self-pity), and it will open greater access to joy in Christ for himself. Note: this process may be hindered if the person is taking antidepressants, as they can have the effect of reducing one's ability to feel love (see Chapter 7, "The Dark Side of Antidepressants").

Serving others is very difficult for people who are depressed. Everything is difficult. But urge them to avoid making decisions on the basis of how they feel. People who are depressed tend to be governed by their feelings. Help them realize that they do not have to be. They can decide to keep moving no matter how low they feel. Remind them that whether it helps them feel better or not, it is our responsibility to serve even while we are suffering. Jesus was involved in evangelism, a prayer ministry, teaching, prophecy, counseling, intercession, and care for a widow—all while hanging on the cross! It is not a sin to feel down, but it is sin to use that as an excuse not to serve.

When a person becomes suicidal, remind him that it is not wrong to think about dying. Every Christian should long to be with Christ. But it is crucial to think about dying or living from a kingdom perspective, which can lead to a genuine desire to actually remain in painful circumstances.

Resources for Helping Those
Struggling with Joylessness

Sermons by Darrell Ferguson:
- "Loving God with All Your Heart" sermon series[152]

Sermons by John Piper:[153]
- ""Spiritual Depression in the Psalms" on Ps.42.

Devotionals from the book, *What's So Great About God?* :[154]

Meditations #**1-20, 34-37,** 46-49, **59**, **62**, 65, **66**, 67, 73, **76, 77, 94-95, 112, 118,** 140, 142, 143, **155**, 166

---

[152] FoodForYourSoul.net. The sermon series are listed in alphabetical order on the "Series Alphabetically" link.

[153] Each of these sermons by John Piper is available at DesiringGod.org in the Resource Library in "Resource Categories by Scripture" (/resource-library/sermons/by-scripture).

[154] Bold numbers represent the meditations that are especially relevant.

CHAPTER NINE:
ANXIETY AND ANGER

Anxiety

Few things can do more harm to both the body and the spirit than intense, prolonged anxiety.

Not all distress is sinful. Jesus was extremely upset at times, and yet was without sin. Evil should bother us. Anxiety becomes problematic when it becomes obsessive and eclipses our joy, or when it turns to worry, sinful fear, or fretting. One sign that this is happening is when the stress begins to cause health problems, such as ulcers or chronic headaches from tense back and neck muscles. God designed us to become tense at times and to be relaxed at other times. When a person is unable to relax, it is evidence that the anxieties of life have eclipsed joy in God.

Receiving a bill you cannot pay, a child bringing home a bad report card, an impossible deadline at work, laundry piling up—those things should cause a degree of tension so that you will be motivated to address the problem. If the purpose of the tension is to drive you to action, however, then once you have taken whatever action you can take, there is no value in remaining tense.

Casting Anxiety on God

The solution to anxiety is to cast it upon the Lord.

1 Peter 5:6-7 Humble yourselves, therefore, under God's mighty hand, that he may lift you up in due time. 7 Cast all your anxiety on him because he cares for you.

Suffering with Humility

The phrase *God's mighty hand* is an Old Testament concept that refers to the sovereign, mighty work of God that results in hardship for His people. Sometimes it is a work of punishment or chastening, sometimes it is a work of amazing deliverance, sometimes a work of provision, sometimes a work of testing. But in each case, it is comes to us as hardship.

The first step in helping a person who is struggling under the mighty hand of God is teaching him to accept it. Teach him not to resist what God is doing. People become tense when they think things are spinning out of control. But things are never spinning out of God's control, and God only does good things. Even when people and Satan are doing evil things, the work God is accomplishing through it is only good—and is far greater than the evil men and Satan are doing.

To accept and even appreciate the mighty hand of God requires humility. Pride resists God's mighty hand, like a baby who does not want to be held—arching his back and struggling in his parent's arms. If your child does that, and for some reason you cannot set him down at that moment, your only recourse is to overpower him and grip him more tightly, which is uncomfortable and distressing to the child. But when the child accepts the idea of being held and snuggles up in his mother's arms, there is not a more beautiful picture of peaceful rest in all the world. When God sends the stresses of life by the dozen and we arch our back and struggle against it, we only make matters worse. Urge the person to humble himself and accept what his Father is doing. Only then will he be able to cast his cares on Him.

Cast Cares on the Lord One at a Time

When asked how he could handle all the stresses of the massive responsibilities that were upon him, George Mueller replied very simply:

> I do not carry the burden. ... It is not only permission, but positive command that He gives, to cast the burdens upon Him. Oh, let us do it! My beloved brothers and sisters in Christ, "Cast thy burden upon the Lord and He shall sustain thee." Day by day I do it. This

morning sixty matters in connection with the church of which I am pastor, I brought before the Lord.[155]

Mueller began his day offloading burdens from his shoulders onto God's, mentioning them specifically and individually, giving them to God. He never carried the burden. Teach the counselee that when God sends difficulties into our lives we must deal with them as much as we are able, but we must not carry them. Let God bear the weight of responsibility for outcomes that are beyond our control or responsibility.

The Big Picture

When we cast all our anxiety on Him, it reminds us of the big picture — the perspective from heaven. The smaller our perspective, the easier it is to become overwhelmed. An unexpected bill, a conflict in the home, or even watching the evening news can be like a small cloud that blocks the entire sun. But when we say, "God, I now offload the weight of this burden onto You. Do with it as You will. I trust You," that kind of prayer has a way of reminding us of how small the burden really is. When you see that "giant" problem sitting there on God's shoulders, suddenly it does not look so massive. In fact, in light of His immensity, the problem shrinks into nothingness. Is God sliding off His throne in helpless dismay because your son brought home an F? Are the armies of angels paralyzed as the kingdom of God grinds to a halt because your health insurance dropped you or you lost your job? Casting our cares on Him provides the "big picture" perspective that delivers us from being overwhelmed.

Humble Yourself

How can we develop this type of mentality? The grammar of 1 Peter 5:7 gives us a clue. The word *cast* is actually a participle (*casting*). Peter is saying, "Humble yourselves … casting all your anxiety on him…." Casting your cares on Him, then, is an outgrowth of humility.

The pride in our hearts is what makes us cling to our worries. "I can handle this myself." And even when it becomes obvious that we cannot

---

[155] George Meuller, "Real Faith," http://hopefaithprayer.com/?page_id=4919.

handle it ourselves, we get no rest from turning it over to God because we know we cannot trust Him to handle it the way we want it handled. Pride says, "I can only rest when I know the outcome will be the outcome I want." Humility says, "I trust God no matter what outcome He deems best. He knows better than I."

This is not easy. The word *cast* is a strong word—it means to throw, heave, or thrust something away from you. Peter does not say, "Lay your cares at His feet" or, "Lay them down at the foot of the cross." He says, "*Throw* them." It takes some effort. It is like trying to throw away Styrofoam packaging material—your cares cling to you because pride wants to hold on to them.

When a person humbles himself and accepts the mighty hand of God on his life, that person can counsel himself:

Psalm 131:1-3 My heart is not proud, O Lord, my eyes are not haughty; I do not concern myself with great matters or things too wonderful for me. 2 But I have stilled and quieted my soul; like a weaned child with its mother, like a weaned child is my soul within me. 3 O Israel, put your hope in the Lord both now and forevermore.

God's Care for You

1 Peter 5:7 Cast all your anxiety on him because <u>he cares for you</u>.

Speak much to the counselee about God's love. In the arms of a kidnapper it is wise for a child to kick and scream. But there is no reason for a baby to resist the tender embrace of a loving parent. The greater our understanding of God's love, the more ability we will have to accept and embrace what He is doing.

- Will I get the job I want? I'm not worried, because Someone who cares for me is in charge of that.
- Will I or my loved one be healed? Someone who cares for me is in charge of that.
- Is it going to rain tomorrow? Fortunately for me, Someone who cares for me is in charge of that.

Thanksgiving

Philippians 4:6-7 Do not be anxious about anything, but in everything, by prayer and petition, with thanksgiving, present your requests to God. 7 And the peace of God, which transcends all understanding, will guard your hearts and your minds in Christ Jesus.

In order for prayer to alleviate anxiety and bring peace to the soul, it must be *thankful* prayer. Thanking God ahead of time for whatever He decides to do in the matter reminds the anxious Christian that God can be trusted. True gratitude, however, is only possible when there is a deep confidence in the goodness of God. Urge the counselee to make a thorough and intense study of God's goodness and His sovereign control over all things. When a soul is convinced that God is in control and He will only do good things, the result is a thankful heart. And as that gratitude is expressed to God, anxiety is driven out by indescribable peace.

Most Christians believe that they are already very thankful to God for all His blessings and gifts. But if their gratitude is not expressing joy, it is inadequate. Make sure the counselee understands that gratitude is not merely being glad something happened. A woman who walks down the street and finds a diamond ring on the ground may be glad that she now has another piece of jewelry. But if the man of her dreams places a ring on her finger and asks her to marry him—that is a much higher level of gladness. The rings may be identical, but the one she receives from the man she loves produces far greater joy because of the meaning behind the gift. If God heals you from a serious illness, or provides a meal and allows it to hit the spot, big gifts and little gifts—it is one thing to simply be glad it happened and say, "Thank You Lord," but it is a much different thing to see the meaning behind that gift and receive it like the woman receives the engagement ring. True gratitude comes when we see the meaning behind God's gifts and receive them as the gestures of His love that they are.

Stress in Decision-Making

The word translated *anxiety* comes from a root that means "to be drawn in different directions."[156] Much of our anxiety comes at the point of making big decisions. Wrong decisions can have severe consequences.

When someone has to make a big decision, teach him how to use wisdom (study the Proverbs, heed counsel from wise brothers and sisters, and strive to choose the option that will be most beneficial for the kingdom of God).[157] Once he has done that, however, he must trust God with the rest. There are times when we simply do not have enough information to foresee outcomes, no matter how much wisdom we employ. This is by God's design. He wants us to trust Him. There are situations in which God's perfect plan requires that we endure a hard outcome of a decision—an outcome that we would avoid if we knew all the facts, so God does not give us all the facts. Understanding this can rescue an anxious person from the tyranny of "what if?" What if I decide the wrong way? What if the economy tanks? What if I become disabled? What if this effort fails?

It is wise to take possible pitfalls into consideration in the decision-making process. If, for example, a potential spouse has a long track record of being humble, Christ-like, and godly; is it possible that he could turn bad in the years to come? Yes, but it is unlikely, and it is a risk worth taking. If, on the other hand, he has led a reprobate life for the last twenty years and has just changed in the last two weeks, there is a significant chance that he will revert to his old ways. A woman would be unwise to marry him.

Many times, however, there are unknowable factors. A person starts a new business, and the office burns down on the day he happens to be changing insurance companies and he loses everything. All of that was unforeseeable. It would be foolish to second-guess the decision to start the business or to entertain a lot of "if only I had…" kind of thinking. If wisdom was followed, then the person can be confident that it was not a

---

[156] Thayer, Greek/English Lexicon of the New Testament.
[157] For a detailed study of wisdom in decision-making see the class titled "Making Wise Decisions" at FoodForYourSoul.net. The sermon series are listed in alphabetical order on the "Series Alphabetically" link.

mistake—even though it seemed to result in disaster. The "disaster" was God's perfect plan.

While apparent, seeming "disasters" happen to believers all the time, for a child of God, real, ultimate disaster never happens (Ro.8:28). Urge the counselee not to allow himself to be pulled apart by the various options he is facing. He must apply wisdom as best he can, make a decision, and then trust God to carry him to wherever He wants him to be in life by means of that decision despite whatever aspects may ultimately prove to be favorable or unfavorable from a human perspective.[158]

Stress in Work

Luke 10:40-42 Martha was <u>distracted</u> by all the preparations... 41 "Martha, Martha," the Lord answered, "you are <u>worried</u> and <u>upset</u> about many things, 42 but only one thing is needed. Mary has chosen what is better, and it will not be taken away from her."

When a Christian's work becomes burdensome, troubling, and upsetting, there are two possibilities:

1) God Has Not Assigned This Task to You

It could be that Martha was turning the meal into more of a production than it needed to be. Sometimes we pile work on our plate that God has not put there, and then we become upset with everyone around us for not helping. How many times has a wife become short with her husband and irritable with the kids because she is scrambling around trying to make the house immaculate before some guest arrives, and the reality is God never required her to have an immaculate house for that guest? Jesus' yoke is easy and light and not burdensome—but the yokes that we place on ourselves tend to be unbearably heavy. We pile responsibilities on ourselves in order to meet the expectations of people whose approval we feel we must have, or simply to meet the expectations of our own prideful ideals for ourselves; and these self-

---

[158] This principle is true especially when those who are in authority over you make a decision on your behalf, such as when your boss says, "I'm sorry, but your services are no longer needed."

imposed tasks take up so much time and energy that we are unable to do the things God has called us to do because we are so busy with all the things we assigned to ourselves. This sometimes results in resentment toward God for requiring far more than we can do—when in reality we would have plenty of time and resources to do what God called us to do if we did only that and nothing else.

2) You Are Serving in the Wrong Way (Not Coming to Christ)

Many of the things that cause stress in our lives, however, are tasks that God *has* assigned to us. And Jesus promised that His burden is easy and His yoke is light (Mt.11:30). Why is it, then, that we often find our task burdensome and stressful? Our God-given tasks become stressful when we do them in a way that is not a drawing near to Christ.

Matthew 11:28-30 <u>Come to me</u>, **all you who are weary and burdened, and I will give you rest. 29 Take my yoke upon you and learn from me, for I am gentle and humble in heart, and you will find rest for your souls. 30 For my yoke is easy and my burden is light.**

The promise is that when we come to Him we will find rest, which means whenever our work becomes burdensome it is a sign that we are not coming to Christ. This is why Jesus praised Mary and rebuked Martha. It was not because Mary was sitting and Martha was working; it was because Mary was attending to Jesus and Martha was ignoring Him. When we do our work with our back to the Lord, it becomes stressful and overwhelming. But when we make all our work a drawing near to Christ, the work itself is restful and energizing.

Teach the counselee who is stressed by his work to make his work an act of fellowship with God. Here are some examples of how to do that:

Appreciate the Importance of Your Work

The importance of a task is not measured by how much money people pay for it, or how prestigious it is in human eyes, or how many people it affects. The only determining factor on the importance of a task is God's calling. If God gave you a task, it is the utmost in importance. If He did not, it is a waste of time. If you become the President of the United States, find a cure for cancer, and achieve world peace, but God did not call you to do any of that; then it is a pathetic, meaningless waste of time. But if the great King of kings and Lord of lords commissions you to scrape gum off the bottom of someone's shoe—that is a high and holy privilege. And if the task is difficult, it is an even greater privilege. It is an honor to be able to do something hard for His sake.

Teach the counselee never to say, "I have to do the laundry," but rather, "I *get* to serve my God in this way! I get to enjoy the grand privilege of serving the King of kings by serving this family that He died for." How ridiculous it is for a Christian housewife to say, "I don't have a job." A woman who is married has been assigned an awesome task—the task of being a wife to her husband in a way that puts on display the kind of love with which the Church honors the great Bridegroom in heaven. If she went from that to being the CEO of IBM or Microsoft, that would be a *huge* step down. God forgive us for how lightly we take the assignments He graciously grants to us.

Look at Work as a Feast

In Malachi 1, God rebukes the priests for carrying on the work He gave them while saying, "What a burden" (Mal.1:13). God goes on to remind them that the ministry He graciously granted them was like a wonderful banquet spread out before them, but they were turning up their noses and sniffing at it contemptuously. Remind the counselee that his God-given tasks are a gift from God that, if done properly, will be delightful and satisfying to the soul like a delicious feast.

Enjoy Working at God's Side

Remind the counselee that when he does the work God has given him, he is walking side-by-side with God. He is actually joining Him in His work. He is working on the same project God is working on. He is in step with Him, working at His side.

Enjoy Being Used by God

Every time a person does something God has called him to do—like wake up in the middle of the night to care for a child, or do that one task at work that is so unpleasant—he is being picked up out of the toolbox and used by the grand Architect of human history to play a role. Oh, how delightful it should be to us to be in His great hand! How excited we should be about getting the nod from the Coach to go into the game in crunch time here in the last days!

Martha's mistake was she was trying to give to God instead of receive from Him. She forgot serving Him was a banquet so it turned into a burden. And when that happens, the result is a self-oriented focus.

40 "Lord, don't you care that my sister has left _me_ to do the work by _myself_? Tell her to help _me_!"

Her self-focus damaged her relationship with her sister and her relationship with the Lord Himself. Burdensome work makes a person irritable with everyone around him, and always results in self-pity. But when we make all our work a receiving from God, a feasting at His banquet table, an enjoyment of being used as a tool in His hand, a joining in partnership with Him in His great work, and a personal enjoyment of His attributes; work will be a drawing near to Christ and will result in rest and renewal for the soul.

Resources for Helping Those Struggling with Anxiety

Devotionals from the book, *What's So Great About God?*:[159]

Meditations #**1-20**, 61, **64-69**, **72**, **76**, **77**, 80, **81-83**, **87**, **89**, 142

Worry

Worry is expecting that God will do something wrong, although worriers usually do not think about it in those terms. Most Christians who struggle with worry do not have a strong sense that God is in control of events. They see future outcomes as mainly depending on people, on nature, on "chance," on themselves—on secondary causes. Even so, worry comes from a distorted view of the nature of God.

---

[159] Bold numbers represent the meditations that are especially relevant.

The two attributes of God that tend to be distorted in the minds of worries are His goodness and His power. Those who always assume bad outcomes in the future either think that God is unwilling to bring good outcomes (lack of goodness) or unable (lack of power).

The Goodness of God

Some worriers think of God as being mostly unhappy with them, like a father who is in discipline mode 90 percent of the time—always finding fault, always disappointed and disgusted with his children, always using the rod. They would say, "I am pessimistic about the future not because I doubt the goodness of God, but because I know I deserve punishment." But in reality they do doubt the goodness of God. They think God's goodness is handicapped by their sinfulness, as if their sin requires God to be mostly harsh rather than mostly kind.

When counseling someone like this, teach the person the following principles:

1) Even though we constantly stumble into sin, God is pleased with us far more than He is displeased. His displeasure over our sin is brief compared to His pleasure in our obedience (Ps.30:5).

2) God's patience is far greater than we can even fathom. He is *extremely* slow to anger and slow to discipline (Ex.34:6).

3) Our stumbling into sin causes compassion in His heart toward us, so that He is even more eager to show us mercy and forgiveness. The psalmists did not pray, "God have mercy on me in spite of the fact that I am so sinful;" they said, "God have mercy on me *because* I am so sinful" (Ps.25:16).

4) Even when God does finally bring the rod, it will accomplish *nothing* but good for us. It is always corrective; never merely punitive. It always benefits us; never harms us. As painful as it is, there is a sense in which it is sweet to us because it is an expression of God's love for us (Heb.12:5-11).

The Power of God

For some worriers the problem is not that they doubt God's goodness or kindness, but rather His power. They think of God as favorable enough toward them, but they do not think of Him as being in control of circumstances and outcomes. They may give lip service to believing God is in control, but when they talk, it is obvious that they really believe outcomes are mainly determined by secondary causes. They think everything is riding on what their spouse does, or what a court decides, or what choices their boss makes. Human agency is at the forefront of their thinking, and God's role is in the distant background.

Remind these counselees that in every action it is both God and human agents who are at work, and God's purposes will far outweigh man's. When Joseph's evil brothers sold him into slavery, they meant it for evil. But God was also at work in that very same action, and God meant it for good (Gn.50:20). And the good God was accomplishing was far greater than the evil that men were accomplishing. Even when men carried out the worst evil man has ever carried out—the murder of the Son of God—God was also at work accomplishing something good, and the good He was accomplishing was far greater than the evil the men were accomplishing. This is true in every event that ever takes place in the life of a Christian. Urge the counselee to take his focus off the human agents involved and put it on the primary Cause behind the action—his loving, heavenly Father.

If the counselee questions whether God really is in control of all things, including the outcome of human decision-making, take him through a study of passages in Scripture that point to God's total control of all things, such as Isa.46:10-11, Ps.135:6, Eph.1:11, Gn.45:5-7,50:20, Acts 4:28, Job 2:10, Lam.3:38, Isa.45:7, Amos 3:6, and 1 Sam.2:6.

Pessimism: Blindness to Blessing

Worriers tend to be pessimists. A pessimist is someone who assumes that, all things being equal, God will generally do that which causes them the most pain. Your husband is ten minutes late picking you up? He was probably in a terrible accident. You just got an unexpected bill—

God most likely will not provide for you. Having a picnic? No doubt God will send rain.

Most Christian pessimists will deny that their view of God is distorted. They will insist their pessimism is realism—the reasonable, rational assumption that follows from observation of past history. But is it really true that past history points in the direction of trouble being more likely than blessing? Not at all. Past history proves that blessing far outweighs trouble. Those who look to the past and see mostly trouble suffer from blessing blindness. Their selective eyesight skips over a thousand blessings and zeros in on one hardship. He will carry a grocery bag to his car in the wind and rain a hundred times, and the bag never breaks. But is he overwhelmed with the kindness of God? Does he think, *Boy, that paper bag could have easily broken and my groceries would have fallen all over the parking lot. Thank you, Lord, for making the bag hold*? No, he takes blessings like that for granted every day and is blind to them. And the one time God has some purpose for the bag to break, it's more than he can handle: "This kind of thing *always* happens to me!"

No matter how much pain a person has experienced, most of the things that have happened in his life have been positive blessings. Just ask him: "How many meals have you eaten? How many breaths have you taken? How many acts of love have been done for you? How many opportunities to love have you been given? How many spiritual resources has God given you access to? How many promises? How many riches in Christ? How high a calling have you received? How faithful has God been?" Even the person who has experienced countless sorrows—if he piled them all up in one stack, that stack would hardly be visible if it were next to the mountain of blessings God has given each one of us.

But the person who resents the pain in his life cannot see the blessings. God will give him a thousand wonderful acts of kindness— big and small—that go completely unnoticed, while he fixes all his attention on one painful thing. People who resent their pain do not appreciate God's kindness, no matter how much of it He showers on them. People like that will enjoy innumerable blessings in a day, but if they have one disappointment, they will go to bed dwelling on that one thing.

Worry is a kind of practical atheism—being an atheist in practice. In fact, for the Christian worry is worse than atheism. The atheist thinks the events of life are random. So if he is afraid of tomorrow because all he has going for him is the luck of the draw, he actually has a valid point. That would indeed be frightening. But for the Christian, who knows that God is in control of what happens, the only way he can be a worrier is to assume that God is generally unkind. The Christian worrier insults the character of God far more than the atheist. If someone does not know you and ignores you, that is a mild insult. But if your own precious child always assumes you will be unkind and do him unnecessary harm, that is a major insult. No child of a perfect God should be a pessimist.

When we say, "We planned our event for Saturday, so I'm sure it will rain" or "With my luck, I will probably hit every red light," what are we saying? Just because I want something to happen, it probably will not? Because I have a particular desire, God will probably do the opposite … and for no other reason than to hurt me? What a distorted view of God! I once received an email from someone about a major decision I was making, and he said, "I'm sure you will do the wrong thing. You will do whatever is expedient and will not show integrity." That really hurt. But to some degree, that kind of attitude toward me may be justified. There have been plenty of times in my life I have failed to do what is right, so it is not inconceivable that someone could assume something like that about me. But to assume that of God? What blasphemy!

Teach pessimists to be alert to God's blessings hour by hour through the day, and to thank God for them continually. The same principle applies to those who are cynical about other people. Teach them to be more alert to the good that God works through people every day, and to be thankful to God for it.

The Solution to Worry

The problem of worry has everything to do with how a person views his heavenly Father. When we worry, it is because of a sense that God is generally unfavorable toward us and He would rather inflict pain than grant joy. He is the type who will hurt you even when it is not absolutely necessary. Deep down the worrier thinks of God as an unpleasant master who has it in for him—or a helpless father who can do nothing about the evil that is being done. Jesus solves both kinds of worry by pointing the worrier to the goodness and power of God (reading this passage out loud to a worrier can have a powerful effect).

Matthew 6:25-34 Therefore I tell you, do not worry about your life, what you will eat or drink; or about your body, what you will wear. Is not life more important than food, and the body more important than clothes? 26 Look at the birds of the air; they do not sow or reap or store away in barns, and yet your heavenly Father feeds them. Are you not much more valuable than they? 27 Who of you by worrying can add a single hour to his life? 28 "And why do you worry about clothes? See how the lilies of the field grow. They do not labor or spin. 29 Yet I tell you that not even Solomon in all his splendor was dressed like one of these. 30 If that is how God clothes the grass of the field, which is here today and tomorrow is thrown into the fire, will he not much more clothe you, O you of little faith? 31 So do not worry, saying, "What shall we eat?" or "What shall we drink?" or "What shall we wear?" 32 For the pagans run after all these things, and your heavenly Father knows that you need them. 33 But seek first his kingdom and his righteousness, and all these things will be given to you as well. 34 Therefore do not worry about tomorrow, for tomorrow will worry about itself. Each day has enough trouble of its own. [160]

Resources for Helping Those Struggling with Worry

Devotionals from the book, *What's So Great About God?* [161]

Meditations #**10**, 37, 41, 61, **62**, **68**, **76**, **77, 81-83**, **87, 89**, 106, 107, 111, 147, 151, 164, 169, 174-180

---

[160] For a detailed study of this passage on worry see the three-part "Overcoming Worry" sermon series at http://foodforyoursoul.net. The sermon series are listed in alphabetical order on the "Series Alphabetically" link.

[161] Bold numbers represent the meditations that are especially relevant.

Fear

Fear of Pain

In the previous section I suggested that worriers are guilty of doubting the goodness of God. Someone may object: "I believe that God is good—but even in His goodness, He may send pain and suffering my way. I am worried—not because I think God will do something wrong—but simply because I am afraid of having to suffer." This sounds reasonable enough at first, but it also reveals a subtle distortion of the person's view of God.

It is not really pain that we fear; it is lack of happiness. If God told you that tomorrow from 3:00-4:00 you will be suffering pain, but it will be the happiest hour of your life, would you be afraid, or would you be excited with anticipation? Very often a woman can hardly wait to give birth to a child—even though she knows it will be tremendously painful. Where there is sufficient happiness, we do not fear pain. What we fear is inability to be happy. If God told you that tomorrow you would suffer no pain at all, but it would be the saddest, most depressed day of your life—that would be terrifying!

When we worry about future suffering, the assumption is that when God brings that suffering He will not also supply access to happiness that is greater than the suffering. That is an incorrect assumption. The Christian always has access to joy that is greater than *any* suffering. The happiness that comes from experiencing the presence of God far outweighs even the most extreme trouble (Hab.3:16-19, Ps.16:11).

It is fitting to experience anxiety when anticipating suffering. Jesus was sweating blood the night before His crucifixion. He was not, however, sweating blood throughout the months and years leading up to the crucifixion, even though He knew it was coming. When one's anxiety is greater than his joy—not on occasion in extreme situations, but as a rule—that person probably does not understand the fact that God never allows suffering without good reason. He may claim to trust God, but deep down he does not really believe that God's reason, whatever it may be, is adequate to justify the degree of suffering He allows.

Teach the fearful person that suffering is to be expected (1 Pe.4:12), that all the suffering God sends is good (Ro.8:28), and that it will never be so severe that happiness will become unreachable (Hab.3:16-19).

When is Fear Sinful?

All worry is sin (Mt.6:34), but not all fear is sin. The emotion of fear is a gift of God designed to protect us. It keeps us from getting too close to a cliff or needlessly exposing ourselves to danger. Frequently, however, it becomes an avenue for sin. When counseling people who struggle with fear, the counselor must first understand exactly when fear is sinful. Fear crosses over into sin when (1) we fear something we are forbidden to fear, or (2) our fear turns into cowardice (that is, it overrides our courage).

Forbidden Fears

There are some contexts in which the very existence of the emotion of fear indicates sin. Scripture gives at least three examples of forbidden fears:

1) Divine Mistakes

No Christian in his right mind would say he believes that God could make a mistake. But as we found in the last section, when a person worries, that person is, in effect, assuming God might do something wrong. This is clearly a sinful misconception of the character of God. To think this way, a person must believe that God lacks either power or goodness.

This type of thinking is more common than one might expect. Christians often disobey God out of fear that if they obey, God may allow some circumstance that will be too much to bear. In your own life, think of how many times you have chosen not to tell the truth, failed to share your faith, or refused to commit to something you knew you should do because of your fear of the consequences. Christians who do that are like the wicked, lazy servant who said to the master, "I knew that you are a hard man.... So I was afraid ..." (Mt.25:24,26).

2) *Irrational Assumptions*

When some type of suffering is likely to occur, it is not wrong to anticipate it and prepare for it. But if it is not likely, then concerning yourself with it is a waste of time and energy. When a woman continually worries that her husband might leave her, even though there are no signs of unfaithfulness, or a man is in continual fear of being fired even though there are no signs of trouble at work, those fears are irrational.

The solution to irrational fear is wisdom.

Proverbs 3:21-26 My son, preserve sound judgment and discernment, do not let them out of your sight; ... 24 [then] when you lie down, you will not be afraid; when you lie down, your sleep will be sweet. 25 Have no fear of sudden disaster or of the ruin that overtakes the wicked, 26 for the Lord will be your confidence and will keep your foot from being snared.

The wise woman or man understands how God tends to operate throughout His world and understands which things are more likely or less likely to happen. Discernment and sound judgment will help protect a person from making foolish decisions that lead to unnecessary suffering.

3) *Loss of a Cherished Idol*

We naturally fear the loss of things that are precious to us. Some things, however, should not be as precious to us as they are. When we realize that we fear the loss of these things, we gain insight into what may be an idol in our hearts.

John 12:42-43 Many even among the leaders believed in him. But because of the Pharisees they would not confess their faith for fear they would be put out of the synagogue; for they loved praise from men more than praise from God.

There is nothing wrong with enjoying praise from men. But if that praise means more than praise from God, it is idolatry. The idolatry in these men's hearts became evident when they had to choose between confessing Christ or clinging to their idol. Their fear was a fear of losing the thing they treasured above God—approval of men.

Jesus said, "Do not be afraid of those who kill the body but cannot kill the soul. Rather, be afraid of the One who can destroy both soul and body in hell" (Mt.10:28). Fearing the wrong thing is evidence that a

212

person does not understand or believe the truth about what is really dangerous—unfaithfulness to God.

Cowardice

Besides being idolaters, the Pharisees Jesus denounced in John 12 were also cowards. Whenever fear overrides courage, it is cowardice. And cowardice is a very serious matter. God's word is clear—cowards go to hell.

Revelation 21:8 But the cowardly ... their place will be in the fiery lake of burning sulfur. This is the second death.

If the government threatens you with torture for preaching the Gospel, it is not sinful to feel uneasy about enduring the torture—as long as you act courageously and go ahead and preach. But if your fear prevents you from doing what is right or pushes you into sins such as lying or worrying, it is cowardice.

When suffering is clearly looming on the horizon, should the counselor say, "Don't worry—everything is going to be all right"? No. The truth is, sometimes when God decides you will have to suffer you can see it coming. The appropriate response is to acknowledge likely pain, which will cause natural feelings of fear, and then to override those feelings with courage (by doing what is right in spite of feelings).

Overcoming Fear

As with any emotion, it is one thing to decide you should not have fear, but it is another thing entirely to rid yourself of it. If you can remember the last time you were afraid, you know that you cannot eliminate fear by simply deciding not to be afraid or by telling yourself there is nothing to fear. When you counsel people who struggle with fear, how can you help them deal with it? By building both their faith and their courage.

Building Faith

The more confidence you have in your caretaker, the less fearful you will be. I remember a time when I was sitting in the living room reading as my young children were playing on the floor. Suddenly there was a clap of thunder so loud it shook the house. All three kids were startled and momentarily stopped what they were doing and looked toward me with great concern. I smiled and said, "Wow, that was a good one!" That put all three at ease and they went right back to playing. They just wanted to know if things were under control, so they looked to see their father's reaction.

We do not have the joy of being able to physically see the face of our Father when we experience frightening trials, but we can look to Him in faith. We can fill our minds with thoughts of His total control and loving care. We can remind ourselves of His faithfulness in the past and His great and precious promises for the future. We can intensify our level of concentration on the imperturbable joy of God and the smile on His face as He watches His perfect plan being carried out, right down to the tiniest details of our lives. It is true that His plan for us often involves suffering, but even in the midst of suffering we can recall His words of comfort:

Isaiah 41:10-14 "So do not fear, for I am with you; do not be dismayed, for I am your God. I will strengthen you and help you; I will uphold you with my righteous right hand.... For I am the Lord, your God, who takes hold of your right hand and says to you, Do not fear; I will help you. Do not be afraid, O worm Jacob, O little Israel, for I myself will help you," declares the Lord, your Redeemer, the Holy One of Israel.

The greatest way to strengthen someone's faith is through the Word of God.

Romans 10:17 ... faith comes from hearing the message, and the message is heard through the word of Christ.

When you are counseling people who are fearful, give them a list of passages such as Isaiah 41 to read when they are afraid. Tell them to read these aloud and have them memorize particular passages. Reading, hearing, or being reminded of God's word can be tremendously calming and reassuring.

Psalm 56:34 When I am afraid, I will trust in you. In God, whose word I praise, in God I trust; I will not be afraid.

Building Courage

Some strong fears simply cannot be eliminated; they must be overcome by courage. Courage is when a person is driven by a desire that is stronger than the desire for safety. For example, a mother might be afraid of heights, but if her baby crawls out onto the roof, suddenly her courage overrides her fear. She will go rescue her baby. Think of a man who is terrified at the prospect of advancing into a hail of gunfire. If he is consumed with the desire to defend his country or to do his job, he will be able to summon the courage. The courageous Christian, acutely aware of what is at stake in our spiritual warfare, has the courage to obey God no matter what the danger.

Seeking courage instead of escape from fear was the Apostles' approach when they faced the incredibly frightening prospect of imprisonment, flogging, and death. In Acts 4, the vicious, dangerous, powerful men responsible for the murder of Jesus summoned the apostles and repeatedly commanded them not to teach or speak at all in the name of Jesus. Think of how terrifying their threats would have been—especially after having just witnessed the crucifixion. Few of us have ever faced threats that terrifying.

The Apostles took these threats seriously. They immediately reported them to the church, and the whole church rushed to corporate prayer. And their prayer began with faith-building affirmations of God's power and sovereignty.

Acts 4:24-29 "Sovereign Lord, you made the heaven and the earth and the sea, and everything in them. 25 You spoke by the Holy Spirit through the mouth of your servant, our father David: 'Why do the nations rage and the peoples plot in vain? 26 The kings of the earth take their stand and the rulers gather together against the Lord and against his Anointed One.' 27 Indeed Herod and Pontius Pilate met together with the Gentiles and the people of Israel in this city to conspire against your holy servant Jesus, whom you anointed. 28 They did what your power and will had decided beforehand should happen. 29 Now, Lord, consider their threats and enable your servants to speak your word with great boldness."

Notice that instead of praying for protection, they prayed for boldness! Instead of seeking the elimination of what they feared, they sought the courage to be obedient in the face of what they feared. And God granted their request:

Acts 4:31 After they prayed, the place where they were meeting was shaken. And they were all filled with the Holy Spirit and spoke the word of God boldly.

The result?

Acts 5:40 [The Sanhedrin] called the apostles in and had them flogged.

They feared being flogged, so they prayed for the courage to obey. God granted their request, and then they were flogged. But look at their response:

Acts 5:41-42 The apostles left the Sanhedrin, rejoicing because they had been counted worthy of suffering disgrace for the Name. 42 Day after day, in the temple courts and from house to house, they never stopped teaching and proclaiming the good news that Jesus is the Christ.

You and I can thank the Lord that the Gospel was proclaimed around the world and passed down to us because those men were more interested in courage than in their own deliverance, comfort, or safety.

**Resources for Helping Those
Struggling with Fear**

Devotionals from the book, *What's So Great About God?*[162]

Fear of trouble – **30**, 41, 46-49, **64**, **66-69**, **76**, 81, **82**, **87**, **89**, 106, 107, **111**, **139**, **147**, **148**, 151, **154**

Fear of man – **30**, 180

Lack of awe/fear of God – **22-30**, **57**, 60, **76**, 103

Fretting

Several times we read in Scripture the command, "Do not fret." Fretting is anxiety over the success or prosperity of evil men.

The Hebrew word translated "fret" (CHARAH) is a fascinating word. When it appears in its normal form it simply means anger. When it appears in the *hithpael* form, however, it is translated "fret." The *hithpael* is a grammatical form that expresses a reflexive idea— something you do to yourself. In this case the action is anger. Fretting is anger that you inflict upon yourself. It is when you get yourself worked up because of the prosperity of evil men.

---

[162] Bold numbers represent the meditations that are especially relevant.

Psalm 37:1,7-8 Do not fret because of evil men or be envious of those who do wrong; for like the grass they will soon wither, like green plants they will soon die away. ... 7 Be still before the LORD and wait patiently for him; do not fret when men succeed in their ways, when they carry out their wicked schemes. 8 Refrain from anger and turn from wrath; do not fret—it leads only to evil.

Proverbs 24:19-20 Do not fret because of evil men or be envious of the wicked, 20 for the evil man has no future hope, and the lamp of the wicked will be snuffed out.

There is a legitimate anger over wickedness. If you are a righteous person, evil should bother you. But when you dwell on it and focus your attention on it so that it begins to dominate your thinking and your emotions, you are fretting.

Both of the above passages connect fretting with envy. You are fretting when you are upset that the wicked are successful while life is so difficult for you. It is distress over the way God is running this world. That attitude can easily turn into an unwitting resentment of God.

The Solution

When counseling someone who is frustrated about the successes of the wicked, teach him to do two things.

Think from an Eternal Perspective

Psalm 37:1-2 Do not fret because of evil men or be envious of those who do wrong; 2 for like the grass they will soon wither, like green plants they will soon die away.

Psalm 73:2-5,16-18 My feet had almost slipped; I had nearly lost my foothold. 3 For I envied the arrogant when I saw the prosperity of the wicked. 4 They have no struggles; their bodies are healthy and strong. 5 They are free from the burdens common to man; they are not plagued by human ills. ... 16 When I tried to understand all this, it was oppressive to me 17 till I entered the sanctuary of God; then I understood their final destiny. 18 Surely you place them on slippery ground; you cast them down to ruin.

Being upset over the success of the wicked demonstrates shortsightedness. Why envy people who have a moment of pleasure and then go to eternal hell? Justice will be done. They are not getting away with anything. Any enjoyment or pleasure they experience will be for this lifetime at most—merely a blink of an eye. Then they will face eternal judgment.

So what is there to envy? The more upset a person gets about the prosperity of the wicked, the more he demonstrates a temporal perspective. From an eternal perspective, the situation is terrible for them and wonderful for the righteous.

Injustice

One of the more common causes of anxiety is injustice. Injustice is a form of suffering, so the beginning point in counseling a victim of injustice is to follow the principles in Chapter 3 (Counseling Those in Pain). For this particular form of suffering, however, some additional principles can be helpful:

Use the Injustice to Increase Love for God

Whenever the behavior of others distresses or disappoints us, it is a wonderful opportunity to increase our love for God, because the attributes of God that are missing in those people become more precious in our eyes. When life is going just fine, and you read a verse that speaks of God as being just, it may not have much of an emotional impact. But when a person suffers injustice, that person has a special ability to appreciate what it is that is so wonderful about justice. More than any of the rest of us, the victim of injustice can see why justice is such a delightful and precious thing. It is only when we suffer injustice that we have a clear perception of the real beauty of this facet of God's glory: His justice. Urge the counselee to take advantage of the opportunity to increase his admiration and delight in a God who is just.[163]

---

[163] This same principle applies to any kind of disappointment we suffer at the hands of men. If a person hurts you by being unreliable, you have increased ability at that moment to appreciate God's faithfulness. If someone lies to you, you have greater ability to love God for His truthfulness. If someone is insensitive, God's compassion is that much sweeter.

Trust in the Promises of Perfect Justice

Psalm 36:6 Your righteousness is like the mighty mountains, your justice like the great deep.

Psalm 37:6 He will make your righteousness shine like the dawn, the justice of your cause like the noonday sun.

Remind the counselee that there is no final injustice for the believer. The Lord will repay everything and make all things right. When we fret over injustice, it is a slap in the face of God because we are assuming He is not going to make things right. It is a grievous sin to accuse God of injustice (Mal. 2:17).

Focus Mainly on What God is Doing, Not on What People are Doing

All our hardships ultimately come from God.[164] Human agents may be involved, and may have evil purposes, but those purposes do not override God's good purposes. In fact, they actually accomplish God's purposes.[165] The good that God is doing is always greater than the evil that men are doing. Urge the counselee to stop paying so much attention to what men are doing and spend more time thinking about what God is doing. Teach the victim of injustice to see the hardship as coming from the hand of his loving heavenly Father.

Imagine you have 2 kids—a 7-year-old boy and a 12-year-old girl. They come to you and say, "There are only 4 cookies left in the jar. Can we eat them?" Normally you would say yes, but it's your daughter's 12th birthday and you were going to surprise her by taking her to her favorite restaurant. You were planning on leaving in a few minutes, and you really want her to enjoy it, so you hate to have her spoil her appetite on a few old, stale cookies.

So you tell them they can have the cookies, but the 7-year-old gets to divide them however he wants. And you know when you say that exactly what will happen. He is going to take all four and leave his sister with none—and that is exactly what happens.

---

[164] Job 1:21,2:10, Lam.3:38, 1 Sam.2:6.
[165] Gn.50:20, Acts 4:28.

So there her brother is, eating four cookies and she gets none. Is that an injustice? In the narrow picture it is—if we consider only the two kids. But if we broaden the picture to include you and the big, surprise dinner, and we take into consideration the fact when the daughter finds out what is happening she is going to throw her arms around you and thank you for making sure she did not spoil her appetite with those cookies—it really is not much of an injustice.

Does that mean what her brother did is OK? No. If you are a good parent, you will deal with him on that and teach him that he should have offered his sister at least two, if not three of the cookies. Your son did not know about your plan, so what he did in taking all four cookies was wrong. So the next day you deal with him on that.

What about Satan? Isn't he involved? Of course he is. In everything that happens, the question is not, "Who is causing this—God or Satan?" The question is, "What is God up to and what is Satan up to? You need to figure out what God is doing and cooperate with that, and figure out what Satan is doing and resist that.

Give Thanks for the Justice You Do Receive

When David experienced injustice, he cried out to God for justice in the second half of Psalm 9 (vv.13-20). But what is fascinating about that psalm is the first half. In the first half David was not receiving any unfair treatment. But instead of doing what most of us do when we receive fair treatment (taking it for granted as a matter of course), David recognized it as an especially wonderful gift from God and praised God for His justice (vv.1-12).

Is the counselee grateful for all the justice God has provided throughout his life? Does he appreciate all the times he was given the correct change, or a fair deal on a sale, or someone represented him accurately, or he was given a full paycheck after a week's work? Or does he only concern himself with justice when it is not there?

**Resources for Helping Those
Who Have Suffered Injustice**

Devotionals from the book, *What's So Great About God?*:[166]

Meditations #**45**, 66-69, **113**, **119**, **136**, **177**, 180

Anger

Just as physical pain is important to alert us to a problem in our bodies, so painful emotions are important for alerting us to the condition of our hearts. Anger is no exception. The things that bring us to anger reveal important information about our spiritual condition.

Not all anger is sinful, but most anger is. Righteous anger is a reaction to an offence against God or others; sinful anger is a reaction to an offence against self. And most of our anger is selfish anger. Righteous anger is a good thing (if you can see a child be abused by his parents and not feel anything, something is wrong in your heart). However, even righteous anger is dangerous. Being in an angry mood makes us much more prone to all kinds of sins, and so we must be very careful even with righteous indignation.

Selfish anger generally has one of two causes: self-importance or blocked happiness.

Self-Importance

Many times an angry response is an indication of an inflated sense of self-importance. We feel we are above having to suffer in certain ways. Our opinions are so important, they should not be contradicted. Our time is so important, no one should waste any of it. Our comfort is so important, no one should inconvenience us. Anger over poor service at a restaurant, over a slow checker at the store, over a debate on some issue you hold dear, or over any other offence, is typically due to inflated self-

---

[166] Bold numbers represent the meditations that are especially relevant.

importance. People who are easily offended are prideful. This kind of anger is rarely seen in young children, because they do not have a great sense of self-importance. If the server at the restaurant overlooks them, or their opinion is taken lightly—the child usually does not become offended, because he is used to being overlooked and taken lightly. He expects nothing different. But as we grow older and our egos inflate, we begin to expect a certain standard of treatment, and anything that falls short of what we think we deserve offends us.

It is usually an exaggerated sense of self-importance that is the culprit behind anger at inanimate objects. Getting angry at a bolt that falls down into the engine, or at a cabinet that gets in the way of your head, or at a copy machine or computer or stop light—anger over the inconveniences of life reveal a heart that assumes it deserves no inconveniences.

The solution to this kind of anger is humility. Anger is fundamentally an expression of love. The person who loves God will be angry when God is blasphemed. The person who loves his daughter will be angry if someone harms his daughter. And the person who loves himself will become angry when he is slighted in some way. Selfish anger exposes the disease of self-love, and so the solution is selflessness and humility. Urge the counselee to use each tinge of anger feelings as a memory cue to direct his thoughts to the greatness and worthiness of God, and his own unimportance in comparison.

Blocked Happiness

Another occasion for selfish anger is when access to happiness is blocked. If a woman believes she must have a certain kind of marriage relationship in order to be happy, then she will become angry at her husband if he blocks her access to that happiness. If a man's happiness is wrapped up in his car, heaven help the person who damages that car.

This kind of anger is very important in helping us make progress in the Christian life, because it exposes a problem that is otherwise very difficult to detect: idolatry in the heart. We are to look to God alone as the source of our joy. If we look to anything else as the source of our joy, we are putting that thing in the place of God, and that is idolatry.

When a counselee has this kind of anger, use it to pinpoint what objects, circumstances, relationships, etc. that person believes he must have in order to be happy. Those are the idols of his heart and they must be deposed. Each tinge of anger over those things being blocked should be used as a memory cue to preach to the soul: "The only true joy-source is the presence of God, and no one can block that!"

Resources for Helping Those Struggling with Anger

Books
The Heart of Anger and the companion volume *Getting a Grip* by Lou Priolo

Devotionals from the book, *What's So Great About God?* :[167]

Anger - 2, **51,** 56, 144, 177

Grumbling – **1-20, 31,** 38, **60-69, 73, 76, 77, 81, 84,** 85, **94-95, 106,** 112, 142, 143, 155, **164,** 178, **179**

Idolatry – **1-20,** 23, 28, **31, 36, 37, 50, 86, 101, 133**

Impatience with people – 86, **88,** 96-99, **104**

Ingratitude – **31, 61-63,** 68, **69, 73, 77, 81,** 83-87, **92, 94-95, 102, 106, 107, 112, 118,** 143, 144, 155, 162

Loving others – **1-20, 25,** 37, **49,** 80, **88, 93, 96-99, 129, 130**

Pride – 38-43, **81**

Selfishness – 37, 49, **88, 93, 96-99,** 101, 173

---

[167] Bold numbers represent the meditations that are especially relevant.

CHAPTER TEN:
PANIC, BIPOLAR DISORDER, AND SCHIZOPHRENIA

Panic Attacks

Panic attacks are periods of intense fear that arise suddenly in times when there is no significant danger present. The heartbeat speeds up, and often there is dizziness or lightheadedness and a sense of needing to leave the room and get some air. Attacks generally begin abruptly, reach a peak within ten minutes, and subside over the next several hours. The panic itself is not voluntary. Telling people to calm down or to get over it will not help. Of course they want to calm down and get over it, but the response of panic is physiological and beyond immediate conscious control.

A friend who struggles with this problem described it this way: "I feel trapped in myself. I feel trapped in despair and gloom, and all I can do is beg for the pain to stop. I don't think a person can really understand this pain until they have experienced it themselves. People around me don't know how to respond when I feel this way—looks of pity, confusion, and annoyance don't help. I have learned to hide this pain—to pretend that I'm fine when I'm not."

Panic attacks are often closely connected to depression. A person becomes depressed, the emotional pain is overwhelming, and a feeling of panic results from the fear that there may never be relief. With every moment that passes, the hope of ever feeling better grows dimmer and dimmer until it is snuffed out altogether. The person feels doomed to unbearable suffering. But the problem is so crippling that there is a sense that "I *must* get better—I *have* to. I can't go on like this!"

Counseling Someone Who Suffers from Panic Attacks

As with other kinds of suffering, begin with genuine compassion and comfort (see Chapter 3). Do not rebuke the person for feeling panic and fear. Reassure him with comforting, soothing, calming words from Scripture. And most importantly, confidently assure the person that you know some biblical principles that *will* help. Offer hope.

If the person struggles with depression, that is a good place to begin (see Chapter 8). The biblical solutions to depression will also be helpful for panic attacks. And the hope of the possibility of recovery from depression can also help.

Explore also how the person is thinking about stress and anxiety in general. Make sure the counselee understands the biblical principles regarding anxiety (see Chapter 9).

The friend I quoted above recovered from her panic problem, and I asked her what it was that helped her. She said primarily the knowledge that it is all right to suffer. "The panic comes from fear that I will not be able to feel better. There is comfort in the fact that I don't have to feel better. I can carry out my calling even while I'm suffering."

She listed six more things that have been helpful to her:

1. I now realize that I'm walking through life, and each thought is a step. I can walk away from fear and panic with each successive thought.

2. I am working on thinking on things above (Col.3:1). When I suffer, I ask myself if I really believe in eternity.

3. God is sanctifying me, making me the woman He wants me to be. He is faithful. He has my best interests at heart. He truly is my Good Shepherd, leading me to peace. "Though he slay me, yet will I hope in him" (Job 13:15).

4. I now am aware that God gives us exactly the amount of pain and pleasure He decides. He will determine all of my suffering, all of my pain—and all of my pleasure. I will not have this power.

5. I am convicted about contentment. To refuse to be satisfied with what God has for me is covetousness and discontent.

6. I have been challenged to see what my idol is.

Then she wrote, "I am tired. Whenever I hear that He breaks us to make us new, I feel I've been broken enough. But I do have a peace in my heart that good times are ahead after the present struggle. I feel optimistic." This was added a few days later: "P.S. God is so quickly healing me of these struggles. I felt renewed even by writing this down." The last words in her note were, "It is over. I am free of the medications, and I am joyful and optimistic."

Bipolar Disorder

"Bipolar disorder" is the new term for the old label "manic-depressive." It is used to describe a person who has major mood swings from extremely depressed moods to extremely elevated moods. The psychological term for the elevated mood is "mania" or "manic episode." According to the DSM IV,[168] a manic episode is "a distinct period of abnormally and persistently elevated, expansive or irritable mood, lasting at least one week." And in order for it to be diagnosed as a manic episode that elevated mood must have three of the following components (four if the mood is only irritable):

1) inflated self-esteem or grandiosity
2) decreased need for sleep
3) more talkative than usual or pressure to keep talking
4) racing thoughts
5) distractibility
6) increase in goal-directed activity or psychomotor agitation
7) excessive involvement in pleasurable activities that have a high potential for painful consequences

In recent years, labels such as *bipolar II* and *hypomania* have been developed to describe people who have emotional ups and downs that are not severe enough to be diagnosed bipolar. This enables psychologists to bill insurance companies for working with people who have normal mood swings.

---

[168] *Diagnostic and Statistical Manual* – the industry standard for diagnosing psychological disorders.

How to Counsel a "Manic/Depressive" Person

The depression aspect is no different from any other depression, so it can be handled the same way (see Chapter 8). The focus of this section, then, will be on counseling the "mania."

What causes mania? The answer to that question depends on whether the reference is to manic *feelings* or manic *behavior*. Manic *feelings* can be caused by a number of medical or spiritual problems, or they may be side effects of certain drugs. Manic *behavior*, on the other hand, has only one cause: the will. Feelings may make certain temptations more difficult to resist, but all decisions are still made by the will. Neither chemicals nor feelings can make a person choose to sin, to act foolishly, or to do anything else.

King Saul suffered from a textbook case of bipolar.[169] His life was characterized by impulsiveness (1 Sam. 13:9-14, 20:30-33), poor judgment (1 Sam. 14), refusal to listen to counsel (1 Sam. 14), irresponsible behavior (1 Sam. 15), temper tantrums (1 Sam. 20:30-33), extreme mood swings (1 Sam. 15:24), rapid cycling—"now I'm not going to kill David; now I am" (1 Sam. 19:6,10), and paranoia (1 Sam. 17:18), and it ended in suicide (1 Sam. 31:4). And God held Saul responsible for all these things. God diagnosed Saul's problem in 1 Samuel 15:23 with one word: "rebellion." Sinful actions are always under the control of a person's will. For help with the manic feelings the counselee should see a medical doctor, as these feelings can arise from various physiological problems. They can also be caused by spiritual problems (see below). The behavior, on the other hand, is always a spiritual issue. No medical problem can cause sinful behavior.

Very often those who have been influenced by psychology have the attitude that says, "As long as I feel this way I have no ability to control my actions." Help the counselee learn not to be governed by his feelings. God does provide us with the strength to resist the impulses of our feelings.

---

[169] I am indebted to Dr. Charles Hodges for these observations about Saul.

Use Biblical Terms

As usual, the psychological labels are unhelpful. The list of symptoms in the DSM IV is a mix of problems that are better addressed individually. I will discuss them one at a time.

Inflated Self-Esteem or Grandiosity

The biblical terms for this are *pride* and *selfishness*. Pride is an inflated sense of self-importance, and selfishness is an inward focus that places one's own immediate desires above the needs of others—or a preoccupation with self without consideration of others.

In some cases, mania may be an attempt to escape depression. A person is depressed, and more than anything he longs to feel better. All his attention is focused inwardly. He is desperate to feel good. Then when a natural upswing in emotions occurs, those good feelings become the focus of all his energy. He tries to make those feelings as strong and long-lasting as possible because he so greatly fears sinking back into depression. The mood has changed, but the root problem (self-centeredness) remains.

Self-centeredness expresses itself differently when moods are depressed or elevated. When the mood is low it becomes self-pity ("poor me"). When the mood is high it becomes abandonment to the impulses of the flesh ("I MUST have this thing I desire").

The solution to pride is humility, and the solution to selfishness is love.

Philippians 2:3 Do nothing out of selfish ambition or vain conceit, but in humility consider others better than yourselves.

Philippians 2:1-11 is a good passage to study for learning humility, because it shows Jesus' example of humility.

Another important key to humility is to turn attention to God. It is impossible to feel any sense of self-importance while beholding the glory of God. Urge the counselee to pursue the 5:1 rule (five thoughts about God for every one thought about self or one's circumstances).

While humility will solve the problem of pride, love will solve the problem of selfishness. Helpful passages for learning to love others are 1 Corinthians 13, Matthew 25:31-46, and John 15:8-17.

Love for others is not Christian love unless it is love that grows out of love for God. Teach the counselee how to love God, and how to love others as an expression of love for God. At this point it may be helpful to go through the Loving God sermon series, with a particular focus on parts 9 and 11, which are about loving others.[170]

Talkative

Being overly talkative is a byproduct of pride and selfishness. Talking too much is a symptom of a heart that thinks, "What I have to say is more important than what anyone else has to say." The solution to this is humility, love for others, and self-control. Take the counselee through the many proverbs on the tongue, with a special focus on gaining these three virtues. Especially helpful is James 3:1-18.

Decreased Need for Sleep and Increase in Goal-Directed Activity

Decreased need for sleep and increased energy to work are not a mental disease; they are blessings from God. When a person feels fully rested after only a few hours of sleep, and he is full of energy and motivation, urge him to use those extra hours in some useful kingdom work.

Racing Thoughts and Distractibility

Inability to focus one's thoughts can be debilitating. When the mind flits from one thought to the next to the next, it prevents the person from being able to pray or to think through a difficult matter that requires concentrated thought. Self-control in the thought life is the most difficult kind of self-control. It is essential, however, for the Christian life.

Very often the counselee will think that controlling his thoughts is impossible. It is crucial that he understand that if he is a believer, self-control of the thought life is possible. It is part of the "all things" that are possible through Christ who strengthens us (Php.4:13). If the counselee does not understand that this kind of self-control is possible for him, he will quickly give up when his mind starts racing.

---

[170] "Loving God from the Heart" at FoodForYourSoul.net. The sermon series are listed in alphabetical order on the "Series Alphabetically" link.

Help the counselee work toward thinking about one thing at a time. If it is time to be thinking about a certain decision that needs to be made, keep the focus on that decision. When other thoughts invade the mind, urge the counselee to jot down a one or two word reminder on a piece of paper so he can remember to think about it later, then return to thinking about the matter at hand.

When the mind is racing, that is an especially good time for prayer. The psalmists speak of pouring out their hearts to God (Ps.62:8). Pouring out one's heart is a special kind of prayer that is not always possible. Many times the heart is dry and empty, and powerful, earnest thoughts and feelings are few and far between. But when the mind is flooded with thoughts and feelings, that is a good time to pour it all out before God in prayer.

Excessive Involvement in Pleasurable Activities that Have a High Potential for Painful Consequences

This is the aspect that causes the most obvious harm in the lives of people who struggle with this problem. During "manic" episodes the person becomes extremely impulsive. It is similar in some ways to drunkenness. The person becomes loud, obnoxious, uninhibited, and reckless. Often there is such irrational optimism that they make poor decisions typified by hasty commitments, foolish investments, spending sprees, and sexual sins.

And even though the mood is elevated, it is dominated by a self-centered focus resulting in irritability. When anyone attempts to restrain the person's impulsivity, or even interrupts his incessant talking, he is easily angered.

Why would an elevated mood cause irritability? Because what seems to be optimism is really pride. The person has become wise in his own eyes, and does not have a posture of learning from others. Once again, learning humility is a key to overcoming this problem. Particularly helpful are the proverbs about being wise in one's own eyes.[171]

---

[171] Pr.3:7, 26:5,12, 28:11, Isa. 5:21.

Lithium

One of the most common treatments for mania has been lithium, administered at near-toxic levels. There are only trace amounts of lithium in the body naturally, and it serves no known function. The prescription for treating mania is hundreds of times the amount normally in the body—between 500 mg and 2000 mg every day. For lithium to work, the levels must be far above normal. For most people, anything above 1.5 mEg/L is toxic (causing speech impairment and confusion), but anything below 1.2 mEg/L has no effect on manic symptoms.

There is no question that high doses of lithium do tend to help people with mania, but the reason is unknown. What is known, however, is that lithium has numerous negative side effects, which commonly include weight gain, mental impairment, memory problems, muscle aches and twitches, weakness, lethargy, and thirst. Consistent with its toxic effects on the nervous system, lithium causes a tremor in thirty to fifty percent of patients, even at therapeutic levels. Tremors can be a warning sign of impending serious toxicity of the brain. EEG studies indicate an abnormal slowing of brain waves in a significant portion of patients routinely treated with lithium. For this reason, lithium has a large non-compliance rate. Forty-three percent of patients stop taking their lithium.[172]

Schizophrenia

Many think of schizophrenia as a "split personality," but technically, the term is much broader. It encompasses all types of insanity—delusions, voices, catatonic behavior, grossly disorganized behavior, hallucinations, etc. The "schism" in schizophrenia is not a division between two personalities, but rather a departure from reality in general.

To this point we have mostly been examining problems that, for the most part, everyone struggles with to some extent. All people have mood swings, anxiety, and discouragement. In one sense, the same could be said about schizophrenia. If insanity is being detached from

---

[172] http://www.sntp.net/drugs/lithium_breggin.htm.

reality, we are all somewhat insane. All of us believe some things that do not correspond with reality, and we all behave in ways that do not correspond to what we know to be true.

As with all the problems covered in this book, schizophrenia is manifested in varying degrees. To the extent that a person can understand, he needs to be taught biblical principles. If he accepts them, they will help.

Even people with extreme mental deficiency can usually understand right and wrong. According to their level of understanding, they are responsible for doing what is right. It may be that even an extremely schizophrenic person understands more than we might guess.

Suppose you go to counsel someone's child, and when you arrive he is huddled in the corner, banging his head against the wall or engaging in some other disturbingly bizarre behavior. Explain to the child that you have something that can help him. Let him know that you can tell him what the Word of God says to do, and that if he listens and does what God commands, he can be better. But if he does not, he will probably be taken to a mental institution and given some very unpleasant drugs. If he is capable of listening and responding, perhaps he will. If not, then you have not done anything to make the situation worse.[173]

The causes of insanity are many. Some are, no doubt, physical. Others are spiritual. Just as physical organs such as the heart or lungs can be destroyed through poor treatment, so a pattern of wrong thinking and feeling can destroy the mind to some degree. And just as a bad lung or heart can be restored and healed, perhaps the same is true of a damaged mind. Nebuchadnezzar recovered from insanity (Daniel 4). We do not know whether God did that by a miracle or by providence, but it may well be that if a person is insane as a result of a hard heart against God, his mind can be restored if he softens his heart.

Do not assume that insanity is caused by sin. It never hurts, however, to urge a mentally ill person—or any person, for that matter—to develop a more responsive, soft heart toward God.

---

[173] If you suspect demonic involvement, the process is the same. Only God has the power to drive out demons, and the power of God flows most powerfully through His Word.

CHAPTER ELEVEN:
GRIEF AND HEARTBREAK

Grief over a major loss, especially loss of a loved one, can be one of the most intense kinds of pain. The permanence of death has a particular way of bringing despair. I have included heartbreak in the title of this chapter because a broken relationship can cause a very similar kind of crushing sorrow and loss as the death of a loved one.

Grief counselors agree on one thing: Nothing can be done about the pain in the short term. Keeping busy or trying to distract yourself during the acute, intense moments of the sorrow may help some, but the pain of a major loss takes time to subside.

In Scripture, grief is always presented as an expected response to a major loss. It affects godly, righteous men and women just as much as anyone else.

The well-known "five stages of grief," popularized by Elisabeth Kübler-Ross's 1969 book *On Death and Dying,* have caused some people to take a mechanistic approach to the grieving process: "You have been in stage two a little too long; now it is time to move on to stage three." Recovery is not like an elevator that takes you from the basement of despair to the penthouse of joy. It is more like a maze where you go forward a bit, move back a few steps, cover the same ground again, and find yourself at the beginning. You set yourself up for disappointment if you think that recovery from grief will be a linear process. It is not. When the Lord takes a loved one away, one must undo the emotional ties that created the loving bond with the deceased, which can feel like disloyalty. Then he must adapt to the loss and learn to live a different life without the loved one. There is no way to make this process either quick or painless.

Recognize Wrong Responses

A great deal of grace and patience should be shown to those who are grieving. However, it is not loving to allow the counselee to continue in any ungodly direction. The following are some wrong responses to grief.

Anger at God

No matter how much pain a person is experiencing, it is never okay to be angry at God. Becoming angry at God is evidence of a horrendous misunderstanding of the character of God. It is an assumption that God has done something wrong, and that a person's own desires are more important than God's. Those who justify anger at God (now popular among Christian integrationist counselors) often do so by saying, "God is big enough to take it." What a foolish argument! God is big enough to take it? God is big enough to handle the behavior of monsters like Adolf Hitler. God is big enough to handle any sin, but that does not mean we are free to commit sin. Regardless of the degree of pain, anger at God is never justified. And where it exists, the twisted conception of God's nature that is causing that anger must be corrected.

Using Drugs and Alcohol to Relieve the Suffering

The pain of sorrow is something we must walk through. Numbing your mind to it will only postpone the pain.

Dropping Out of Life

When a person is faced with extreme pain, there is a temptation to use that as a reason for indulging in self pity, which can become a habit that continues the rest of his life. One who gives in to this temptation uses his pain as an excuse to no longer function as a Christian in the church or in his family or in the world. God has not given us that option.

Blaming Yourself

In the case of the death of a loved one, it is fairly common for people to begin picking through the past for things they did wrong, thinking through regrets—even thinking of things they did that may have affected the circumstances surrounding the person's death. *"If only I had (or had not) ..."*

God is sovereign over the past, and we should not second-guess His plan. Even in the case where the grieving person *did* do something wrong, once he repents of that sin, it is over, and he must forget what is behind and press on toward what lies ahead. Psychotherapists are notorious for making people relive past failures and reopen past wounds. This is not done out of cruelty, but out of the belief that the solution is in repairing the subconscious. Scripture, however, does not point us to the past for the solution. We are to be looking to the future, not obsessing about the past, as if we could somehow heal ourselves by wallowing in old pain.

Blaming Other People or Circumstances

If a loved one was killed in a car accident, family members might be plagued with "If only's." If only my brother hadn't asked for a ride ... if only my son hadn't been using the truck ... if only the other driver had been watching ... if only he hadn't gotten the phone call that made him five minutes later.... There are a thousand reasons that the person was in a particular place at a particular time in those particular circumstances. The One who orchestrated every detail is the sovereign Lord, who was accomplishing His purposes.

Experiencing Guilt Over Not Feeling Sad Enough

It is impossible to predict how a tragedy will affect a person emotionally. Sometimes deep, acute pain never comes, even for a close loved one. A person might begin to wonder, *Why am I not more sad? Maybe I didn't love him properly ... maybe something's wrong with my emotions....*

How about this—maybe God is showing you great mercy and kindness. There is no required amount of grief over a loss. It could be that you have such a firm faith in God's plan that your emotions are driven by your faith in Him more than by your loss.

Another misconception is the idea that if you ever stop mourning or if you do not show enough sorrow, then you are somehow forgetting or abandoning the memory of the loved one. God wants you to begin the work of untangling those emotional ties and move on. If God wanted you to remain as attached to the person as you were in the past, He would not have taken him away.

How Can You Help Someone Who Is Grieving?

Begin by applying the principles on compassion and suffering covered in Chapter 3.

When the grieving counselee is open to conversation, sharing biblical principles will help more than anything. He may need help understanding which reactions are wrong and which are not. The responses in the section above are wrong. There is nothing wrong, however, with feeling pain and experiencing deep sorrow—even for a long period of time. There is nothing wrong with crying out loud in public.[174]

Strive to turn the counselee's attention to the one Treasure that cannot be lost. Again—five thoughts about God's reliability and eternality for every one thought about the loss.

---

[174] It is not good that our culture has privatized grief. In Scripture, grief seems intended to be a community affair.

PART 3
BEHAVIOR PROBLEMS

CHAPTER TWELVE: ADDICTION

For the counselee who struggles with addiction, begin with the principles from Chapters 4-6. The material in this chapter is designed to supplement those chapters with principles directly related to addiction.

The World's Definition

Addiction is commonly defined as a condition involving *tolerance* (requiring an ever increasing dosage to achieve the same effect) and/or *dependence* (withdrawal symptoms when use is discontinued).[175] The psychological term that has been coined to encompass both tolerance and dependence is *neuroadaptation*, which, predictably, locates the entire problem in the brain.

It is no surprise, then, that many believe addiction is caused by substances (nicotine, alcohol, etc.). It is possible for a substance to have properties that cause an intense craving for more. And it is also possible that some people are born with a predisposition to be especially weak in regard to certain kinds of sins. But neither the craving nor the predisposition is, of itself, an addiction. No substance can *cause* addiction, because the decision to indulge in a behavior is an act of the will. No drug can make someone decide to take it, and no activity has the power to make someone decide to engage in it. (If it did, no one would ever become free from an addiction.)

For the believer, slavery to sin is voluntary.

---

[175] The world's definitions of addiction not only ignore the spiritual aspect, but they fail to explain addictions that do not involve chemical substances, such as gambling (most gambling addicts do not suffer physiological withdrawal symptoms or require ever-increasing "doses" of gambling).

Romans 6:16 Don't you know that when you offer yourselves to someone to obey him as slaves, you are slaves to the one whom you obey?

One becomes a slave to either sin (or righteousness) by allowing himself to be subject to it. But even then his will is still intact. His life will be dominated by whatever or whomever he allows to influence his will.

For a Christian, no one particular sin is impossible to resist (Php.4:13, 1 Cor.10:13), however, it is possible for a Christian to voluntarily re-enslave himself to a defeated foe:

2 Peter 2:19 ... a man is a slave to whatever has mastered him.

God's Definition

The biblical term for addiction is *bondage*, or *enslavement*. Titus 2:3 speaks of the problem of being addicted to much wine. The word translated "addicted" (*dedoulomenos*) comes from the word "slave" (*doulos*). A person is enslaved to a behavior when that behavior is seemingly impossible to quit. Normally, when people experience severe negative consequences for some behavior, those consequences are enough to make them stop. Enslavement is when a person will continue to indulge in the behavior in spite of such consequences. He is resolved to stop, wishes he could stop, but fails.

Enslavement to anything other than righteousness is sin. We are not to be mastered or controlled by anything (1 Cor.6:12, 2 Pe.2:19). Paul went to great lengths to make his body his slave for fear that even after having preached to others, he himself might be rejected by God (1 Cor.9:27). Part of the fruit of the Spirit is self-control, so all failure to exercise self-control is sin; whether it is a forbidden behavior, such as sexual immorality, or a neutral behavior, such as shopping or drinking coffee. Any habit, then, that continues even after an effort to quit, is addiction/enslavement.

Instead of using the unhelpful and inaccurate psychological terms (neuroadaptation, tolerance, and dependence), perhaps a better definition of addiction is this:

Addiction (enslavement) is when a person keeps deciding to do something that he wishes he would not do

Conflicting Desires

When you counsel someone with a bad habit, do not say, "If you really wanted to quit, you would." That is not a valid assumption. It is possible to want to quit but to also have powerful impulses that seem impossible to resist.

Galatians 5:17 ... the [flesh] desires what is contrary to the Spirit, and the Spirit what is contrary to the [flesh]. They are in conflict with each other, so that you do not do what you want.

Jesus said, "The spirit is willing, but the flesh is weak."[176] We all have conflicting desires. In most cases, the reason a person seeks counsel is that he sincerely *wants* to be rid of his addiction. He wants to be rid of it because of the negative consequences, yet he finds himself enslaved by his craving—like the drunk in Proverbs 23:31-35 who is confused, dizzy, being beaten, and yet says, "When will I wake up so I can find another drink?"

2 Peter 2:22 Of them the proverbs are true: A dog returns to its vomit....

Not only will dogs return to their vomit—they will even eat it! What could be more repulsive—or foolish—than re-ingesting something your stomach has already rejected? That is what these kinds of sins are like. They bring incredible pain into a person's life, yet he goes right back to them time after time.

The World's Solution

The world's main way of dealing with enslaving habits is mainly through Twelve Step programs (such as Alcoholics Anonymous), which can be summarized under four headings:

- Admit you have no control over your habit.
- Clean up your life morally.
- Look to a higher power for help.
- Try to make amends.

---

[176] Mt.26:41 NAS.

There are some very good things that can be said about this approach, and those who struggle with addiction are understandably drawn to Twelve Step programs. Everyone in the group understands what you are going through. You are not judged or looked down upon. The people are compassionate, and yet firm. They will tend to see through lies and phoniness, which creates a genuine, open, honest atmosphere. Instead of sermon-length discourses, advice is kept mostly to very practical, very simple advice that is closer to bumper-sticker length. And the advice comes from human wisdom, so it seems very reasonable. No faith is required.

Even many churches have modeled their efforts after the world's Twelve Step approach. The popular Celebrate Recovery program takes the principles of the Twelve Steps and connects them to the wording of the Beatitudes. For example, step two in the Twelve Steps is "believe that a power greater than ourselves could restore us to sanity." In Celebrate Recovery, that principle is attached to the Second Beatitude: "Blessed are those who mourn, for they will be comforted" (Mt.5:4).

If the world discovers a principle that is biblical, it makes good sense to embrace that principle. There is a danger, however, in taking human wisdom that is not biblical and adjusting the terminology to make it sound biblical. Such is the error that is so common in the integrationist approach—drawing principles from the world's human wisdom and dressing them up with biblical language, rather than drawing the principles directly from the Scriptures.

Some of the principles in the Twelve Step programs are quite biblical, and for that reason many people have been helped through those programs. There are, however, some unbiblical principles as well. Beginning with the world's solutions and attempting to adjust them to fit Scripture often leads to error, because the foundational, underlying assumptions are not compatible with the truth of God's Word.

Evaluating the Twelve Steps

*Step 1: We admitted we were powerless
over our addiction*

Celebrate Recovery attaches this principle to Romans 7:18, "I know that nothing good lives in me, that is, in my flesh. For I have the desire to do what is good, but I cannot carry it out." In the Celebrate Recovery system, this corresponds to the first beatitude: "Blessed are the poor in spirit."

Step 1 of the Twelve Steps may sound similar to Romans 7:18 and Matthew 5:4 on the surface, but the principles are actually quite different. The Twelve Step program is very closely tied to the disease model of addiction.[177] The following is taken from some Narcotics Anonymous literature: "Our first step [is to] admit powerlessness over it. That admission is the foundation upon which our recovery is built. Our experience with addiction is that when we accept that it is a disease over which we are powerless, such surrender provides a basis for recovery through the Twelve Steps."

The key word is "powerless." Dr. Howard Fields, Director of the Wheeler Center for the Neurobiology of Addiction, states,

> Most people tend to think of addiction as the result of a weakness of character or a moral failing, but as the biological mechanisms that produce drug dependence come to be better understood, researchers are learning to think of addiction as a brain disorder...
> I don't believe an addict is responsible for being addicted. I believe they've been victimized by the drug and by circumstances that are largely beyond their control.[178]

In an interview on the subject, Fields stated that punishing an addict for his actions is akin to putting cancer patients in jail for having cancer. Alcoholics get drunk only because "some unconscious force makes

---

[177] The language about alcoholism being a "disease" was mostly metaphorical when AA was first developed, but in recent years there has been a shift from thinking of alcoholism as being similar to a disease in some ways to regarding it as an actual, organic disease of the body.

[178] Howard Fields, Wheeler Center for the Neurobiology of Addiction.
http://www.ucsf.edu/foundation/impact/archives/2000/10_fields.htm.

them take that fifth or sixth drink even when they know they shouldn't. This is a disease, not a crime."[179]

Steps four through six have the appearance of taking responsibility, but the underlying assumption is that the addiction is a disease, outside of the person's control, and that assumption limits the addict's responsibility for his behavior.

Dr. Fields goes on to say something very telling: "When we come up with effective treatments, then the public at large will begin to believe this. That's what happened with depression."[180] Do you see the implication of what he is saying? The assumption is that if a drug can be found to have an effect, that will be proof the behavior was caused by a disease and is not anyone's fault.

That is a logical fallacy. The fact that a drug may have some effect is not proof or even evidence to suggest the problem had a physical cause. If a person becomes angry out of selfish pride and then takes a sedative to alleviate his anger, that does not mean the anger had a chemical or biological cause. It had a spiritual cause. The fact that a physical manifestation of a spiritual problem can be affected by a drug says nothing about the cause.

The message of the Twelve Step groups is one of hopelessness. If you are an alcoholic, you will always be one. Even if you have not had a drink for thirty years, you are still as much an alcoholic as ever and you will be until the day you die. That is not the gospel. Our message is a message not of powerlessness, but of power, redemption, and transformation. Paul says to the *former* drunks in Corinth:

1 Corinthians 6:9-11 Do you not know that the wicked will not inherit the kingdom of God? Do not be deceived ... drunkards ... will [not] inherit the kingdom of God. 11 And that is what some of you <u>were</u>.

Is there such a thing as a former drunkard? Yes! Some of the Corinthians used to be "alcoholics," but they are no longer. And the solution was not simply quitting—it was transformation.

---

[179] Fields, "Alcoholism: Vice or Disease? A Conversation with Howard Fields, Part 1 of 3" ucsf.edu/news/2007/04/3811/fields.
[180] Fields, http://www.ucsf.edu/foundation/impact/archives/2000/10_fields.htm.

1 Corinthians 6:11 But you were washed, you were sanctified, you were justified in the name of the Lord Jesus Christ and by the Spirit of our God.

If there is one thing Christians are not, it is "powerless" against sin. We have access to divine power and can do all things through Christ (Php.4:13).

Step 2: ... came to believe that a power greater than ourselves could restore us to sanity.

Step 3: ... made a decision to turn our will and our lives over to the care of God as we understood Him.

Christians do, of course, believe that a greater power can restore sanity and that we should turn our lives over to Him. However, there is a reason for the vague terminology in the Twelve Step program. There is no mention of the Lord Jesus Christ because that would imply the higher power has to be Jesus Christ. The reason for the words "power greater than ourselves" is to make the point that *any* god will do. It does not have to be Jesus Christ. It does not have to be the God of the Bible. It does not have to be a god who has any particular power or ability. It does not even have to be a god that actually exists, because it is not the god who changes you; it is merely the *belief* in a god that helps, according to this approach.

The Christian message is quite the opposite. Placing one's faith in a false god or a demon or Satan masquerading as an angel of light (all of whom are higher powers to be sure) will not lead to recovery. And faith in the true God brings recovery through power that comes not from the faith, but from God.

Step 4: ... made a searching and fearless moral inventory of ourselves.

Is that a good thing to do? Yes, as long as moral deficiencies are seen as sin against a holy God, and not an unfortunate disease that causes a person problems.

Most Twelve Step adherents see this step as an effort to clean up their act morally the best they can. But will a vague belief in a random higher power and an effort to shore up moral weaknesses be enough to transform a sinful heart into holiness? Not a chance.

Steps 5-12

The underlying assumption of a disease model of addiction, combined with the confusion over whether the power to change comes from the act of believing (regardless of the object of faith), or from Christ alone (the only valid object of faith), hinders what would otherwise be very helpful principles in the other steps. For example, step five is to admit to God, ourselves, and others the exact nature of our wrongs. Admitting culpability is a crucial aspect of repentance, but how can a person admit culpability for his sin while at the same time insisting it is a disease over which he has no control? And what good is it to confess to a god who has no authority to forgive nor power to redeem?

No restoration can take place until there has been true repentance, and repentance is not merely turning from a sin; it is turning from a sin back to Christ. Turning from an addiction to a false god is not repentance. Nor is it repentance to confess to having a disease. And where repentance lacks genuineness or thoroughness, the rest of the steps are undermined. Steps six and seven involve asking God to remove our "shortcomings." That is a good request, but apart from true repentance it will not happen.

Human Wisdom Cannot Transform the Heart

Thousands of people have had success at quitting a habit as a result of Twelve Step recovery groups. This is most likely due more to the exposure and accountability of the meetings than to the steps themselves. Continual encouragement and accountability can be quite helpful. Most participants know from experience that people who do not keep going to the meetings are much more likely to relapse than people who do.

Encouragement and motivation from other people are very helpful in modifying behavior, but apart from biblical principles of transformation they cannot change the heart. That is why as soon as someone stops going to the meetings, he tends to fall back into his old habits. The Twelve Steps do nothing about bondage to the flesh. In fact, they often simply enable a person to exchange one bad habit for a less troublesome one. Drunks go from being hooked on alcohol to being hooked on nicotine, caffeine, or sugar. Life becomes more manageable, but the bondage to the flesh remains.

God's Solution

In the war against the flesh, most of our failures are due to our general position of weakness in the overall war. We tend to focus on wanting to win individual battles with temptation, but individual battles are rarely won when fought from a position of disadvantage in the overall war. The focus of this section, then, will be on how to gain a position of strength in the overall war.

Break the Power of Idolatry

The attraction of sin comes from the soul's belief that happiness and satisfaction will come from that sin (see "Diagnosing the Desires" in Chapter 4). An essential part of worship is looking to God as the only source of joy and satisfaction, so looking to anything else is idolatry (Jer.2:11-13). Looking to something for your joy and satisfaction is worship because it places that thing in the place where only God belongs—giver of joy.

The first step in gaining a position of strength in the war, then, is to depose the idol. This is done by convincing oneself of two facts:

1) The pleasure of sin is temporary, fleeting, and unsatisfying. When it is over it leaves emptiness and depression, not joy.

2) The experience of God's presence will be thoroughly satisfying and more delightful to the soul than the pleasure of sin.

When the soul sees a particular sin as the source of satisfaction of the thirst of the soul, then every time that sin is resisted, it will feel like a loss—like the person is missing out on something good. As long as resisting feels like a loss, there will not be significant victory. The person must come to the point where the nearness of God's presence really is so much more delightful and desirable than the sin that when temptation is resisted it feels like gain rather than loss.

The first twenty meditations in the book "What's So Great About God?"[181] are designed to re-train the soul to prefer the presence of God over the pleasures of this world. It may be helpful to have the counselee read and pray through at least one of those meditations per day for three weeks, and discuss them with you when you get together.

A More Powerful Attraction

John Piper began his message in the 2004 Desiring God Conference with an illustration about the solar system. The massive sun stands at the center and holds all the planets in their proper courses. Even Pluto, 3.6 billion miles away, is held in orbit by the powerful gravitational pull of the sun.

> So it is with the supremacy of Christ in your life. All the planets of your life—your sexuality and desires, your commitments and beliefs, your aspirations and dreams, your attitudes and convictions, your habits and disciplines, your solitude and relationships, your labor and leisure, your thinking and feeling—all the planets of your life are held in orbit by the greatness and gravity and blazing brightness of the supremacy of Jesus Christ at the center of your life. And if He ceases to be the bright, blazing, satisfying beauty at the center of your life, the planets will fly into confusion, and a hundred things will be out of control, and sooner or later they will crash into destruction.[182]

In the Christian's struggle against sin, love for God must be at the center. If love for God is lacking, the sun is effectively removed from the solar system and all the countless strategies, tips, and tricks for

---

[181] The book is available for free download at TreasuringGod.com in the "Articles" section of the Resource Library. Resources are listed in alphabetical order. Scroll down to "W" for "What's so Great about God?" Hard copies of the book can be purchased at WhatSoGreatAboutGod.com.

[182] John Piper, "Sex and the Supremacy of Christ," [sermon on line]; (Desiring God Ministries, 2004, accessed 11 November 2006); available from http://www.desiringgod.org/ResourceLibrary/EventMessages/ByDate/184_Sex_and_the_Supremacy_of_Christ_Part_2; Internet.

resisting temptation are like so many rockets, trying to nudge Jupiter back into orbit.

The pull of an addiction on the heart can feel like an inescapable "tractor beam," and the only way out is to be pulled in another direction by a more powerful force—desire for the presence of God, fueled by delightful experiences of His presence in the past. For more on how to do this, see the sermon series, "Loving God with All Your Heart."[183]

Fight desire with desire. Override desire for sin with desire for something better. Thomas Chalmers called this "the expulsive power of a new affection." Cravings for the pleasures of sin will be expelled by craving for the nearness of God.

Increase Faith

The solution to all spiritual problems is sanctification (being made more holy). For example, it was through the washing of sanctification that the former addicts in Corinth overcame their addiction to alcohol (1 Cor.6:11). Sanctification is accomplished by grace through faith. Only God's grace can transform the heart, and only faith can give us access to that grace. Every sin we ever commit is due to lack of faith. God promises that His way will be more satisfying than the pleasure of sin. Satan promises the pleasure of sin will be worth whatever it costs us spiritually. We choose one or the other based on who we believe. The most basic key to overcoming an enslaving sin is to increase one's faith in the great and precious promises in God's Word.

The three basic ways of increasing faith and gaining access to more grace are Scripture, prayer, and fellowship. For a summary of the basics of how to have a daily routine of Scripture, prayer, and fellowship that will result in spiritual growth and increased faith, see "The Basics of the Christian Life" series.[184]

---

[183] FoodForYourSoul.net. The sermon series are listed in alphabetical order on the "Series Alphabetically" link.
[184] ibid.

Exposure

For the person caught in an enslaving sin, the spiritual discipline that tends to be most neglected is fellowship. Sin always pushes us toward privacy and away from intimacy, because intimacy in relationships involves exposure. And where there is sin, exposure is terrifying. Very often a person will be willing to do anything to be free from his sin *except* expose his sin to others. And yet without help from others, the battle will be lost.

Attempting to win the war against an enslaving sin singlehandedly is as foolish as a single soldier attempting to win World War II by himself. The person with an enslaving sin has already proven that he does not have enough strength on his own to win the war. It is hard enough to win a war when you start out on equal standing. But if the person is enslaved, he is starting the war behind the bars of the enemy's prison camp. Clearly the enemy has the upper hand. If there are powerful forces out there who are willing to form an alliance and help the person, and that person refuses that help, he cuts himself off from one of the most important means of grace and dooms himself to failure.

Of all the things you will call the counselee to do, this will probably be the hardest. The shame of enslavement to a sin makes people say, "I'm not ready for that. I'll do anything else—electric shock therapy, I'll shell out big money for some program, I'll do anything you ask—just please do not make me confess my sin to people in the church." Yet in many cases it is this step that will determine success or failure.

No Christian has the option of privacy. Privacy is worshipped in our culture, and that has infected the Church. Each person wants to function as his own, personal PR firm so he can control how each person thinks of him. But the Church, as Christ designed it, is not a place for privacy. God calls us to love one another with intimacy, and intimacy cannot coexist with privacy. If a person's only interaction with the body of Christ is at a surface level, he is sinning against God, against the church, and against himself. If the counselee does not have close relationships with people in the Church, exhort him to join a small group—not only to gain victory over his enslaving sin, but to be obedient to God's Word. Confront the counselee with the following commands in God's Word:

Shared Emotions

Romans 12:15 Rejoice with those who rejoice; mourn with those who mourn.

That command requires knowledge of one another—several layers of knowledge. First, it requires that we know what is happening in each other's lives. You cannot mourn with someone who is mourning unless you know he is mourning. And you will not know that by sitting in the same room with him in the worship service. Most people can manufacture a pretty good smile for a couple of hours on Sunday morning at church. The same goes for rejoicing with those who rejoice. When people have special things happen that bring them great joy, it will not come to you by osmosis. Obeying this command requires knowledge of what is going on in that person's life. We all understand how hard it is when someone has to go through some terrible sorrow alone. But it can also be very hard for people to go through some great joy alone. When there is something you have longed for or strived for years to obtain and you finally get it, but no one knows your life well enough to know what a great joy that is—that can be very lonely.

Romans 12:15 requires us to know each other at the level of knowing the details of each other's lives. But that is only the beginning. Knowledge of the events of someone's life will not touch your emotions unless you love that person. The deeper your love, the more your emotions will be affected by theirs.

Confession of Sins

James 5:16 Therefore confess your sins to each other and pray for each other so that you may be healed. The prayer of a righteous man is powerful and effective.

This is not a command for a few people in the church who happen to have real close friends. It is a command that is binding on every person who names the name of Christ. This requires close, trusted friendships, which come only through considerable time, effort, and energy.

Much of the power behind the grip of enslaving sins is secrecy. It was David's desire for secrecy that drove him to multiply his guilt through a cover-up that involved the murder of an innocent man. Satan can prevent the enslaved sinner from access to the grace he needs to be free. Once that secrecy is given up, the grip of the sin is far less powerful. When the sin is finally confessed and no longer has to be hidden, there is an amazing sense of relief and freedom. The shame and humiliation the person so dreaded turns out to be much less than what they feared. In fact, in many cases confession causes others to admire the person who is so honest, and it opens up avenues of ministry to people who are struggling with sin.

Ministry to others is another reason why close relationships are so important. There are people in the church who need help out of some sin, but they will never get that help until they can confess it, and they will never have the courage to confess until they see you do it. Putting up a façade of holiness does no one any good. We think that will make people be impressed with us, but more often it just makes people either suspicious of us or intimidated by us. They may or may not be impressed with the façade, but either way they will not be comfortable opening up with you.

Most people understand the importance of accountability in escaping enslaving sin. It is not enough, however, to simply ask a friend to keep you accountable. No one can "keep" another person accountable. Accountability works not when someone else keeps you accountable, but rather when you make yourself accountable. Where there is not a willingness to make oneself accountable, all the questions from an accountability partner about how you are doing can be easily deflected with vague answers or flat out lies. The addict must initiate accountability rather than putting it on the shoulders of the accountability partner.

A Lifestyle of Exposure

Ephesians 5:11-13 Have nothing to do with the fruitless deeds of darkness, but rather expose them. 12 For it is shameful even to mention what the disobedient do in secret. 13 But everything exposed by the light becomes visible.

2 Corinthians 4:2 We have renounced secret and shameful ways; we do not use deception ... by setting forth the truth plainly we commend ourselves to every man's conscience in the sight of God.

Even where there is a pattern of honest accountability with a trusted friend, over time the degree to which that motivates can diminish. When a person has an understanding response time after time, eventually the fear of confession decreases and the benefit of accountability is diminished. So beyond direct accountability to an individual or small group, there must also be a lifestyle of exposure. It is foolish for an addict to have long segments of time when no one knows where he is or what he is doing. His credit card statements and bank activity should be an open book to his spouse or close friend. If a man struggles with looking at porn on his computer, he should have a window on his office door and have the monitor visible from the window. And he should utilize monitoring software that sends an email to his spouse or friend showing any questionable websites he has visited.[185]

Carry Each Other's Burdens

Galatians 6:2 Carry each other's burdens, and in this way you will fulfill the law of Christ.

God did not design you with enough strength to be able to handle the Christian life on your own. As Josh Harris says, "Lone rangers are dead rangers. Without the encouragement, rebuke, exhortation, prayers, and spiritual gifts of others, your burden will be too heavy to bear. And others' burdens will be too heavy for them to bear without your help."[186]

Once again, this requires close friendships. You cannot bear a person's burdens if you do not know what his burdens are. Nor will that person be much help in carrying your burdens until you have built a deep enough friendship that he is not only aware of what is happening in your life, but he understands your particular points of weakness and vulnerability. Some people need gentle tenderness. Others need a good, swift kick in the seat of the pants. Tailor-made grace requires thorough knowledge.

Keep in Step with the Spirit

Galatians 5:16 So I say, walk by the Spirit, and you will not gratify the desires of the flesh.

The power of the flesh is broken only when a person walks by the Spirit. The imagery of walking points to progression of steps. This underscores

---

[185] Covenanteyes.com, PCPandora.com.
[186] Joshua Harris, *Sex Is Not the Problem (Lust Is): Sexual Purity in a Lust-Saturated World,* 131.

the moment-by-moment aspect of the Christian life. When people become caught up in an enslaving sin, very often they become so focused on the particular behavior they are trying to escape that they forget about the importance of the thoughts. They think of steps toward or away from God in terms of actions. To think this way is to be oblivious to most of the steps one takes in life.

Job 31:1-4 I made a covenant with my eyes not to look lustfully at a girl. 2 For what is man's lot from God above, his heritage from the Almighty on high? 3 Is it not ruin for the wicked, disaster for those who do wrong? 4 Does he not see my ways and count my <u>every</u> <u>step</u>?

Job understood that each thought and each lustful glance is a step. Every moment our thoughts take us another step in some direction. The addict resolves with all his heart to never engage in a certain behavior again, but when temptation hits he falls immediately, and is mystified as to why. He does not understand that after allowing the mind to run unhindered in a sinful direction, he should expect to end up in the place toward which he has been traveling. Gaining control of actions will not happen apart from self-control in the thought life. This is why the sinner is called to repent not only of his ways, but also of his thoughts.

Isaiah 55:7 Let the wicked forsake his way and the evil man his <u>thoughts</u>. Let him turn to the Lord, and he will have mercy on him, and to our God, for he will freely pardon.

Repentance must be thorough. When there is a willingness to give up a behavior, but an unwillingness to let go of the thoughts—that is not repentance. Urge the counselee to repent of sinful thoughts, and to strive to walk step-by-step, thought-by-thought with the Holy Spirit. This means thinking in ways He desires us to think, as revealed in His Word.

Romans 13:14 Clothe yourselves with the Lord Jesus Christ, and do not think about how to gratify the desires of the flesh.

Thoughts are like a big snowball balanced at the top of a steep hill. Once they begin rolling in a certain direction, it is nearly impossible to stop them. To prevent runaway thoughts, the process must be stopped at the earliest stages. For more on how to do this see, "Correcting Wrong Thoughts" in Chapter 6.

Resources for Helping Those
Enslaved by Addictions

For Accountability

Accountability Form: There is an accountability form on the "Forms and Surveys" page in the Resource library of TreasuringGod.com. Urge the counselee to modify the form, deleting questions that are not relevant for his situation and adding questions that he knows he needs to answer on a weekly basis. Urge him to commit to fill out the form each week and give it to you or another accountability partner.

Monitoring Software: Use monitoring programs to expose Internet use to an accountability partner.[187]

Bible Study: Setting Captives Free

SettingCaptivesFree.com is a ministry devoted to helping people out of enslaving sins. It is an outstanding online Bible study designed to help the counselee learn how to take such delight in the presence of God that he prefers it above the pleasure of sin. The person going through the study does one lesson on-line each day, and is assigned a mentor who communicates with the counselee via email throughout the study. The study is available for the following enslaving sins:

- **Pornography and sexual sin**—"The Way of Purity"[188]
- **Homosexuality**—"Door of Hope"[189]
- **Teens struggling with sexual sin**—"Purity Challenge"[190]
- **For spouses of those struggling with sexual sin**—"A United Front"[191]

---

[187] Covenanteyes.com, PCPandora.com.
[188] settingcaptivesfree.com/courses/way-of-purity/
[189] settingcaptivesfree.com/courses/door-of-hope/
[190] settingcaptivesfree.com/courses/purity-challenge/

- **Overeating**—"The Lord's Table"[192] and "The Lord's Table for Children"[193]
- **Anorexia and bulimia**—"In His Image"[194]
- **Drinking**—"New Wine"[195]
- **Gambling**—"Higher Stakes"[196]
- **Smoking**—"The Breath of Life"[197]
- **Self-injury**—"By His Wounds"[198]
- **Anxiety, depression, and fear**—"The Cross-Centered Mind"[199]

Devotionals from the book, *What's So Great About God?*:[200]

Meditations #**1-20**, **31**, 32, **76**, **131**, 133

---

[191] settingcaptivesfree.com/courses/united-front/

[192] settingcaptivesfree.com/courses/lords-table/

[193] settingcaptivesfree.com/courses/lords-table-for-children/

[194] settingcaptivesfree.com/courses/his-image/

[195] settingcaptivesfree.com/courses/new-wine/

[196] settingcaptivesfree.com/courses/higher-stakes/

[197] settingcaptivesfree.com/courses/breath-of-life/

[198] settingcaptivesfree.com/courses/his-wounds/

[199] settingcaptivesfree.com/courses/cross-centered-mind/

[200] Bold numbers represent the meditations that are especially relevant.

CHAPTER THIRTEEN:
SEXUAL SIN

Sexual behavior reveals what is in a person's heart, and for that reason Scripture speaks about it often. In Colossians, Paul equates sexual sin with covetousness and idolatry:

Colossians 3:5-6 Put to death, therefore, whatever belongs to your earthly nature: sexual immorality, impurity, lust, evil desires and greed, which is idolatry. 6 Because of these the wrath of God is coming.

Married or single, your behavior in this aspect of your life waves a flag that signals the allegiance of your heart.

The material in Chapters 4-6 is crucial to understanding how to counsel a person who struggles with sexual sin. Begin with the material in those chapters as well as the material in Chapter 12 (escaping enslaving sin). Beyond that, some very helpful passages of Scripture for dealing with sexual sin are Proverbs 5-7 and 1 Corinthians 6.

Homosexuality

Great care must be taken when using the word, "homosexual" because in the Bible it means one thing, but in our culture it means something very different. Biblical references to homosexuality focus on *behavior*. But most people in our culture use this term to refer to what they call a sexual orientation and what the Bible calls temptation. According to our culture, if you are tempted to commit homosexual acts, you *are* a homosexual—regardless of how you behave. Biblically speaking a person is not homosexual unless he or she actually engages in homosexual behavior. This is important because when we say, "Homosexuality is a sin," what the world hears is that it is a sin to even be tempted. Without question, homosexual behavior (which includes indulging sexual thoughts) is sin (Ro.1:26-27, 1 Cor.6:9, Lv.18:22). It is not a sin, however, to have an "orientation" (that is—it is not a sin to be tempted—as long as one fights against that temptation). Jesus Himself was tempted, and yet was without sin (Heb.4:15).

Most Christians have no idea which people in their church struggle with strong temptations toward homosexuality. This is no surprise. If you struggled with that temptation would you tell anyone at church? Most Christians who struggle with this particular sin (and often other kinds of sexual sin) carry on the war in lonely isolation. Sadly, it is not uncommon to hear people in churches making jokes and derogatory remarks about homosexuals. Sexual sin is one of the most difficult sins to overcome, and requires more outside help from others than most sins. Those who need help the most are the least likely to have it. Make it your goal to do your part in reversing this problem. A person fighting against sexual sin—including homosexual sin—is to be commended, not looked down upon. The great problem in the Church is the people who are not fighting against the sin in their lives. If a person is repentant, our role is to come alongside him and help him gain victory.

Some people, from the time they first begin to experience sexual attraction, for no reason they are able to discern, find themselves drawn to people of the same sex. They do not want to feel that way, and they do everything they can to shift their attraction to the opposite sex in order to be normal. They beg God to take the temptation away from them, but instead it becomes stronger and stronger. What are people like that supposed to do? What about a man, for example, who begins to develop a friendship with another man but then a sexual attraction develops? Should he cut off the friendship with no explanation?

An Inside Look at the Struggle

The following is a letter I received from a woman in a former church who wanted to confess her struggle:

> I really need to ask some questions, but I have been avoiding these particular ones for a lot of reasons. But I feel very alone in my struggle, desperate actually, and I guess I hardly have anything to lose by asking. To be honest, life right now seems almost too unbearable, and I feel guilty for my lack of strength. Even though I am constantly trying to reorient myself to an eternal perspective, comfort is still so often elusive. What kind of witness is that?

I've struggled for a long time with being gay. It seems so unlike the "average" sin or struggle. Just about any type of sin I can think of—greed, gossip, self-centeredness, discontent … all of those are things I hate and want to be rid of. Even when I'm tempted to indulge in them I hate that they are a part of me in any way.

But this, being gay, I cannot understand why it is wrong. I believe the Bible is clear that it is, so I have committed to rejecting the lifestyle, but it so often makes me sad.

You say the feelings are not wrong but just the actions. So can I be in love with someone of the same sex and be pure? Is sex the only thing restricted? What about any level of affection? Is hugging a friend okay but not someone I'm attracted to? How do I draw the line?

In college I was shocked to hear a Christian tell me that there was "nothing wrong with being gay." I questioned it, but you can't believe how happy I felt at the prospect of it possibly being okay. It was like an impossible dream come true. So I let myself be open to a relationship, which eventually did come. I would have given anything for this person, including my own life.

And then I started going to Church and realized that the pro-Christian gay arguments really did seem to be a bit of a stretch (which I had a sense of all along but still hoped), and eventually saw that I had to choose between this relationship or faith in God.

I also realized that since our time here on earth is so short in comparison with eternity, how could I choose now over then? If it really was grieving the Holy Spirit, how could I continue to walk this road away from Him? So I made my choice and that's what led to my conversion.

This past year has been so hard, trying to keep a friendship while also ending the relationship the way it was. I have been trying to hold on and let go at the same time without knowing quite what the boundaries should be. Meanwhile, she was faced with the same decision and chose against God. Given how much I love her this grieves me in a way I cannot even express, and not only do I grieve for her soul, but for the fact that we have become so different from each other.

She doesn't understand practically anything that I'm passionate about. Almost all meaningful topics of conversation are off limits.

I think I can imagine the pain of a divorce … if I could have married her I would have (I hope this is not too unsettling to your stomach).

Now it feels like the tearing apart of my own limbs … in fact, I think that would hurt less. Today what had me down is that she said she is going to date again. Now that she is moving on it should be easy to let go. But I'm feeling the pain of separation all over again. I knew the reality, but today it became even clearer. I can feel the blade that cuts us apart all the more.

I don't understand why it has to be this way! I have decided to obey God regardless of whether I understand, but I wish I could see some reason for it. At least all other sin looks like sin.

I feel like a terrible witness, especially if my sorrow over the whole matter is seen. People who knew me before I was saved think my reasoning is crazy. I'm shooting myself in the foot, and besides, who would want to serve a God that's so demanding and narrow and painful? Is it any wonder I don't see any fruit from witnessing?

And Christians would understand my reasoning and applaud my turning away from sin, but it is surely a strange and sinister thing to struggle with in the first place, and what does my sadness say about the forgiveness I've received? Ungrateful! How can I hold on to something so evil with such longing? I feel isolated because I have so many secrets.

I guess I'm paying the price for my sin … I know I deserve it. My path led me into deep and very dark sorrow (though mostly after repentance). When will the light come? I feel like I might not last. Can you maybe pray for me in the next couple of days? I feel so low I wonder if I can bear it.

I include this letter so you will understand that not all homosexuals are the people marching in the gay pride parades. If there is anything but compassion and love in your heart toward the woman who wrote this letter, you have serious work to do in your heart to become a competent counselor. Once a person has repented there should be no stigma of any kind—even if the struggle continues—no matter what the sin.

Part of the problem stems from the fact that some people teach homosexuality is the worst sin there is—in a class below all other sins.

This theory is based on the idea that homosexuality appears at the bottom of the downward spiral described in Romans 1.

First, it is true that homosexuality is highlighted in that chapter, but nothing in the chapter indicates that homosexuality is the most evil of all sins. More likely it is included because homosexuality is such a clear example of a sin against natural revelation, which is the focus of Romans 1.

Secondly, those who say it is at the bottom of the downward spiral need to read this chapter more closely. First, sinful man gave himself over to worshiping the creation rather than the Creator ...

Romans 1:26-27 Because of this, God gave them over to shameful lusts. Even their women exchanged natural relations for unnatural ones. 27 In the same way the men also abandoned natural relations with women and were inflamed with lust for one another. Men committed indecent acts with other men, and received in themselves the due penalty for their perversion.

Is that the end of the process? No. The downward spiral continues...

Romans 1:28-31 Furthermore, since they did not think it worthwhile to retain the knowledge of God, he gave them over to a depraved mind, to do what ought not to be done. 29 They have become filled with every kind of wickedness, evil, greed and depravity. They are full of envy, murder, strife, deceit and malice. They are gossips, 30 slanderers, God-haters, insolent, arrogant and boastful; they invent ways of doing evil; they disobey their parents; 31 they are senseless, faithless, heartless, ruthless.

Is there a level of depravity that appears lower in the downward spiral than homosexuality? Yes, there is, and it is characterized by greed, envy, pride, disobedience to parents, and gossip. There is no stigma in the church attached to people who have repented of pride or gossip but are still tempted by it. In fact, if they face temptation but resist it, we admire them. It should be the same for those who struggle with any sin.

Homosexuality is unusual in that only a very small percentage of the population is even tempted by it. If you struggle with prejudice against homosexuals, keep in mind how often you fall to whatever sin you do happen to struggle with. If the enemy went after you in the area of homosexuality, you would have just as much trouble fighting that as you do with whatever besetting sins do exist in your life.

What Causes Homosexual Attraction?

The same sinful heart that produces sins such as gossip and pride produces the sin of homosexual behavior (which includes fantasies). But what about the attraction? What makes a person open to this particular temptation?

As with everything else, the world wants to blame it all on the brain. As of yet, however, no neurological cause has been discovered. Nor has any sociological cause. There are millions of people who lacked a role model of the same sex, or had a negative relationship with the same-sex parent, or who were sexually abused as a child, and it did not cause any homosexual urges at all.

Is it possible that some people are born with a tendency toward homosexuality? Perhaps. We know that the sex drive is something people are born with, and we also know there are such things as birth defects. Some people are born with physical deformities; some are born with mental deficiencies. It seems that practically any part of a person's makeup—including the sex drive—could possibly be defective from birth. It could be the way they were born, or it could be a result of something that happened to them. There could be emotional factors, environmental factors, physical factors, or spiritual factors. There are many possible causes of susceptibility to various sins, but there is only one cause of the decision to engage in the actual behavior, namely, the will.

The good news is, you do not have to know what caused the susceptibility in order to help the person. God's grace is powerful enough to overcome any weakness, no matter how or why it came to be.

The Way Out

Most people are tempted with some kind of sexual perversion. For some people it is homosexuality, for others it is pornography, for some it is a desire to engage in sexual activity or fantasy while single, for others it is a desire to engage in sexual activity or fantasy with someone other than his or her spouse. A woman can be tempted to be unresponsive sexually to her husband. A man can be tempted to use his wife as a tool for his own pleasure without concern for her pleasure. Whenever Satan sees a powerful, God-given desire intended for good, he makes every attempt to pervert it for evil and lead people into sin. What can we do to help a person who wants out of sexual sin? Escaping sexual sin is the same as escaping any other sin. Diagnose the various problems in the heart, and takes steps to bring each aspect of the inner man into line with biblical standards (see Chapters 4-6 and Chapter 12).

For targeted, day-by-day help in overcoming homosexual temptation, urge the counselee to go through the "Door of Hope" online Bible study.[201]

Resources for Helping Those Struggling with Sexual Sin

For Accountability

Accountability Form: There is an accountability form on the "Forms and Surveys" page in the Resource library of TreasuringGod.com. Urge the counselee to modify the form, deleting questions that are not relevant for his situation and adding questions that he knows he needs to answer on a weekly basis. Urge him to commit to fill out the form each week and give it to you or another accountability partner.

Monitoring Software: Use monitoring programs to expose Internet use to an accountability partner.[202]

Bible Study: Setting Captives Free

SettingCaptivesFree.com is a ministry devoted to helping people out of enslaving sins. It is an outstanding online Bible study designed to help the counselee learn how to take such delight in the presence of God that

---

[201] http://www.settingcaptivesfree.com/courses/door-of-hope.
[202] Covenanteyes.com, PCPandora.com.

he prefers it above the pleasure of sin. The person going through the study does one lesson on-line each day, and is assigned a mentor who communicates with the counselee via email throughout the study. The study is available for the following enslaving sins:

- **Pornography and sexual sin**—"The Way of Purity"[203]
- **Homosexuality**—"Door of Hope"[204]
- **Teens struggling with sexual sin**—"Purity Challenge"[205]
- **For spouses of those struggling with sexual sin**—"A United Front"[206]

Devotionals from the book, *What's So Great About God?*:[207]

Meditations #12-14, **17-20**, 23, **31**, 32, 36

---

[203] settingcaptivesfree.com/courses/way-of-purity/
[204] settingcaptivesfree.com/courses/door-of-hope/
[205] settingcaptivesfree.com/courses/purity-challenge/
[206] settingcaptivesfree.com/courses/united-front/
[207] Bold numbers represent the meditations that are especially relevant.

CHAPTER FOURTEEN: SELF-DESTRUCTIVE BEHAVIOR

When is it Wrong to Harm Your Body?

The most common argument for why a Christian should not engage in unhealthy behavior is to say that our bodies are the temple of the Holy Spirit (1 Cor.6:19); therefore, we should not harm them. But why would that apply to smoking, alcohol, and drug use, but not to missionaries who go where there are terrible diseases and poor health conditions or hostile natives with spears? It would be difficult to find many people in the Bible who put their bodies in harm's way more than Paul, the writer of 1 Corinthians 6:19. So the argument that he was referring to physical harm runs aground. The conclusion Scripture draws from the fact that your body is the temple of the Holy Spirit has to do with spiritual things, not physical things.

The point is not—Your body is the temple; therefore, do not do any physical harm to it.

The point is—Your body is the temple; therefore, do not *defile* it with sexual sin.

No passage of Scripture forbids self-injury or unhealthy behavior altogether. Therefore it is not always wrong to do harm to your body. It is only wrong to do harm with a wrong motive, or harm that violates other biblical principles, such as the principles of stewardship or servanthood.

The Stewardship Principle

In Luke 19 Jesus told a parable about a nobleman who, before leaving to be appointed king, entrusted a sum of money to his servants and said, "Put this to work until I come back." The king represents Jesus, and the servants stand for believers. Your King has given you a wide variety of resources—including your body—and he expects you to put it to work for His purposes until He returns (see Luke 19:12-13).

1 Corinthians 6:19-20...You are not your own; 20 you were bought at a price. Therefore honor God with your body.

Everything, including your body, belongs to your Owner, the Lord Jesus Christ. You are only a steward of your body as well as everything else He has entrusted to you. You will be rewarded or punished according to what use you made of the body entrusted to your care. If you abuse it or fail to take care of it so that it becomes an ineffective tool for God's work, that is poor stewardship.

Inviting disease and early death through excessive smoking, obesity, starvation, heavy drinking, or reckless behavior squanders the physical resource God has entrusted to our care (not to mention the squandering of financial resources on increased healthcare costs).

The Servanthood Principle

Matthew 20:28 The Son of Man did not come to be served, but to serve.

Jesus was a servant, and He lived that way as an example for us (Jn.13:15). We are here to serve. So if we do so much unnecessary harm to our bodies that we cannot serve effectively, we have failed in our responsibility. God expects a man to take care of his family, but if he does something that causes him to die early, he leaves them without a provider. God calls us to help those in need. But if we become so rundown, so obese, or so out of shape that we cannot help anyone do anything, we are not profitable servants. Does it have a significant impact on your ability to serve if you are five pounds over your ideal weight? No. But if you become so out of shape that you cannot help a friend move, you have become a less effective servant.

Motives

Great men and women of the faith have allowed all kinds of horrible injuries to be inflicted on their bodies for the sake of the gospel. Where the gospel can be advanced through suffering, injury, or even death, it may be worth it. But inflicting injury or harm upon oneself for the sake of gaining attention or pity, being in control, self-loathing, or to gain some benefit that is not worth the harm being done—all are bad motives.

Self-Loathing

In Chapter 4 (diagnosis) we learned to always ask the counselee about the thought process leading up to sinful behavior. I once asked that of a counselee who had been cutting herself, and her response was as follows:

> You asked about the thoughts leading up to, during, and after [cutting]. Usually it is fueled by anger toward self. Maybe it is anger at someone else and then directed at self, but somehow it all comes back to self. Guilt, shame, anger, and a huge sense of neediness and emptiness all combine to create such a state of distress that it feels like something has to be done about it.

The inner attitude that drives this kind of behavior is something to which most of us can relate. Usually it is not carried to the extreme of self-mutilation, but feelings of self-loathing are very common. A person falls to a besetting sin again and again and becomes disgusted with himself—feeling like garbage. The same thing frequently happens with people who have been abused. Even if they did nothing wrong and were simply the object of someone else's sin, it is still common for them to experience guilt and self-loathing.

Self-loathing is tricky, because it is so often disguised as humility or repentance. The proper response to sin is one of sorrow, grief, and disgust. But obsessively dwelling on our own sinfulness is not a righteous response. Work to shift the counselee's attention from himself to God.

The world looks at the problem of self-loathing and thinks the solution is self-love, self-esteem, and self-forgiveness. But those "solutions" only make the problem worse. The problem is *too much* focus on self. Increasing thoughts about self will only make matters worse—even if they are positive thoughts. Do not counsel the self-loather by going on about how wonderful he is. The truth is, with regard to the sin in his life, he is not very wonderful. God is wonderful. Urge the counselee to think five thoughts about God for every one thought about himself.

The biblical term for self-loathing is self-condemnation, and the solution is in 1 John 3:19-20.

1 John 3:19-20 This then is how we know that we belong to the truth, and how we set our hearts at rest in his presence 20 whenever our hearts condemn us. For God is greater than our hearts, and he knows everything.

When the heart condemns, the solution is to remember that God does not condemn those who are in Christ (Ro.8:1), and God's judgment trumps ours. If our heart says, "Condemned" and God says, "Justified, forgiven, and accepted," His judgment is valid and ours is invalid. The idea of self-forgiveness is, first of all, absurd. Forgiveness cancels a debt by absorbing the loss so a relationship can be restored. None of that makes any sense if done to oneself.

Secondly, telling the person to forgive himself will only make matters worse. His whole problem is that he thinks *his* assessment of himself is what matters, rather than God's. So telling him that the solution is for him to forgive himself only perpetuates that false belief.

When there has been a failure, thoughts about oneself should be limited to the following:

1) Discover what went wrong so it can be avoided in the future.
2) Discern what virtues are missing so the person can strive for progress in those areas.
3) Consider the best path to recovery.

How to Recover from Failure

Keep Fighting!

For steps one and two above refer to Chapters 4-6. Regarding step three, remind the counselee that the battle is not over. As long as he is still breathing, the war is still on. When we stumble into a sin, the enemy does not sit back and declare victory. He is looking for a far greater victory. When we are down, he pounces. After we fall to a sin, he ramps up his attacks. He wants to use our discouragement and grief to persuade us to lower our defenses, and let him wail away with his accusations. He kicks us when we are down, and he whispers in our ear, "Don't even think about defending yourself. You know you deserve this." How do you combat the accusations of the accuser of the brethren when everything in you agrees with what he is saying about you?

Study the Cross

1 John 1:9 If we confess our sins, he is faithful and just and will forgive us our sins and purify us from all unrighteousness.

Why does a self-loather have a hard time accepting God's forgiveness? Because of pride. Self-loathing is an attitude that focuses mainly on self, which is the essence of pride. Accepting forgiveness requires humility. Pride wants to do something to make up for the wrong that was done. Accepting forgiveness requires admitting that nothing can be done (on our end) to undo what was done, and we are completely at the mercy of the one against whom we sinned. Proud people cannot accept forgiveness, because to do so they have to admit not only their sin but also their helplessness.

Urge the counselee to study the sacrifice Jesus made for his sin, so he can be convinced that Jesus' payment was adequate. When a person will not forgive himself for something, it is because he does not truly believe Jesus' payment for that sin was sufficient; he feels that he somehow needs to add to what Jesus paid.

Hebrews 10:17-19 "Their sins and lawless acts I will remember no more." 18 And where these have been forgiven, there is no longer any sacrifice for sin. 19 Therefore, brothers, since we have confidence to enter the Most Holy Place by the blood of Jesus ...

If God has forgiven our sin, no further sacrifice is necessary. It is impossible to have higher standards than God, and it is impossible to be holier than God. But that is what a person is trying to do when he wants to add additional punishment for his sin beyond what Jesus has already paid.

In John 13 Jesus was making a point about the fact that unless a person is washed by Christ, he cannot be saved.

John 13:9-10 "Then, Lord," Simon Peter replied, "[wash] not just my feet but my hands and my head as well!" 10 Jesus answered, "A person who has had a bath needs only to wash his feet; his whole body is clean. And you are clean...."

If the person you are counseling is a believer, he has been cleansed "by the washing of regeneration"[208] and he is clean.

Acts 10:15 "Do not call anything impure that God has made clean."

Set Your Mind on Things Above

Look at your situation from a biblical point of view. What does the Bible say about God's attitude toward a repentant sinner? Jesus told a three-part parable, recorded in Luke 15, that answers this question in a dramatic way. What happens when a woman finds her lost coin that she has turned the house inside out looking for? She rejoices! What happens when a shepherd finds one stray lost sheep? He rejoices! What happens when one of a man's sons takes off and plunges into a profligate, sinful lifestyle, but then comes to his senses and returns in repentance? The father throws a huge party, runs out to meet him, and before the son can even speak, wraps his arms around him and rejoices! That is God's attitude toward us when we repent of our sin. He loves repentant sinners. He loves the contrite.

Isaiah 57:15 For this is what the high and lofty One says—he who lives forever, whose name is holy: "I live in a high and holy place, but also with him who is contrite and lowly in spirit, to revive the spirit of the lowly and to revive the heart of the contrite."

Make sure that the person you counsel has a proper understanding of God's attitude toward him and his failures.

Remember: God Can Redeem Anything

God never throws up His hands and says, "This person's life is a hopeless mess. I'll just have to put him on the shelf for the rest of his life." Any situation can be redeemed. God can fully restore anyone from any fall. Just knowing that can help a person persevere.

At his peak, Tiger Woods was regarded as the greatest golfer in the world, and one of the things that set him apart from the rest was his

---

[208] Titus 3:5-6 NAS.

ability to recover from a bad hole. Every golfer, including Tiger Woods, sometimes gets a terrible score on a hole. When that happens, most golfers become flustered and do poorly the rest of the round. They think, *It is no use; my score is shot now,* and just hack their way through the remaining holes. But Tiger Woods had an amazing mental toughness. Very often after a disastrous hole or two he would come back and win the tournament. Understanding the importance of resilience is helpful in golf—but much more so in spiritual matters of eternal significance. Everyone fails. The critical question is not whether you will fail, but how well you recover. Even in the face of numerous lost battles, the war can be won if you keep fighting.

Don't Universalize the Problem

On the one hand, we need to admit our sinfulness and accept the suffering that comes along with it as being something we simply must deal with in this life. But on the other hand, we must not get carried away when we talk about our sinfulness. Being weak in one area does not mean that you are weak in every area. You may be lacking in self-control, but that does not diminish the work of the Holy Spirit within you in other areas, such as compassion or zeal for His name or desire for holiness. It is not humility to disparage your spiritual life across the board, ignoring the work of the Holy Spirit in other areas of your life. The Christian life should be an exercise in joyfully expressing gratitude for the fact that God is making us more and more righteous every day.

2 Corinthians 3:18 And we, who with unveiled faces all reflect the Lord's glory, are being transformed into his likeness with ever-increasing glory, which comes from the Lord, who is the Spirit.

Resources for Helping Those Struggling with Self-Condemnation

Devotionals from the book, *What's So Great About God?*[209]

Meditations #**59**, **123**, 157, 158

---

[209] Bold numbers represent the meditations that are especially relevant.

Cutting and Self-Mutilation

Remember the woman who was asked to share her thoughts leading up to this behavior at the beginning of this chapter? This is the rest of what she said:

> For some it is a way of trying to change the emotional distress into physical distress—something you can see, something you can control, something you deserve, maybe even something that can show others how you feel, though most cutters are very secretive. There are also those who cut because they feel dead, almost like they don't exist. Pain makes them feel more alive. For many, the pain of cutting is not very great, some might not even feel it. For me, I felt the pain of it, but right afterward I didn't feel any pain at all (pain causes endorphins to be released, so maybe that has something to do with the "high" associated with cutting). I usually felt a sense of satisfaction and greater control over my emotions after having done it. I also found that it dulled my emotions overall. After I stopped I seemed to become much more emotional in general, with regard to both happiness and sadness. I would say that cutting is a quick fix that doesn't last. It stifles the possibility of seeking real healing, it suppresses emotional pain, and it is addictive.

Ask the counselee if self-mutilation is a way of handling overwhelming emotions. If so, teach the counselee how to find comfort in God. Emotions usually become overwhelming when there is something that we feel we *must* have in order to be happy, and we do not have that thing. Explain to the counselee that his desire comes from an appetite for joy that will not be fulfilled by that thing he so desperately wants. But it can be fulfilled by delightful experiences of the presence of God. The "Loving God with all Your Heart" sermon series,[210] and the first twenty devotionals in the book "What's so Great about God" are designed to help with this. Another good resource is the "By His Wounds" online Bible study.[211]

---

[210] FoodForYourSoul.net. The sermon series are listed in alphabetical order on the "Series Alphabetically" link.

[211] http://www.settingcaptivesfree.com/courses/his-wounds.

Anorexia, Bulimia, and Overeating

Anorexia is the practice of starving oneself in order to be thin. No matter how thin the anorexic becomes, she feels fat and wants to be thinner.

Bulimia is the problem of binge eating followed by purging. Bulimics will eat massive amounts of food in one sitting and then eliminate it by means of vomiting or laxatives.

Overeating is routinely eating more calories than are burned, resulting in ongoing weight gain.

All of these problems generally have several other emotional components.

For anorexics:
- false standards of beauty
- unbiblical attitudes toward food
- obsession with physical appearance
- elevating the ability to control body size to the level of an idol

For bulimics and other overeaters:
- idolatry of food (looking to food to satisfy the hunger of the soul)
- lack of self-control
- unbiblical response to failure

One thing they all have in common is an obsession with food. When you refer to the problem, it is best to refer to it as a food obsession or idolatry, rather than an eating disorder. The terms anorexia and bulimia make the problem sound like a disease or defect in the brain, rather than a sin problem that can be redeemed. She does not have a disease or a mental disorder—she has simply gotten into a habit of being obsessed with food.

Once again, the beginning point is to discover at what point the person's thinking departs from the right path. Then work to correct the problems in the heart (Chapter 6) and help her overcome the addiction to this behavior (Chapter 12).

The Proper Attitude toward Food

Adjusting one's attitude to align with God's Word will help both the under-eater and the overeater, because both problems come from an unbiblical attitude toward food.

Correcting a Negative Attitude toward Food (Anorexia)

Anorexics tend to view calories as an enemy. Carbohydrates, simple sugars, fatty foods—all enemies. This attitude is supported by our culture, which regards these things as generally unhealthy. They are not unhealthy. They are wonderful gifts from God. Fat and sugars are crucial for good health, and perform many essential functions in the body. Fat is needed for absorption and storage of various vitamins, so having too little fat creates health problems. Every action God calls us to do in His service requires energy that comes only in the form of calories. And beyond the health necessity, sugar and fat also make food enjoyable, which is also an important spiritual reality. There is an entire book of God's Word devoted to showing the importance of enjoyment of life (Ecclesiastes).

Ecclesiastes 2:24-25 A man can do nothing better than to eat and drink and find satisfaction in his work. This too, I see, is from the hand of God, 25 for without him, who can eat or find enjoyment?

God wants us to enjoy Him through the blessings of life, and food is a key part of that. So are work and family.

Ecclesiastes 3:22 So I saw that there is nothing better for a man than to enjoy his work,

Ecclesiastes 9:9 Enjoy life with your wife, whom you love, all the days of this meaningless life that God has given you under the sun-- all your meaningless days. For this is your lot in life and in your toilsome labor under the sun.

Ecclesiastes 5:19 Moreover, when God gives any man wealth and possessions, and enables him to enjoy them, to accept his lot and be happy in his work--this is a gift of God.

Ecclesiastes 6:2 God gives a man wealth, possessions and honor, so that he lacks nothing his heart desires, but God does not enable him to enjoy them, and a stranger enjoys them instead. This is meaningless, a grievous evil.

And when you go through life depriving yourself of life's pleasures, unless you have some good reason for doing so, that deprivation, in itself, is meaningless.

Ecclesiastes 4:8 There was a man all alone; he had neither son nor brother. There was no end to his toil, yet his eyes were not content with his wealth. "For whom am I toiling," he asked, "and why am I depriving myself of enjoyment?" This too is meaningless-- a miserable business!

Ecclesiastes 6:6 even if he lives a thousand years twice over but fails to enjoy his prosperity. Do not all go to the same place?

Ecclesiastes 8:15 So I commend the enjoyment of life, because nothing is better for a man under the sun than to eat and drink and be glad. Then joy will accompany him in his work all the days of the life God has given him under the sun.

This is consistent with the New Testament message as well:

1 Timothy 6:17 Command those who are rich in this present world not to be arrogant nor to put their hope in wealth, which is so uncertain, but to put their hope in God, who richly provides us with everything for our enjoyment.

1 Timothy 4:1-4 The Spirit clearly says that in later times some will abandon the faith and follow deceiving spirits and things taught by demons. 2 Such teachings come through hypocritical liars, whose consciences have been seared as with a hot iron. 3 They forbid people to marry and order them to abstain from certain foods, which God created to be received with thanksgiving by those who believe and who know the truth. 4 For everything God created is good, and nothing is to be rejected if it is received with thanksgiving,

Abstaining from food as an end in itself violates the fact that food is good, and is to be received gladly with thanksgiving. Throughout history God has used feasting as a key component of worship, because He wants worship to be a joyful experience of receiving goodness from God, and feasting is a perfect picture of that.

Deuteronomy 14:22-26 Be sure to set aside a tenth of all that your fields produce each year. 23 Eat the tithe of your grain, new wine and oil, and the firstborn of your herds and flocks in the presence of the Lord your God at the place he will choose as a dwelling for his Name, so that you may learn to revere the Lord your God always. 24 But if that place is too distant and you have been blessed by the Lord your God and cannot carry your tithe (because the place where the Lord will choose to put his Name is so far away), 25 then exchange your tithe for silver, and take the silver with you and go to the place the Lord your God will choose. 26 Use the silver to buy whatever you like: cattle, sheep, wine or other fermented drink, or anything you wish. Then you and your household shall eat there in the presence of the Lord your God and rejoice.

That is just one of many examples in the Old Testament law where eating and enjoyment of eating were a key part of worship.

Gluttony vs. Proper Enjoyment of Food

To the anorexic, almost all enjoyment of food feels like gluttony—which raises the question, where is the line between the kind of feasting God wants us to enjoy and sinful gluttony?

There are two kinds of gluttony. One is overeating (routinely eating so many more calories than are burned that ongoing weight gain occurs). The "ongoing" part is important. God made our bodies to fluctuate somewhat in weight. We found above that the reasons weight gain is problematic are because obesity hinders servanthood and stewardship. So if those are the reasons weight gain is bad, then it is only bad if it is enough weight to cause those problems. Gaining five or ten pounds does not prevent a person from helping others in need, nor does it create health problems. If a person's weight fluctuates up and down 10 pounds, but never more than that, then that person is maintaining a relatively steady weight and is not overeating.

The other kind of gluttony is looking to the food rather than God as the source of joy and satisfaction. This is idolatry regardless of the amount of food consumed. If an anorexic eats one little scrap of food per day, starving herself to death, but each time she eats that little scrap she is looking to it for her joy and satisfaction without reference to God, she is guilty of gluttony. But if she enjoys a feast as an expression of God's love, and her enjoyment of the feast is an act of fellowship with God, then it is not gluttony, even if she gains a few pounds.

Nothing is Unclean

In the time of the Mosaic Law, certain foods were forbidden for Jews because they were ceremonially unclean. Jesus abolished that system in Mark 7:19, and when Peter refused to eat some of those non-kosher foods on the basis that they were unclean, God said, "Do not call anything unclean that God has made clean" (Acts 10:15, 11:9). Most anorexics think of food as being unclean—not ceremonially like Peter, but they just have an adversarial relationship with food. Calories are the enemy. When Someone who is good gives you a good gift as a gesture of His love, you should not regard that gift as the enemy. Urge the counselee to constantly preach to her soul, "Do not call unclean what I have made clean."

Acts 14:17 He has shown kindness by giving you rain from heaven and crops in their seasons; he provides you with plenty of food and fills your hearts with joy.

Correcting an Idolatrous Attitude
Toward Food (Overeating)

Eating too much food is usually a symptom of trying to get out of food that which it cannot provide. Food can supply energy, nourishment, sustenance, and pleasure, and can serve as an occasion for fellowship. God did not design food, however, to provide fulfillment, encouragement, refuge or relief from suffering, depression, boredom, or anxiety. When we try to get those things out of food, all we get is weight gain.

Help the overeater to understand the relationship between appetite and desire. Appetite is the ache of emptiness, and desire is the impulse to fill that emptiness. The problem comes when there is a desire disorder in which a person craves something that will not satisfy the appetite. If a person had some wires crossed in his brain so that every time his stomach was empty it made him crave water instead of food, he would drink and drink and never be satisfied. And in the same way, when the soul craves the presence of God, and the encouragement, strength, joy, peace, fulfillment, etc., that come from experiencing the presence of God, but that appetite becomes interpreted as a desire for food, the result is overeating. When desires match up with appetites, then once the appetite is fulfilled, the desire diminishes. A person becomes dehydrated, has an intense desire for water, and then, once the body becomes sufficiently hydrated, the thirst disappears. When the desire for food does not diminish even when the stomach is full, it is usually a sign that the appetite does not match the desire. When the soul thinks that food is the solution to boredom, for example, hunger never goes away because no matter how much food is consumed, the boredom remains.

The solution to desire disorder is to retrain the soul to desire that which will satisfy its appetites. Simply saying "no" to food will not, in itself, solve the problem. Desire will only increase more and more until you give in. When there is a craving for food that does not arise out of actual hunger, the soul is confused and must be corrected. Urge the counselee to preach to his soul in those moments: "You are hungry, but not for food. Food cannot satisfy this craving, because it is an appetite of the soul, not the body. And the only thing that can satisfy the cravings of the soul is the presence of God."

For some people, the cravings of the soul have been interpreted as hunger for food for so long that they actually feel it in their stomachs. Discerning actual hunger pangs can be difficult. This is especially the case in a wealthy culture where food is so abundant. Many people have not felt an actual hunger pang in months. They eat whenever they have a craving, so they never actually come to the point where their bodies actually experience real hunger.

In her book *The Weigh Down Diet*, Gwen Shamblin provides some practical insights on how to discern actual hunger pangs. (Please note: I do not endorse Gwen Shamblin's current teachings. Her doctrine was sound at the time she wrote *The Weigh Down Diet*, but later she denied the Trinity and is currently a heretical false teacher.) God designed the human body such that if we eat only when we are actually hungry, and stop eating as soon as we are full, we will not gain weight. Obesity is generally the result of either eating when one is not actually hungry, or continuing to eat past full.

The amount of food the body needs varies from person to person depending on factors such as levels of activity and metabolism. The process of discovering how much food a particular person needs is fairly simple. Have the person pay careful attention to what he eats each day and weigh himself every morning when he wakes up, using a scale that shows tenths of pounds. He can then cut back on the amount he eats each day until there is a drop in weight. At that point he knows the amount of food his body needs. Eating slightly less than that will result in gradual weight loss.

In some cases the amount of food needed may be very little— perhaps even half the amount he is accustomed to eating. Urge the counselee to eat the amount of food his body needs, and when there are cravings for additional food, strive to discover which appetite of the soul is being misinterpreted as hunger for food.

So the first principle is: Don't try to get from food something that food is not designed to provide. The second principle is this: Do get from food that which food is designed to provide. It is important to learn to enjoy food properly. There is a connection between eating food and God filling the heart with joy.

Acts 14:17 He has shown goodness ... by providing you with plenty of food and filling your hearts with joy.

The proper way to enjoy food is to interpret all the pleasures associated with it as samples of what it is like to be in the presence of God. Just as food satisfies the body, so nearness to God satisfies the appetites of the soul. That is why God so often compares Himself to food in Scripture. So when you eat something really tasty and it just hits the spot, you remind yourself, "That's what happens to my soul when I experience the presence of God." When the food gives you strength and energy and takes away that empty feeling in your stomach, you tell your soul, "That's what would happen to you if you were to experience the presence of God right now. You would have strength and those feelings of emptiness and dryness would be gone."

And beyond the fact that food illustrates a spiritual reality, it is also a gesture of God's love. When something tastes good or a meal is delightful for one reason or another, our ability to enjoy that is an expression of God's love, and it is crucial that it be interpreted as such. When we receive it as a gesture of love, and respond to God with feelings of gratitude, that exchange is fellowship with God. And the simple act of eating a meal is transformed into worship.

This should have two effects on the overeater. First, it should greatly increase enjoyment of eating. Instead of the mere enjoyment of taste, now the person will have that pleasure plus the much deeper pleasure of communion with the living God. Because the eating is now worship, it can and should be enjoyed with as much enthusiasm as possible.

The second effect should be a decrease in the enjoyment of overeating. The joy of worship applies while eating food that the body needs. Once the stomach is full, however, and eating is no longer appropriate, it is no longer possible for the eating to be worship or fellowship with God, since it is not God's desire that we overeat. The more the person enjoys communion with God while eating when hungry, the less desirable overeating will be.

Resources for Helping Those Struggling with Eating Problems

Online Resources:

Overeating—"The Lord's Table" [212] and "The Lord's Table for Children" [213]
Anorexia and Bulimia—"In His Image" [214]

Suicide

If a person has threatened suicide, he is most likely in terrible emotional pain. Comfort and strengthen the counselee using the principles from Chapter 3. Offer the person hope and remind him that suicide is murder, and that there are consequences on the other side of the grave that will be so severe that it will not be worth it.

If a believer commits suicide, he will go to heaven. But make sure the person understands that if he is willing to commit the sin of suicide, there is no guarantee that his salvation is genuine. Indeed, it is quite likely that it is not genuine. And if it is not, the suffering in hell will be far worse than the suffering he is trying to escape in this life. And even if he is genuinely saved, there will be a severe consequence on Judgment Day that will be so severe that he will wish he had not committed suicide.

While compassion is crucial whenever someone is suffering, it is also important not to allow the counselee to use suicide to manipulate you. Some counselees will threaten suicide because they know if they do so, they can call you any time, day or night, and have an instant companion who will listen and talk for as long as the counselee desires. Threatening suicide is threatening sin, and should not be rewarded. Be compassionate, but also point out the sin of threatening suicide, and do not allow the counselee to control your life with his threats. If he does end up killing himself after an occasion when you did not have the time

---

[212] http://www.settingcaptivesfree.com/courses/lords-table.
[213] http://www.settingcaptivesfree.com/courses/lords-table-for-children.
[214] http://www.settingcaptivesfree.com/courses/his-image.

to talk to him, that is not your responsibility. Be willing to make sacrifices to help those in pain, but be careful that your sacrifices do not cause you to neglect other things the Lord has called you to do.

PART 3 PHYSICAL PROBLEMS

In this section there is only one chapter (Fibromyalgia), because the discussion of this issue will set forth principles that apply to other physical problems.

CHAPTER FIFTEEN: FIBROMYALGIA

What Is Fibromyalgia?

Fibromyalgia is a condition that has no apparent cause, in which a person experiences pain throughout the body for at least three months at a time. Most patients (80 to 85 percent) are middle-age females who experience tenderness in several areas of the body. The name given this disease is simply a translation of the symptoms into Latin: *fibro* means "connective tissue," *my* means "muscle," and *algia* means "pain." If a person complains of muscle pain in the connective tissue and doctors cannot discover a cause, she is diagnosed with fibromyalgia ("muscle pain" in Latin).

For about a hundred years doctors have been searching to discover the causes, and to date have been unable to do so. Diagnosis is based completely on the reports of the patient, so fibromyalgia does not follow the classic definition of disease (which requires objective evidence of dysfunction or abnormality in body tissue).

As yet, there is no generally accepted theory regarding either the cause or the treatment of fibromyalgia. Perhaps the most popular theory is that it is a sensory amplification syndrome—a defect in pain processing in which the brain accentuates pain signals. That theory seems plausible, although there are no scientific facts to support it.

This disease has no known cure, so the focus is on relief of symptoms. A staggering number of treatments have been tried and sometimes have had a placebo effect, but without long-term results. There is no generally agreed-upon treatment. Many researchers have recently suggested that adequate sleep and specific exercises may provide some relief. Pain medication is also commonly used.

The normal pattern is for the symptoms to fluctuate but not to become progressively worse. (The fluctuation is not affected by treatment.)

How to Help

Counsel for Suffering in General

For people who come to you with any physical problem, do two things: 1) urge them to follow sound medical advice from a good doctor, and 2) teach them the biblical response to suffering (see Chapter 3).

Show Compassion

Do not dismiss the suffering simply because fibromyalgia is not a disease according to the classic definition. Whatever the cause of fibromyalgia, there is no question that the pain is real—just as real as pain caused by a physical disease.

Counsel for Anxiety

One thing is certain—fibromyalgia is related to the way a person deals with stress. Onset of symptoms is often connected to some type of stress, and the way the body is affected is related to how that stress is handled. A high percentage of fibromyalgia sufferers also suffer from depression and emotional problems. According to three separate studies, disability resulting from fibromyalgia appears to be related to pay scale and job satisfaction. The less a person likes her job and the less money she makes, the more likely she is to miss work due to fibromyalgia.

To effectively help people who have to live with the pain of fibromyalgia, it is important to teach them how to respond correctly to suffering. In addition to the material in Chapter 3, the following may be helpful:

- Shift their focus from the symptoms to the God who sent the symptoms (Dt.32:39).
- Take the emphasis off of relief. It is fine to ask God for relief, but people should never demand it or think they must have it to be happy. Instead, they should put their hope in the Lord and spend what little energy they have on applying biblical principles rather than merely seeking relief.

- Ask questions that guide them toward the truth: "Is it correct to say that God is in control, and He does only good things? God could have prevented this; why didn't He?" Help people who are suffering see what is happening to them as the intentional, purposeful work of their loving heavenly Father.
- Show them how it is possible to minister to others while suffering (Jesus ministered even while on the cross).
- Help the counselee develop true contentment even in the midst of suffering.

PART 4: RELATIONSHIP PROBLEMS

CHAPTER SIXTEEN: CODEPENDENCE

The World's Definition

Codependence is not a disorder listed in the DSM IV, and the question of whether it should be regarded as a clinical disorder is a matter of controversy among psychologists. Clearly, however, it describes a problem that many people have. The following is a typical list of symptoms:

1. My good feelings about who I am stem from being liked and accepted by you.
2. My own hobbies and interests are set aside and my time is spent sharing your hobbies and interests.
3. My fear of rejection determines what I say or do.
4. My fear of your anger determines what I say or do.
5. I use giving as a way of feeling safe in our relationship.
6. I put my values aside in order to connect with you.
7. I value your opinion and way of doing things more than my own.
8. My clothing and personal appearance are dictated by your desires and I feel I am a reflection of you.
9. I'm not aware of how *I* feel; I'm aware of how *you* feel.
10. I'm not aware of what *I* want. I ask what *you* want.
11. My social circle diminishes as I involve myself with you.
12. My mental attention is focused on manipulating you to do things my way.
13. The dreams I have for my future are linked to you.
14. Your struggle affects my serenity. My mental attention is focused on solving your problems or relieving your pain.
15. My mental attention is focused on protecting you

16. My self-esteem is bolstered by solving your problems.
17. The quality of my life is in relation to the quality of yours.

God's Definition

Once again, the world's label "codependent" is unhelpful because it takes a wide variety of characteristics and lumps them all together under a single heading. The biblical terms for this list of characteristics fall into four categories: fear of man, thinking on earthly things, selfishness, and love.

Fear of Man

Fear of man describes any situation in which a person cares so much about the opinions of people that the desire for their approval dominates his thinking or drives him to make ungodly choices. Items 1-7 in the list are symptoms of fear of man, and items 8-11 describe the obsessive thoughts that result from fear of man.

When you counsel people with these characteristics, point out to them that fear of man is the opposite of trust in God, and it is a trap.

Proverbs 29:25 **Fear of man will prove to be a snare, but whoever trusts in the Lord is kept safe.**

Ironically, those who fear man generally do so out of a strong desire to be kept safe. A woman, for example, may desperately try to ensure that her worst fear (being left alone) is not realized. She conforms all her beliefs and opinions to whatever makes the man she is with willing to stay with her. This is her way of keeping herself safe from the dreaded condition of being alone. Show her from Proverbs 29:25 that rather than ensuring her safety, she is actually making herself vulnerable to a snare.

It is a slap in the face of God when we are more concerned about human opinion than God's assessment, and we have no right to do so.

Isaiah 51:12-13 **"I, even I, am he who comforts you. Who are you that you fear mortal men, the sons of men, who are but grass, 13 that you forget the Lord your Maker, who stretched out the heavens?"**

The more the heart moves from fear of man to fear of God, the more the thought life will move in that same direction, and the obsessive thoughts will diminish.

Resources for Overcoming Fear of Man

- Four-part sermon series: "Fear of Man"[215]
- Book: *When People are Big and God is Small* by Edward T Welch
- Book: *Pleasing People: How Not to be an "Approval Junkie"* by Lou Priolo

Selfishness

Item 12 indicates another problem altogether—simple selfishness disguised as concern for another person. All efforts at manipulating others for one's own benefit rise out of selfishness.

The solution to selfishness is humility and selfless love. For help on teaching humility see "Correcting Wrong Attitudes" in Chapter 6.

Love

The remaining items in the list (13-17) are not symptoms of a disease or mental disorder at all. In fact, they are marks of Christian love! If the counselee has these "problems," encourage him to be grateful to God for the good things God has placed in his heart. We all have personalities that make us more prone to certain sins, but those same personality characteristics make certain aspects of righteousness come more naturally to us. Urge the counselee to maintain and strengthen his love for others.

---

[215] FoodForYourSoul.net. The sermon series are listed in alphabetical order on the "Series Alphabetically" link.

Keep Separate Issues Separate

Don't let the world dictate the categories of your thinking. When someone comes to you and says, "I have a problem with codependency," it is a mistake to assume all of the seventeen symptoms listed above apply to the person. The person may have a problem with obsessive thinking, but not with manipulation or selfishness. He may have a fear of man rather than fear of God, but none of the other problems. Or he may simply have godly love, but someone has told him it is codependency. As always, ask questions about what goes on in his mind, and discover where his thinking goes off track, if at all.

CHAPTER SEVENTEEN: MARRIAGE[216]

Counseling a Couple

In most cases the ideal is to counsel the couple together. Perhaps the most difficult task in helping a troubled marriage is moving the focus from what my spouse needs to change to what I need to change. One way to move in that direction is to ask both husband and wife to describe the ideal marriage. In some cases they may need help at this point, as those in very troubled marriages tend to have drastically lowered ideals for marriage. Their ideal may be little more than behaving in a polite, cordial way toward one another or a house with no yelling. If this happens, offer suggestions. "What about strong, passionate, soul-satisfying love? Wouldn't you also like that? How about intimacy or joy in one another?" Help them develop the highest, most appealing description of a marriage that they possibly can.

Now turn to the husband and ask this question: "When you picture this ideal marriage, what changes would have to happen *in you* for that to become a reality?" The question is not what changes must take place in his wife, or what changes must take place in their relationship, but specifically what changes in his character, behavior, affections, etc. would have to take place in order for him to reach the place of that ideal husband. Write down the things he says. Now ask the wife if there are any especially important things he missed. Write those down as well. Now speak to the couple about which one or two items on the list are the highest priority to be addressed (offering biblical guidance where

---

[216] Most of the principles in this chapter also apply to anyone who is having problems with someone they live with, such as a roommate or family member.

necessary). Next, go through the same process with the wife, to find out what areas she feels she needs to change.

From this point the counseling is mostly a matter of helping the husband reach his goals, and helping the wife reach hers (see Chapters 4-6 and 12).

Counseling an Individual

The Root Problem: Selfishness

Most marriage problems are easy to diagnose. The culprit is almost always selfishness. One or both partners become focused on how he or she is being treated; resentment, anger, and self-pity build, and the result is a host of relational problems, such as poor communication, arguing, and lack of affection. In Chapter 8 (Depression) we found that self-pity causes the heart to put up blinders that block out all blessings and notice only hardships. In much the same way, selfishness in a relationship blinds the selfish person to all the good the other person is doing, and only failures to love are noticed. The selfish wife will be oblivious to fifty acts of consideration by her husband, but will notice the five times when he lacked consideration. The result is she feels he is *always* inconsiderate.

Sadly, much that is written on Christian marriage only exacerbates this problem. Books that say, "Romance her, and she will give you what you want," or, "Show him respect, and he will give you the love you desire" only feed into the problem of selfishness. Giving good treatment to your spouse for the purpose of getting your spouse to treat you better is not love. It is manipulation. Teaching couples how to manipulate each other only feeds the root problem of selfishness.

If the disease of selfishness is not addressed, no amount of addressing the symptoms will heal the marriage. For example, most books on marriage devote a significant section to how to improve communication. Couples who have poor communication, however, rarely need information on how to communicate more effectively. They are generally capable of clear communication already (if you, as a counselor, can understand what they say to you, then you know they are capable of clear communication). The reason their communication with each other is poor is not due to lack of *ability*, but rather lack of *willingness*. When there is anger or resentment, the heart refuses to offer the courtesy of clear communication. The angry partner will say something in cryptic form, not caring whether he is being clear. In most cases, when that same person explains what he was saying to the counselor, not only can the counselor understand what he is saying, but his wife can as well. She may be shocked— "I didn't know that's what you meant!" Why could she not understand during their argument, but she is able to understand now in the counselor's office? Because the husband is showing the counselor the courtesy of being clear in his communication. There are some couples who really do need instruction on how to communicate more clearly, but in most cases the problem is one of willingness, not ability. And the unwillingness is a symptom of selfishness. If a couple is fighting, the solution will not come from tips on communication clarification or annoyance avoidance.

James 4:1,2 What causes fights and quarrels among you? Don't they come from your desires that battle within you? 2 You want something but don't get it.

If a wife is angry with or resentful toward her husband, that anger is not caused by his failures. It is not caused by his insensitivity, or forgetfulness, or cruelty. The cause of the anger is a desire in the wife that is being blocked by the husband. There is something she feels she *must* have in order to be happy, and the husband is either blocking it or failing to provide it. The solution is not for the husband to begin providing it. The husband should do all he can to bring her joy, but no matter how much he does for her, the problem of anger will not be solved as long as her focus remains selfish. Whenever a person's focus is on how he or she is being loved, rather than on loving others, there will always be disappointment, resentment, frustration, anger, and unhappiness. When a person turns his attention toward how well he is being treated, he will inevitably become hyper-sensitive to unkindness and blind to kindness. (Think about it—how many people didn't buy you flowers today? 6 billion! Even if there were a hundred wonderful acts of kindness shown to you today, the list of kind actions that were not shown to you today is infinite, and so as long as your focus is on what is not being done for you, you will be unhappy.)

Furthermore, joy does not come mainly from receiving love anyway. Joy comes from loving.

The word translated "want" in verse 2 is a strong word. It is often translated "lust," and it refers to any powerful desire (not just sexual desire). It may be a lust for respect, a lust for affection, a lust for kind words, a lust for consideration—any desire that is elevated to "must have" status. When a "must have" desire is unfulfilled, there will be anger.

James does not proceed to give tips on how to satisfy desires or lusts. Instead, he denounces the type of behavior that characterizes living for lusts. He calls it friendship with the world and spiritual adultery. The solution he gives is not manipulating people to meet our "needs" (lusts). Rather, the solution is humility.

James 4:4-6 Adulteresses! Don't you know that friendship with the world is hostility toward God? So whoever wants to be the world's friend becomes God's enemy. ...6 Therefore He says: God resists the proud, but gives grace to the humble.

The solution is humility—selflessness—dying to self.

When a couple comes for counseling, the one who took the initiative to seek counseling has some objective in mind. The first step should be to discover what that objective is. Though a person may be reluctant to come right out and say it, the objective is very often this: "I'm seeking counseling because my spouse is making my life intolerable, and I want you to help me get my spouse to change." If you, as a counselor, confirm that goal by collaborating to change the spouse, you will do more harm than good.

Should a Christian have the goal of changing his or her spouse? Yes! We should have the goal of changing everyone with whom we have influence. The command to encourage one another is a command to change discouraged people into encouraged people. The command to strengthen one another is a command to change weak people into stronger people. All of the influence we have with people should be used to bring that person along in the process of sanctification (being made more like Christ). And the more you love a person, the greater should be your desire for them to make spiritual progress. Anyone who is not striving to change his or her spouse into closer resemblance of the image of Christ is living in disobedience.

Careful consideration must be given, however, to motives. Why are you trying to change your spouse? Is it because you love your spouse and you deeply desire your spouse's highest joy, and you know that joy is found in increased righteousness? Or is the motive selfish—you want to change your spouse so that your life will be more pleasant?

Changing Yourself: Three Virtues

If a person's motive for changing someone else is a desire for righteousness and joy then that person will be just as concerned about changing himself as he is about changing others.

However, making the shift from focusing on others' sins to focusing on one's own heart is very difficult. It is not uncommon for a counselor to explain this principle to a counselee and for them to nod and say, "Yes, yes, I know all that. I understand that. Absolutely, I agree. I understand." But a few minutes later they return to talking about how poorly they are being treated. Each time the counselee reverts back to living for the goal of being treated better, interrupt and say, "That kind of thinking will cause you nothing but anger and misery." Most people revert back to selfish thinking without even realizing it, so it must be pointed out to them each time.

Some people will give up the goal of selfish manipulation of their spouse only if they are convinced that the counselor will pursue it for them ("I'll stop nagging my husband if you'll start"). As long as the heart believes its joy is dependent on the spouse changing, selfishness will prevail in the motives. Convincing the person that joy comes from nearness to God's presence alone usually requires a great deal of repetition.

When the person is finally convinced, he or she will begin asking, "How can I experience His presence in that way?" For a detailed answer to that question, refer to the "Loving God with all Your Heart" sermon series.[217] But for a starting point, explain to the counselee that all unrepentant sin blocks this kind of nearness to God. So the priority for the counselee must be to fight against his own sin, and to pursue righteousness. And the areas of righteousness that are most often missing in marriages are contentment, forgiveness, and love. The path to joy in marriage comes mainly from increasing in those three virtues.

---

[217] FoodForYourSoul.net. The sermon series are listed in alphabetical order on the "Series Alphabetically" link.

Explain to the counselee that whenever someone sins against us, two different parties are at work: that sinner and God. The sinner is doing evil and God is doing good. When he comes home late from work again without a phone call, or she belittles him or scolds him like a child—those hardships are coming from God. The sin is not from God, but the hardship created by that sin is from God. And the good that God is doing is far greater and far more significant than the evil the sinner is doing. Teach the counselee to have five thoughts about the good God is doing for every one thought about the evil that sinner is doing. The first step to contentment is focusing attention on the goodness and trustworthiness of God in all the suffering He sends.

Secondly, point out the fact that enduring undeserved suffering in a Christ-like way is something God will reward (1 Pe.2:20). Some people can handle all kinds of suffering in other areas of life, but for some reason they think they are not supposed to have to suffer in their marriage. Help them understand that marital suffering is suffering for Christ. If the person is refraining from divorce out of obedience to Christ, then the ongoing suffering is in the category of suffering for Christ. And when we suffer for Christ we are instructed to rejoice and be exceedingly glad because great is our reward in heaven (Mt.5:12)!

Remind the counselee that suffering is inevitable. In a fallen world there is no such thing as a love relationship that does not involve suffering. (Nor is there such a thing as suffering-free singleness.) It is fine to ask God for relief from the suffering He sends, however, as long as the person feels that relief is the only way he can have joy, relief remains an idol in the heart.

The first step in marriage counseling is bringing a person to the point of saying, "Lord, I do not want anything other than what You want for me." This is difficult. When a woman comes to you, for example, and she is a wonderful wife and her husband is a terrible husband, your natural inclination is to focus your attention on her husband. But that will be counterproductive. If you commiserate with her, you push her in the opposite direction she needs to go. You encourage her to be less content rather than more content. It may seem unreasonable to address her spiritual problem of lack of contentment when she is trying hard to be a good wife and her husband is not trying at all. But this is the greatest gift you can give her. It is her only path to happiness. Teach her to pray, "Lord, You have given me the same thing You have given every other married woman—a man who hurts his wife. Obviously it is my request that he do so less and less, but I willingly accept Your will and Your timing." The same is true for a husband whose wife is not trying. He may feel that the problems in the marriage are ninety-five percent her fault, and only five percent his. And he may be right. But still, the best thing you can do for him is to help him change his five percent.

Resources for Contentment

Devotionals from the book, *What's So Great About God?*[218]

Grumbling – **1-20, 31,** 38, **60-69, 73, 76, 77, 81, 84,** 85, **94-95, 106,** 112, 142, 143, 155, **164,** <u>178,</u> **<u>179</u>**

Ingratitude – **31, 61-63,** 68, **69, 73, 77, 81, 83-87, 92, 94-95, 102, 106, 107, 112, 118,** 143, 144, 155, 162

Forgiveness

Every unforgiven offense adds to resentment. Some people have a mountain of resentment that is comprised of hundreds of thousands of offenses over 20 or 30 years. And that resentment makes it impossible for the spouse to do anything that makes the person happy. Suppose a man works too much and his wife resents it. Finally she blows up at him, so he tries to change. He rearranges his work schedule in a way he thinks will make a big difference. Now he is coming home late twelve nights a month instead of twenty. From the wife's point of view, nothing has changed, because resentment, like self-pity, causes a person to be blind to what is good, and to only see what is bad. She will see nothing but those twelve nights he is still late. Every night he is late, every minute he is late, she is building up more resentment and thinking, *nothing ever changes.*

---

[218] Bold numbers represent the meditations that are especially relevant.

Each offense, no matter how small, must be dealt with as it happens; otherwise there will be an accumulation of resentment that will eventually destroy love and make closeness both undesirable and seemingly impossible.

Think about it. What can your spouse do about a pile of 500 past sins? He can apologize and repent of the last one that set you off, but you will not be satisfied with that, because nothing has been done about the other 499. He can talk with you and discover another 200 complaints, and try to do something about all those, but that still leaves 300. When you allow things to build up so that your heart hardens against your spouse, you are putting your spouse in a hole with no way out.

The real issue is not how godly your spouse is. It is how patient and forgiving you are. When you love someone, you tend to cut him slack and you do not see his faults. When you resent someone, you tend to notice every failure and are blind to any good that he does.

For the purposes of this discussion, I will define patience and forgiveness as follows:

Patience: Keeping a soft heart toward a sinner, showing kindness and refusing to become angry or vengeful.

Forgiveness: Putting the matter in the past once and for all, and offering a completely reconciled relationship to the sinner.

By these definitions, it is not possible to forgive someone who has not repented. However, it is always possible to be patient, regardless of whether there is repentance.

When patience or forgiveness are difficult, it is because we have lost sight of how patient God has been with us, and how much we have been forgiven (Mt.18:21-35).[219]

---

[219] For a detailed study of forgiveness see the six-part sermon series titled "Forgiveness" at FoodForYourSoul.net. The sermon series are listed in alphabetical order on the "Series Alphabetically" link.

Resources for Forgiving Others

Devotionals from the book, *What's So Great About God?*:[220]

Meditations #**86**, **88**, 93

Love

Very often a wife complains about her husband coming home late, or failing to listen to her, or not being romantic enough, or not spending enough time with her; but then when the husband does more of those things, she is not satisfied. This is because what the wife really wants is not more time or more romance or more listening; what she wants is love. And if the husband disciplines himself to crank out more of the activities of love without actually loving her (desiring her and delighting in her), it will not be satisfying to her heart even if he spends 24 hours a day with her. In the same way, if a wife speaks respectfully to her husband, serves him, shows kindness to him, etc., but does not desire him or delight in him, it will not be satisfying to him.

This is a difficult point in counseling, because most people believe that they love their spouse, and all that is needed is to learn to express that love a little better. If the problem is lack of actual love, however, then the problem will never be solved through attempts at improving in expressions of love.

Desire and delight for others is increased when desire and delight for God is increased. Urge the counselee to go through the Loving God sermon series.[221]

Resources for Loving Others

Devotionals from the book, *What's So Great About God?*:[222]

Meditations #**1-20**, **25**, 37, **49**, 80, **88**, **93**, **96-99**, **129**, **130**

---

[220] Bold numbers represent the meditations that are especially relevant.
[221] FoodForYourSoul.net. The sermon series are listed in alphabetical order on the "Series Alphabetically" link.
[222] Bold numbers represent the meditations that are especially relevant.

Changing Your Spouse

As noted above, the goal of changing one's spouse, if the motive is to increase the spouse's joy in Christ, is an excellent goal. But motives must be carefully examined because where motives are selfish, results are poor.

Selfish Motives Sabotage Progress

Practically every woman in marriage counseling says the same thing: "He keeps saying he will do this or that, but nothing ever changes." In many cases, it is her selfish motives that are actually slowing his spiritual progress. If she truly desires his highest joy, and makes that clear to him, he will tend to be responsive to her efforts to bring it about. But if her main objective is to satisfy her selfish desires, he will tend to go into a posture of guarding himself ("If she isn't going to watch out for my interests, I need to"). He will then tend to resist her efforts, because he sees them as a threat to his joy.

Selfish Motives Make Progress Unsatisfying

Spiritual progress is slow. Even after a wonderful day of sanctification, we remain almost as sinful as we were the day before. That is going to be true every day for the rest of your life, and it is true for your spouse as well. Looking for overnight transformation in your spouse is like the teenager who lifts weights for one day and then stands in front of the mirror looking for his new muscles. When motives are selfish, the rate of change is always too slow to satisfy.

Furthermore, whenever we look to any earthly thing, including a spouse, in a covetous way (an attitude that says, "I must have this in order to be happy"), we doom ourselves to dissatisfaction, because no earthly thing can satisfy the thirst of the soul. When we think of an earthly thing or circumstance as a joy source, that is idolatry because God is the only joy source. God is the only spring of water that can satisfy the thirst of the soul, and when we look to anything else to satisfy that thirst, we not only commit idolatry (putting an earthly thing in the place of God), but we find that earthly thing to be a cistern that cannot hold water (Jer.2:11-13). So the person who looks to his or her spouse for joy will always be disappointed.

Husbands

The biblical model for men to help their wives in the process of sanctification is found in the example of the Lord Jesus Christ.

Ephesians 5:25-26 Husbands, love your wives, just as Christ loved the church and gave himself up for her 26 to make her holy, cleansing her by the washing with water through the word.

Whatever spiritual struggles the wife has—whether it be lack of respect, moodiness, selfishness, anger, laziness, an enslaving sin, or any other spiritual problem, the solution is to apply the Word of God to her heart. This can be done by counseling her directly, helping her find good preachers to listen to or authors to read, or helping her make connections with another godly woman who can disciple her and pray with her.

Wives

When there is an unbelieving spouse, most often it is the husband. This is such a prevalent problem that a significant section of the Bible is devoted to addressing it—1 Peter 3:1-6. Though the passage speaks of winning an unbelieving husband, it stands to reason that the principles would also apply to winning a believing husband who is acting like an unbeliever in some area.

1 Peter 3:1-2 Wives, in the same way be submissive to your husbands so that, if any of them do not believe the word, they may be won over without words by the behavior of their wives, when they see the purity and reverence of your lives.

If the man is open to listen and is receptive to words, she should use words and tell him the glorious truths of the gospel. But when he becomes unreceptive to her words (which is very common) she must endeavor to win him *without words*. She must devote herself to a pure, reverent lifestyle, and be submissive and respectful. She must strive to attract him into the kingdom of God with her inner beauty.

1 Peter 3:3-6 Your beauty should not come from outward adornment, such as braided hair and the wearing of gold jewelry and fine clothes. 4 Instead, it should be that of your inner self, the unfading beauty of a gentle and quiet spirit, which is of great worth in

God's sight. 5 For this is the way the holy women of the past who put their hope in God used to make themselves beautiful. They were submissive to their own husbands, 6 like Sarah, who obeyed Abraham and called him her master. You are her daughters if you do what is right and do not give way to fear.

What about a husband who claims to be a believer but acts like an unbeliever? You cannot know for sure what is in a person's heart. Only God can perfectly judge whether someone is saved. So to the degree that he acts like an unbeliever, this principle applies—the wife should try to win him over without words by the purity of her life.

Abuse

Every married person is an abuse victim. Anyone who lives in the same house with a sinner is an abuse victim (some more than others, of course).

How should you counsel a victim of severe abuse? All of the principles previously covered about suffering still apply. In the case where a woman or the children are in danger of death or serious injury, I think it is appropriate for her to leave. That is a personal opinion, not based on any particular Bible passage, but it is consistent with biblical principles. For example, in the Old Testament God called His people to submit to the king. Yet when Saul was trying to kill David, it was appropriate for David not only to flee but also to deceive Saul and the high priest so he could escape, and even to eat the sacred Bread of the Presence. In Matthew 12, Jesus seemed to sanction what David did. So when life and limb are at significant risk, it is appropriate to flee. It is not appropriate to take revenge or to show disrespect, but it is appropriate to flee.

The Bible never sanctions separation without divorce, so to "leave" means to divorce.[223]

---

[223] For a detailed study of divorce, see the sermon series "Divorce and Remarriage" at FoodForYourSoul.net. The sermon series are listed in alphabetical order on the "Series Alphabetically" link.

Problem Solving

Many marriages never improve—not because the couple doesn't know what is wrong, and not because they don't know what they are supposed to be doing—but because they never take the time to be intentional about making changes.

The book of Proverbs teaches us general principles of success in life, with the implication that it is wise to make plans.

Proverbs 20:18 Make plans by seeking advice.

Proverbs 15:22 Plans fail for lack of counsel, but with many advisers they succeed.

Proverbs 21:5 The plans of the diligent lead to profit as surely as haste leads to poverty.

God requires us to be good stewards of our lives and to live wisely. Wise people make plans. It is not wise to fly through life by the seat of your pants making all your decisions as you go. God has given you a life to live. This is a gift of immeasurable value. Your life is in your control, but only as a steward. It does not really belong to you, but it has been entrusted to your care. Your duty as a Christian is to live in the most excellent way possible. Just as you should brush your hair and not be a slob so as to glorify God in your appearance, in the same way your life should not be disheveled. This is also true of your marriage. Urge the counselees to have a marriage planning retreat at least once every six months.

Instructions for a Marriage Planning Retreat

Meal 1

Start by asking each other, "How could I improve?" Write down your major concerns, then pick the top five or so and rank them in order of importance to address. Some issues can wait six months until the next planning retreat. Others must be handled right away.

Once there is a consensus on the top five, write those on a new piece of paper—one for the husband and one for the wife. Now put those papers away, and just enjoy each other and do something fun together until the next meal.

Meal 2

The goal now is to take an organized approach to addressing the top five issues.

We all tend to go through life with a vague awareness of things that need our attention. We think, *I need to get organized ... our marriage needs attention ... we have to get our budget together ... I need to exercise ... I must spend time with the kids...,* but they never happen because we fail to set specific goals. The purpose of your time together at this second meal is to set goals. The more specific they are, the better. Avoid vague words such as "improve," "cut back," "give more energy to," etc.

Vague goal: I want to get in shape.
Specific goal: I want to work out twenty minutes a day, five days a week.

Vague goal: I want to spend more time with the kids.
Specific goal: I want to devote a full hour just to the kids at least four days a week.

Vague goal: I need to be more romantic.
Specific goal: We will go on a date at least once a month.

Once all the goals have been written down, put the paper away and enjoy each other until the next meal.

Meal 3

Plan the steps to reaching your goals. For example, if your goal is to have family devotions every night, you need to decide:

- Who will plan it and lead it?
- Where will it take place?
- How are you going to find good material to use?
- By what date will this material be purchased?
- Who will be in charge of getting the family together?

- What will you do when the phone rings during devotions?
- What about nights when you are out or have guests over?

If your goal is to go on a date once a month, you will need to determine:

- Who will plan the date?
- How will you make sure that money is set aside?
- What has to take place on the date for it to be successful? How will that be achieved?
- If the date will be on the last Friday of the month, on what day will you plan it?

Even if your goal is to study the Bible for thirty minutes each morning, several decisions need to be made:

- What will you study?
- What materials will you use?
- What about days you oversleep?

Writing down your plan of action will help clarify your thinking and enable you to modify or eliminate unrealistic goals.

The last step is to determine when you will go back over this list to see how you are doing. It is a good idea to check up on yourselves about a week after your planning retreat.

It takes doing this a few times to get the hang of it. Most couples, on their first planning retreat, tend to set far too many goals and set them way too high. Remember these two principles:

1. The more minor the adjustment to your lifestyle, the greater your likelihood of success.

2. The fewer changes you make, the greater your likelihood of success.

The value of this approach is that it relieves much of the concern that "If I pursue selflessness, maybe my spouse will never change." You know that at the retreat you will hear your spouse ask, "How can I improve?"

It also eliminates the "need" to nag each other between planning retreats. When an issue arises, you know you will have a chance to address it at the next planning retreat, so you can overlook it for now. This eliminates the great majority of both verbal nagging and suppressed nagging that turns into resentment.

Most of your complaints end up not even being brought up at the planning retreat, because by the time the planning retreat rolls around you realize they are insignificant or you forget them altogether. So instead of little things building into an imposing mountain of resentment, they begin fading into oblivion.

It is nice if the planning retreat can take place somewhere special, however, make sure to think of the planning retreat as work, not as a vacation. If you have the goal of enjoying yourself, then you have expectations for the retreat other than the purpose for which it is intended. If it falls short of those expectations, then you may be disappointed and become upset. The purpose of the retreat is to solve problems, not create new ones.

Resources for Marriage Counseling

- Building a Joyful Marriage sermon series[224]
- Marriage Builder class—audio[225] as well as summary brochures on each topic (available from the Agape Book Store). It may be a good practice to have the couple read the brochure on the topic they need and underline the five statements that they find most poignant. The underlined portions can be discussed at the next counseling session.
- The Art of Marriage DVD series

---

[224] FoodForYourSoul.net. The sermon series are listed in alphabetical order on the "Series Alphabetically" link.
[225] ibid.

APPENDIX 1:
PROMISES TO TRUST WHEN...

It is by trusting in God's promises that we overcome the world and its defilements and participate in the divine nature.

1 John 5:4 This is the victory that has overcome the world, even our faith.

2 Peter 1:4 He has given us his very great and precious promises, so that through them you may participate in the divine nature and escape the corruption in the world caused by evil desires.

Success in the Christian life comes through trusting God's promises. But which promise for which circumstance? The following list is nowhere close to comprehensive, but it does offer some suggestions for which promises go with which circumstances.

Items in **bold** are virtues to be gained from trusting the promise, items in *italics* are sins/challenges/struggles to be overcome through trusting in the promise. Spiritual progress is always by faith, so make heavy use of these promises in counseling.

****

Anger over
Unfulfilled/Blocked Desire

Anger over an unfulfilled or blocked desire is due to a failure to believe that the joy that is available directly from God at that moment would be enough to satisfy the soul. The following promises will help correct that.

Ps.63:3, Isa.55:2, Ps.63:5, Ps.37:4

Anger can also be a sign of pride—the assumption that you deserve better treatment than Jesus received. Jesus pointed out that no servant is greater than his master, we should therefore wash one another's feet (Jn.13:14-16), and we should expect to be betrayed even by friends (v.18) and persecuted by enemies (15:20). But we can also expect reward if we respond with love.

Lk.6:28-35

Answered Prayer

Lk.11:13, Mt.7:7-8, Ps.50:15, Ps.145:18, Jer.29:12, 1 Jn.5:14

Anxiety/Worry

Ps.23:1-6, Mt.6:25-34, Php.4:4-7, Ps.121:7-8, Ps.46:1-4

Boredom

Ps.89:15-16, Ps.16:11, Ps.36:7-8, Ps.63:5

Comfort

Php.2:1-2, Ps.23:4, Jn.14:18, Mt.28:20, Ps.30:5, Lam.3:31-33, Isa.30:18, 2 Cor.4:16-18, Ro.8:18, Ro.8:28, 2 Cor.1:3-5, Dt.32:4

Complaining

Isa.55:2, Ps.63:5

Contentment in God's Nearness

Ps.16:11, Ps.63:3,5; Isa.55:2, Ps.37:4, Ps.73:27-28, Jn.14:18, Ps.10:17, Ps.91:1, Ps.36:8

Courage

Heb.11:24-26, Ps.118:6-7, Ps.112:1-10

Desire for Earthly Things Above God

Ps.63:3, Ps.37:4, Isa.55:2, Ps.63:5, Ps.4:8

Discouragement in Suffering (see Suffering)

Disappointed in People

Every time you are disappointed with a person, the feeling of frustration is due to the longing in your soul for people to behave as they should (faithfulness). The stronger your frustration, the greater your appetite for faithfulness. And the greater your appetite for faithfulness, the more delighted you should be that God is faithful. Every time a person does something that upsets you, let it cause you to rejoice over a God who is not like man.

Nm.23:19

Desire for God

Ps.89:15-16, Ps.16:11, Ps.36:7-8, Ps.63:5

Discontent (See Contentment)

Depression/Despair/Losing heart)

Ps.23:4, Ps.3:3, 2 Cor.4:16-17, Gal.6:9

Discouragement over Loss

Joel 2:25, Lk.18:28-30, 2 Chm.25:9

Discouragement over Opposition

Jas.4:7, 1 Pe.5:8-9

Discouragement over My Sin

Micah 7:8-9, 1 Jn.2:1,12, Ro.8:34, 1Cor.1:8-9, Heb 4:14-16, Isa.55:6-9, Ps.32:5-7, Isa.57:15-19, Zeph.3:17, Heb.12:5-6, Ps.41:4,11a, Ps.103:8-12

Encouragement

Ps.23:4, Ps.3:3, Php.2:1-2, 2 Cor.4:16-17

Escape from Temptation (see Temptation)

Eternal Perspective

Isa.65:17-19, Rev.21:4, Heb.6:18-20, 1 Jn.3:2-3

Evangelism/Missions

Lk.16:9, Pr.24:11-12

Favor in the Eyes of God

Ps.5:12, Ps.103:13-14, Zeph.3:17, Ps.11:7, Ps.17:15, Lk.11:13

Fear of Circumstances

Ps.121:7-8, Ps.34:7, Lk.21:16-18, Ps.46:1-4,

Fear of Man

Jn.14:18, Ps.10:17, Php.1:27-30

Forgiveness of Others

Mt.6:14

Fretting Over God's Name Being Dishonored

Ps.46:10, Isa.46:10, Rev.5:13

Generosity

Lk.6:38

Greed/Stinginess (See Generosity)

Guidance

Ps.23:3, Jer.16:21, Isa.57:17-19, Isa.58:9b-11, Isa.30:19-21, Ps.25:12-14, Ps.48:14

Honor

1 Sam.2:30, Ps.34:5, Ro.2:7-10

Joy in Suffering (See Suffering)

Justice

NOTE: Some have said, "Never ask God for justice, because we all deserve hell." It is true that we all deserve hell, but it is wrong to conclude that we should therefore not seek justice from God! God does not mix accounts. The issue of what you deserve for some sin is separate from whether you are being treated unfairly by some person, and Scripture very often calls us to seek justice from God when we are being oppressed or mistreated. The point is not so much to desire the punishment of our oppressors, but rather for God to make things right and repay us in some way for what was taken from us.

Ps.37:6, Ps.9:7-9, Ps.11:7, Ps.33:5, Ps.36:6, Ps.72:2, Ps.103:6

Laziness

Eph.6:7-8, Gal.6:9, Mt.16:27, 1 Cor.15:10, 1 Cor.15:58

Loneliness

John 14:18, Ps.10:17

Losing Heart/Despair

Ps.23:4, Ps.3:3, 2 Cor.4:16-17, Gal.6:9

Loss (See Discouragement over Loss)

Love for People

BELIEVERS
1 Cor.12:7, Mt.25:34-40,
UNBELIEVERS
Lk.6:35
THE NEEDY
Pr.19:17

Low Desire for God

Ps.89:15-16, Ps.16:11, Ps.36:7-8, Ps.63:5, 1 Chrn.28:9b, Jer.29:13, Mt.7:7, Jas.4:8, Mt.6:6

Lust (See temptation)

Motivation

Eph.6:7-8, Gal.6:9, Mt.16:27

Optimism (Obedience and godliness are within my reach!)—See also Favor in the eyes of God

Isa.45:19, Ps.103:13-14, Dt.30:11-14, Zeph.3:17, Php.4:13, Ez.11:19, Eph.2:18, 1Cor.1:8-9, Ps.25:14, Ps.37:23-24

Overwhelmed by Circumstances

Ps.121:7-8, Ps.8:4, Isa.46:4, Ps.33:17-21

Peace in Your Heart

Zeph.3:17, Ps.36:7-8, Php.4:4-7

People-Pleasing

When we desire praise from men we should look instead to the promises of praise from God.

1 Cor.4:5, Ro.2:7-10, Ro.2:29, 2 Cor.10:18, Jn.5:44, 1 Sam.2:30, Mt.25:21, Mt.25:34-35

Persecution

Mt.5:10-12

Perseverance/Preservation (see also Strengthening and Pessimism)

Isa.40:31, Isa.46:4, 2 Thes.3:3-5, 2 Cor.1:21, Ro.14:4, 1 Cor.1:8, 2 Tim.1:12, 1 Pe.1:3-5, Ez.11:19-21, Jude 24-25, 1 Thes.5:23-24, Php.1:3-6, Jer.31:31-34

Pessimism (Obedience will be too hard)

Isa.45:19, Ps.103:13-14, Zeph.3:17, Php.4:13, Ez.11:19, Eph.2:18, 1Cor.1:8-9, Ps.25:14

Prayer

1 Chm.28:9b, Jer.29:13, Mt.7:7, Jas.4:8

Protection

Ps.121:7-8, Ps.34:7, Lk.21:16-18, Ps.91:11-12

Refuge

Ps.91:2-4, Ps.46:1, Ps.59:16, Ps.2:12, Ps.5:11, Ps.9:9, Ps.14:6, Ps.17:7, Ps.18:2, 30, Ps.31:19, Ps.34:22, Ps.36:7, Ps.71:3, Ps.118:8, Ps.119:114, Ps.142:4-5, Ps.27:5

Rest (see also strengthening)

Ps.23:2, Ps.91:1, Ps.4:8

Restoration

Ps.51:17, Pr.24:16, Hos.6:1-3, Mic.7:8-9, Ro.11:29, Jer.15:19, Isa.55:6-9, Ps.32:5-7, Isa.57:15-19, Ps.23:3, Ps.19:7, Lam.3:31-33

Strengthening/Being Sustained

Php.4:13, Isa.45:5, Ps.18:1, Ps.18:32, Ps.28:7, Ps.29:11, Ps.46:1, Ps.59:9, Ps.59:16, Ps.68:35, Ps.73:26, Isa.30:15, Isa.41:10, Isa.40:29, Isa.40:31, 2 Cor.12:9, Isa.46:4, Lk.11:13, Ps.41:1-3, Ps.55:22

Success

Pr.15:19

Suffering (Discouragement)

1 Pe.4:13, Job 23:10, Ro.8:28, Ps.41:1-3, Jas.1:2-4, Lam.3:31-33

Temporal Perspective (See Eternal Perspective)

Temptation

Ps.63:3,5, Isa.55:2, Ps.37:4, 1 Cor. 10:13, Heb.11:24-26, Ps.36:8, 2 Sam.12:8b, Jas.4:7

Trust for Needs

Mt.6:25-34, Mt.6:33

Trust in God's faithfulness

Isa.37:32

Turmoil in Your Heart

Zeph.3:17, Ps.36:7,8

Vindication (See also Justice)

Ps.27:6, Ps.23:5, Ps.37:5-6, Isa.54:17, Mic.7:8-9, 1 Cor.4:5

Vitality/Health (Spiritual Thriving)

Jer.17:7-8, Ps.1:3, Isa.58:9-11

Weakness (See Strengthening)

Worry (See Anxiety/Worry)

Warnings

Warnings Against...

Failure to Persevere

1 Cor.15:2, Col.1:22-23, Heb 3:14, Ro.11:22, Heb 3:12-15, Mk.16:16, Heb.4:1,7,14, Heb.6:4-7,11-12, Heb.10:23-39, 2 Pe.3:17, Rev.3:11, Heb.12:15,25, Jn.15:6-11, 2 Pe.2:20-21, Ro.11:20-22, 1 Tim.1:18-20, 2 Tim.2:12, Rev 22:19, Ex.32:33, Mt.18:34-35, Lk.12:46, Mt.25:30, Ro.8:12-13, 1 Ti.3:6, Col 2:19, 1 Tim.4:1, Mt.24:10, 1 Tim.5:15, Ez.33:12-20, (See also Ez.18:24-26 and 3:20,21), 1 Cor.9:27-10:14, 1 Co.5:5, Rev.2:17,3:5,12, 21, Rev 21:7, Mt.5:13, Mk.9:50, Lk.14:34

Sin in General

Romans 6:16

Sexual Sin

Job 31:1-4, Pr.5:3-23, Pr.6:26-35, Pr.7:22-27, Ecc.7:26

APPENDIX 2:
TOPICAL INDEX FOR
DEVOTIONALS HOMEWORK

The problems of the human heart are solved by increasing love for God. And love for God is increased when His attributes are personally experienced. The devotional book, *What's So Great About God?*, is designed to help the reader experience 76 different attributes of God. The meditations on those attributes are numbered 1-180. The index below lists the particular meditations that may be helpful as a homework assignment for the counselee who is struggling with the particular issue listed before the number.

The numbers in bold are the ones that are particularly relevant or important.

Addiction (see Enslaving Sin)
Anger – 2, **51,** 56, 144, 177
Anxiety – **1-20**, 61, **64-69**, **72**, **76**, 77, 80, **81-83, 87, 89**, 142 (see also Worry)
Approval (God's) – 45-49, **52, 54**, 62, 69, 78, **86**, 90-92, 104, 153, 172, 180
Boredom – **1-20**, 33, **44, 65, 76**, 134
Burnout – **1-20**, 33, **35**, 44, **64, 70-73, 76, 105**
Comfort – 7-**10, 76, 77**, 80, 82
Complaining (see Grumbling)
Covetousness – **1-20**, 23, **31, 36, 50, 87**
Craving Compassion – **1-20, 46-49**, 52, 66, **76, 77, 80**, 142, 143, **171**
Critical of Others (see Faultfinding)
Depressed – **1-20, 34-37**, 46-49, **59, 62**, 65, **66**, 67, 73, **76, 77, 94-95, 112, 118**, 140, 142, 143, **155**, 166
Disapproval (man's) – 66, **69**, 180
Discouragement over Failure – **46, 53, 54-56, 59**, 60, **78, 79, 86, 104, 105, 123**, 160

Distant from God – **1-20, 48, 51**, 59, 62, 65, 73, **75-77**, 80, **81, 86, 92, 102, 107-110**, 111, **118**, 121, **122, 123, 124, 126**, 129, **140**, 141, 142, 144, 146, **150-153,** 160

Enslaving Sin – **1-20, 31**, 32, **76, 131,** 133

Favor (God's) – **1-20**, 46-49, **53**, 54, **67-69**, 77, 81, **87**, 100, **123**, 129, **139, 153**, 157-159, 169, 172, 180

Failing Health (see Getting old)

Faultfinding – 88, **96-99, 113, 157**, 161

Fear of Trouble – **30**, 41, 46-49, **64, 66-69, 76**, 81, **82, 87, 89**, 106, 107, **111, 139, 147, 148,** 151, **154**

Fear of Man – **30**, 180

Forgiveness (God's) – 46-49, **51-56, 59, 78, 79, 86, 90, 123**, 157-159, **172**

Forgiving Others – **86, 88**, 93

Getting Old – 32, 33, **34**, 35, **76**, 165

Gossip – 113, 125

Gossip (victim of) – **125**, 180

Guidance – 114-123

Guilt – 46, **51-54**, 78, 79, **86, 104, 152**

Grumbling – **1-20, 31**, 38, **60-69**, 73, **76, 77, 81, 84, 85**, **94-95, 106**, 112, 142, 143, 155, **164**, 178, **179**

Healing (Spiritual)/Restoration – **1-20,** 72-74, **76, 78, 79, 86**

Idolatry – **1-20**, 23, 28, **31, 36, 37, 50, 86, 101,** 133

Impatience with People – 86, **88**, 96-99, **104**

Ingratitude – **31, 61-63**, 68, **69, 73, 77, 81, 83-87, 92, 94-95, 102, 106, 107, 112, 118**, 143, 144, 155, 162

Injustice (victim of) – **45**, 66-69, **113, 119, 136, 177**, 180

Lack of Awe/Fear of God – **22-30**, 57, 60, **76**, 103

Lack of Brokenness over Sin – **18-19, 52, 54-56, 57, 59, 79**

Lack of Desire for Scripture – **1-20, 65**, 73-76, **124-128,** 132

Lack of Hope – **5**, 12, **17-20**

Lack of Love for Others (see Loving others)

Lack of Meaning in Life – **1-20**, 44, 62, **76**, 83, 122, 134

Lack of Motivation – **4, 9**, 35, **70**, 73-75, 90, 163

Laziness – 39, 40

Legalism – 39, 93, 170

Loneliness – **13, 17-20, 48, 65, 66**, 68, **69, 81**, 92, **102, 134**, 140, 144, 167, **168, 169**

Love for the World – **1-20**, 23, **31**, 32, **36, 50, 101**